STARCHILD I and II

A Re-Discovery of Stellar Wisdom

and

Lights of the Veil

Melusine Draco

Published in 2016 as Starchild I and II
Starchild I originally published by ignotus press in 2000

A CIP catalogue record for this title is available from the British
Library.

Cover pictures:

Front: The Eagle Nebula

Back: The Pillars of Creation :

NASA

Mélusine Draco's highly individualistic teaching methods and writing draw on historical sources supported by academic texts and current archaeological findings; endorsing the view that magic is an amalgam of science and art, and that magic is the outer route to the inner Mysteries. Author of several titles currently published with John Hunt Publishing including the best-selling six-part Traditional Witchcraft series; two titles on power animals – *Aubry's Dog* and *Black Horse, White Horse*; *By Spellbook & Candle: Cursing, Hexing, Bottling and Binding*; *The Dictionary of Magic & Mystery*; *Pan: Dark Lord of the Forest*; *By Wolfsbane & Mandrake Root: The Shadow World of Plants and Their Poisons* and *The Secret People* published by Moon Books; *Magic Crystals Sacred Stones* and *The Atum-Re Revival* published by Axis Mundi Books. She is also Principal of Coven of the Scales and the Temple of Khem.

Website: http://www.covenofthescales.com
Website: http://www.templeofkhem.com

Blog: http://melusinedracoattempleofkhem.blogspot.com/

Facebook: https://www.facebook.com/Melusine-Draco-486677478165958
Facebook: http://www.facebook.com/TradBritOldCraft
Facebook: http://www.facebook.com/TempleofKhem
Facebook: http://www.facebook.com/TempleHouseArchive
Facebook: http://www.facebook.com/countrywriterscraft

"May you enter favoured, and leave beloved."
[an ancient Egyptian blessing]

CONTENTS:

Foreword

In 2000 I published *Starchild: a Re-Discovery of Stellar Wisdom'* It had taken ten years to write and encapsulated what I'd learned on the path up to and beyond Initiation into the Mysteries – it was a catharsis of all the jumbled and fragmentary magical and mystical information collected in the brain, purged and then drawn together to make a coherent whole. It was, I thought at the time - either through arrogance or ignorance - my *Magnum Opus*.

Sixteen years later I have put the finishing touches to *Starchild II: Lights of the Veil*, which demonstrates that the path of the Initiate is never ending in terms of learning. *Starchild II* does not render *Starchild I* obsolete – it is an extension of that original understanding - an affirmation, if you like. The first book was created out of the wisdom of the ancient Egyptian world and while the second emerged from more recent wider-reaching discoveries, it has revealed how our mystical roots have sprung from different strains of the same panspermiac seed.

The past sixteen years have seen tremendous breakthroughs in science, archaeology and astronomy, and have merely strengthened the belief that mankind's true quest for knowledge, wisdom and understanding still lies along the Path of the Initiate. *Starchild II* uses the old stellar-wisdom to pull all the various esoteric threads together and examine them under a spiritual microscope. Panspermia was an idea of great antiquity, implying that the seeds of life are inherent in the Universe ... we can now see that it also carries all the magic and mystery of the stars.

MD

Starchild I

A Re-Discovery of Stellar Wisdom

Introduction

**Starchild guarantees that your attitude to religion and magic will
never be the same again – whatever your belief.**

In that old Hollywood classic, *Now Voyager*, Bette Davies' concluding
lines to her married lover are: "Don't let's ask for the moon. We have the
stars." An innocuous enough little romantic phrase that appears in
countless books of cinematic quotations, but what does it really mean?

On one hand (and that which probably came into the mind of the
scriptwriter), was why strive for the unattainable when you can settle for
a reasonably acceptable or effective alternative. One the other hand (and
the thought that would occur to the mystic), it could also mean why go for
the familiar and safe when you can reach out to infinity.

It is perfectly reasonable to feel that the stars are far away and too
remote for us to contemplate. More often than not, our view of the
heavens is obscured by cloud or, in urban areas, light pollution. The stars
do not offer up their energies for examination on a regular basis like the
moon (monthly), or the sun (quarterly), because this is an annual cycle – a
gigantic cosmic carousel that endlessly circles Polaris, the Pole Star. The
stars are pretty enough – occasionally spectacular – but they offer very
little by the way of a magical or devotional focus.

Or do they?

It depends on how you like your magical energies served, I suppose. If you like plain, wholesome fare with few surprises; if you prefer a satisfying but unchanging recipe in your ritual; or if adventure plays no part in your quest, then stellar magic isn't for you. The pursuit of stellar wisdom is, literally, as old as Time. It has its roots in all the ancient creation myths – the primordial, indigenous forces, later classed as 'demonic' by later conquerors and invaders, and those great social innovators, the incoming priesthoods.

Stellar magic reaches from the inner chthonic planes of the Earth to the out limits of Space. And this isn't one of those screwball theories that conveniently align known facts to fit the hypothesis. In The Magic Furnace, cosmologist Marcus Chown, explains how every particle which makes up this world of ours originated in a 'magic furnace' somewhere in outer space and is still playing out its part in the cosmic drama that began some 15 billion years ago.

"The iron in our blood, the calcium in our bones, the oxygen in our very breath – all were forced in blistering furnaces deep inside stars, and blown into space when those stars exploded and died," writes Chown. "We are connected directly to the most dramatic and awe-inspiring of cosmic events – everyone of us is stardust made flesh."

Melusine Draco

CONTENTS

Part One – Divine Funeral Pyre
"Every man and every woman is a star."
Liber AL Vel Legis pt 1 v.3

And then there was only the silence of the stars, and space, and blackness and a void which was and is, and is to come, for in the end is also the beginning, and this void, being Nothing, could not be created, and this void, being Nothing could not be destroyed, and this void being Nothing, is and was and will be, and this void, being Nothing, is not, was not and will not be. It exists and does not exist forever, has existed and has not existed forever, will exist and will not exist forever; no words can describe that Nothing which is perceived and yet not perceived We are separate from that Nothing, and we judge time as a series of events. Were we One with that Nothing, there could be no Time.

[*The Devil's Maze,* Gerald Suster]

This planet of ours is doomed, even if the Earth doesn't suffer a cataclysmic collision with an asteroid – or our own pollution doesn't get us first. Not during the next century, nor even by the next millennium, but sometime within the far distant future, our Sun will die.

In astronomical terms, this 'yellow dwarf' star is barely middle-aged and located some 25,000 light years from the centre of the galaxy. It is held together by gravity, which is constantly trying to pull everything down into its centre: if that gravitational pull was unopposed, it would crush the sun to a mere speck in less than an hour, turning it into a black hole. The fact that such a catastrophic event has not taken place is due to another, equally powerful force within the solar interior, which counteracts gravity.

This state of cosmic equilibrium, however, will not last forever. At some stage the supply of the Sun's natural resources will run out; the core will shrink and the heat will increase; the outer layers will expand and cool – the Sun will become a 'red giant' star, 100 times brighter that it is today. Its heat will be so intense that the Earth, along with the Moon, Mercury, Venus and Mars, will be incinerated and probably totally destroyed. The outer planets Jupiter, Saturn, Uranus, Neptune and Pluto *may* survive, but only Saturn's moon, Titan, seems to have the right ingredients to sustain life despite its cold and rather noxious atmosphere.

This solar funeral pyre will only last for a relatively short time before the core collapses and the Sun dwindles to a very small, feeble star known as a white dwarf. Gradually it will fade to become a cold, dead globe – a black dwarf ... attended by the ghosts of its surviving family. And this is not some science fiction fantasy, it is *scientific reality* based on the observations of eminent physicists, cosmologists and astronomers, such as Fred Hoyle, Stephen Hawking, Patrick Moore and Brian Cox. Regardless of the fact that these events lie so far in the future that we need not concern ourselves with them, it does raise one very important question for us to ponder.

Where, we *must* ask ourselves, does 'God' – of the past, present or future – come into all this? Because there is no power in the Universe, either spiritual or temporal that can prevent this *natural* phenomenon from taking place. Faced with the inevitable destruction of our solar system, it is enough to force even the most blinkered of believers to question the existence and omnipotence of any Supreme Being. At first glance it would seem that astro-science *has* indeed finally put the last nail in God's coffin.

As Andrew Norman Wilson observed in *God's Funeral, 'Even a fervent religious believer must, if honest, confront problems in relation to faith which were not necessarily present for those of earlier generations.'* The truth can't be resisted, of course, but the religious establishments have made martyrs out of those who challenged those early beliefs: *'Reacting furiously to the notion that the earth was not the centre of the universe, nor man the most important being on earth'.*

Nevertheless, however much we might like to deny it, evidence of God or more correctly – the 'Creator' – or what is left of Him/Her/It, *is* out there. This may not be the benevolent, divine presence of the religious textbooks, but current space exploration produces a more reasonable argument for the continuing existence of god-power from the *scientist's* point of view, rather than from the theologian's. By facing up to the inevitable destruction of our planet by natural forces, rather than confirming the *non-existence* of God, science actually proclaims long and loud that there is proof of the everlasting, regenerating life. Eliphas Levi wrote:

Without faith, science leads to doubt; without science, faith leads to superstition. Uniting them brings certainty, but in so doing they must never be confused with each other. The science of the Qabalah makes doubt, as regards religion, impossible, for it alone reconciles reason with faith by showing that universal dogma, at bottom is always and everywhere the same, though formulated differently in certain times and places, is the purest expression of the aspirations of the human mind, enlightened by a necessary faith ...

Levi formulated much of what we recognise in today's esoteric teachings and enables us to see that in every religious symbol from the collective unconscious, the occult sciences of the Qabalah, ritual and ceremonial magic, and the *Hermetica* of Hermes Trismegistus (the 'Thrice Great Thoth'), brings out the true and the false, separating the realities and the counterfeit to provide us with a religion for the future.

The Qabalah can be seen as the mathematics of human thought; the algebra of faith as it were; solving all problems of the soul as equations, by isolating the unknowns. Magic is the science of the magi, utilising the knowledge of secret and particular laws of nature that produce and conceal hidden forces. Hermetica is the science of nature hidden in the hieroglyphics and symbols of the ancient world ...

From the earliest development of human myth, the stars have been symbolic of the Old Gods of that ancient world. We are talking, of course, about those powerful Creation deities, the majority of whom were later made redundant by incoming priesthoods. Apart from recording the annual changes in the position of the stars, however, early man would have quickly realised that those distant pinpoints of light, had no dramatic or immediate effect on his life on Earth, in the same way as the Sun or Moon. Nevertheless, the remote stars were universally viewed as being the dwelling place of the Mighty Dead, or even a form of manifestation of individual deities.

From the historical and religious perspective, variations on the theme of the Creation of the world, its Destruction, and the subsequent origins of mankind, generally fall into two easily identifiable categories: those concerned with the origin of things, and those connected to periodic ceremonies which were performed to ensure the continuity and wellbeing of the people. The earliest recorded cosmogonies were an amalgam of thought and imagery that reflected the religious needs of emerging civilisation, and the continuing influence of the primitive folklore of its ancestral beliefs.

The earliest examples of Creation myths are those of Mesopotamia and Egypt, which chronicle the world emerging from the chaotic waters to bring in what is often described as a 'Golden Age' at the dawn of time. The Egyptians viewed this as *zep tepi*, the 'First Time', starting with Atum emerging from the waters of Nun and beginning the work of Creation on the primeval hill, known as the Mound. These myths are cosmogonies in the literal sense, since they refer to the beginning of the *cosmos* (i.e. the known world of the time) and the diverse relationships of the gods, but contain little reference to the creation of mankind itself. Although Khnum fashioned humans from clay on his potter's wheel, the Egyptians, with their early beliefs reflecting a return to the stars after death, were obviously less pre-occupied with earthly human creativity than the neighbouring Mesopotamians and Hebrews.

By contrast, the Mesopotamians focused more on the beginning of civilisation and mankind, than on the origins of the cosmos, with one legend describing Enki creating humans out of clay to act as servants of the gods. The most famous of the Creation myths, however, is the Babylonian *Enuma elish* that reflected the Egyptian concept of exalting the gods. Much later Hebrew Creation myths, detailed in the first three chapters of the *Book of Genesis*, exercised a profound influence upon later Western thought and culture. This priestly tradition plagiarised the idea of primordial waters from earlier cosmogonies but did not have the world being created out of Nothing, as later theologians maintained: a watery chaos existed *before* the Hebrew's god's act of Creation. Early Yahwist tradition concentrated on the creation of mankind (drawing on earlier Egyptian and Mesopotamian myths), whereby the later Hebrew god created the first man (Adam) out of the earth, and woman (Lilith) from the primordial slime.

Parallel concepts of identifying the gods with the stars and the observation of the constellations can also be traced to the Babylonian Creation myth, the *Enuma elish,* where Marduk *'created stations for the great gods, fixing their astral likeness as constellations. He determined the year by designing the zones* [zodiac]: *he set up three constellations for the 12 months'* [*Man, Myth & Magic*]. Mesopotamians regarded the movement of the stars and planets as the 'writing of heaven' and from it evolved the development of astrology as a means of divination. The casting of horoscopes fuelled the idea that human destiny was controlled by the stars; an idea that much later spread rapidly throughout the Graeco-Roman world.

For the Egyptians, however, those stars 'which grow not weary' have *always* had immense significance in their culture. The circumpolar stars that never set in the west, were identified as 'the Imperishable Ones' and, according to the Pyramid Texts, the kings were raised up to heaven to join their company on death, to be free from change or decay. As we have seen from previous chapters, this association of the stars with the revered dead has a longstanding tradition in Egypt, which is revealed on the ceilings of the many tombs that were painted with stars, or the image of the arched sky-goddess depicted on the lids of the coffins and sarcophagi.

The hieroglyph of the five-pointed star represented the celestial 'world beyond the tomb' while the five-pointed star in a circle [an image so familiar in modern paganism] was the symbol for the place in the sky where the sun and the stars re-appeared after having been invisible, according to the Pyramid Texts. In later times it came to represent Otherworld – celestial or subterranean, i.e. the *dwat* and Amenti.

The ancients also identified their gods and goddesses with specific stars and planets. To the Sumarians, the planet Venus corresponded to the goddess Inanna, then 'Lady of Heaven', while the Babylonians knew her as Ishtar. As the Evening Star she was seen as a fertility goddess, associated with love and luxury – as the Morning Star she presided over war and carnage. Her symbol was a star of eight or sixteen rays. The Mesopotamian god of the Underworld, Nergal, who was also associated with war and pestilence, was identified with the planet Mars.

To the Egyptians, the constellation Ursa Major suggested a ritual object used ceremonially in 'the Opening of the Mouth' as part of the Osirian funerary rites. It also represented the thigh of a sacrificial animal and therefore connected to Set; while some sources have linked the constellation of Draco with the 'Mother of Set', Nut. The distinctive constellation of Orion was first attributed to Sah, and later as 'the glorious soul of Osiris', holding a deep significance in Egyptian belief because of their continuing traditional connection between the stars and the dead.

Sothis (or Sirius), the 'Dog Star' was originally identified with Sopdet, and later Isis, but more importantly, it was associated the annual flooding of the Nile. The calendar, having been based on the date of the heliacal rising of Sothis near the sun at the Summer Solstice, coinciding with the commencement of the Inundation. Ancient texts also assign other planets to the various gods – Jupiter with Horus 'who limits the two lands'; Mars with Horus of the Horizon; Mercury with Sebegu (a god associated with Set); Saturn with Horus 'bull of the sky'; and Venus ('the one who crosses' or 'god of the morning') with Re or Osiris.

Although the Egyptians had both civic and astronomical calendars, it is almost impossible to fix precise dates in the chronology of the history of the Nile Valley. That said, as Raymond A. Wells points out in *Astronomy Before the Telescope*, more than six millennia ago, man's primal gleanings from the night sky crystallised into a variety of myths that formed the basis of Egyptian religion. *'Since its principal deities were heavenly bodies, the priesthood mastered the ability to predict the time and place of their gods' appearances ...* **Many of these achievements were already in place before the unification of Upper (Nile Valley)** *and Lower* **(Delta)** *Egypt.'* [Author's emphasis. MD]

During the Old Kingdom, the belief that mortals were reborn among the circumpolar stars led to the continued depiction of stars on the ceiling of the tombs as an important part of the funerary art of the day. As Wells also makes a point of explaining: *'The mythology of the sky goddess Nut giving birth to Re, catalysed both time-keeping and calendar development, endowed the concept of divine royalty, and instituted the matrilineal inheritance of the throne.'*

One of the utterances from the Pyramid Texts exhorts the sky goddess, Nut, to spread her protective body over the deceased so that he might ascend to join those already placed among the Imperishable Stars. The funerary rites with their attendant deities were regarded as microcosms of the universe itself, and just as Nut spread her star-spangled body over the earth, so she stretched herself over the dead. Even when the stellar beliefs of early Egypt were merged into the later solar and lunar cults of Atum-Re and Osiris, the practice of stellar decoration continued throughout the rest of the empire's history.

The Greeks accredited the Egyptians with recognising the existence of the movement of the stars, and the earliest detailed records are the 'diagonal calendars' or star-clocks, also painted on the wooden coffin lids of the early Middle Kingdom. These calendars consisted of 36 columns, listing 36 groups of stars referred to as 'decans' into which the night sky was divided. Each decan rose above the horizon at dawn for a period of ten days every year.

This system, however, was also flawed, since it did not take into account the fact that the Egyptian year was always around six hours short, adding up to a difference of 10 days every 40 years. Because of this 'slippage' it is doubtful whether these Middle Kingdom star-clocks were ever considered to be a practical measure of time, nevertheless this was another integral ingredient of tomb decoration, if only paying symbolic lip-service to the Old Ways.

The astronomical knowledge of the early priests and architects is further confirmed by examples of the ceremony of *pedj shes* ('stretching the cord'), first recorded on a granite block during the reign of the Dynasty II ruler, Khasekhemwy (c2686BC). This method was reliant on the sighting of Ursa Major and Orion, using 'an instrument of knowing' (*merkhet*), which functioned on the same principle as the astrolabe, and a sighting tool (*bay*) constructed from a central rib of a palm leaf. Although many later texts described the *pedj shes*, it has been suggested that this, like all the old stellar religion's symbolism, had become mere ceremony and that in practice the temples were simply aligned in relation to the river, the *British Museum Dictionary of Ancient Egypt* tells us.

The Pyramid Age

As recent popular histories have revealed, the Great Pyramid was almost certainly aligned with the stars and, along with the Sphinx, are literally 'oriented' (that is, they faced due east, the direction of sunrise at the equinoxes. The shafts in the King's and Queen's Chambers in the Great Pyramid demonstrate the stellar alignments of all four shafts in the epoch of 2500BC. The northern shaft in the Queen's Chamber is angled at 39 degrees and was aimed at Kochab (Beta Ursa Minor) in the constellation of Ursa Minor. The southern shaft angled at 39 degrees 30, was directed at Sirius in the constellation of Alpha Canis Major.

In the King's Chamber, the northern shaft, angled at 32 degrees 28, was directed at the ancient Pole Star, Thuban (Alpha Draconis) in the constellation of Draco. The southern shaft, angled at 45 degrees 14, focused on Al Nitak (Zeta Orionis), the brightest and lowest of the three stars in Orion's Belt. In their book, *The Orion Mystery*, Bauval and Hancock also demonstrate that the three stars in Orion's Belt might possibly correspond to the faulty diagonal line of the Great Pyramid (of Cheops) and the second Pyramid (of Chephren), with the third Pyramid (of Mycerinus) being off-set slightly to the east. *'The first two stars* (Al Nitak and Al Nilam) *are in direct alignment, like the first and second Pyramids, and the third star* (Mintaka) *lies off-set somewhat to the east of the axis formed by the other two.'*

The Egyptian word for pyramid (*mer*) means 'place of ascent' or more correctly 'what goes [straight] up from the *us*' (a word of uncertain meaning), the suggested ascending being done by the dead Pharaoh as he was transported into the sky to spend eternity among the Imperishable Ones. The development of the pyramids, of which there are some 80 (although many are now reduced to piles of rubble), began after 3000BC and culminated in the colossal structures known as the Giza Group that were built between 2600-2500BC. After that, pyramid building went into decline, with ever-smaller structures being built.

Some of the later (and grossly inferior) pyramids are nevertheless significant in that they contain fine examples of the Pyramid Texts: the set of magic spells dating from prehistoric times, giving a safe passage to the Pharaoh into the sky. Many of the texts describe the journey of the king to the Other World, situated in the sky beyond the eastern horizon, and his activities upon arrival. Judging from the formation of the texts, it is significant that the king could not rely on any divine assistance from the gods during his journey but, armed with the magical power of the texts, he might overcome the hazards of his final trials before joining the Sun-god in his daily travels across the sky.

According to Professor I E S Edwards (*The Pyramids of Egypt*) for most part, the Pyramid Texts were certainly *not* inventions of Dynasties V and VI, but had originated in much earlier times. *'It is hardly surprising, therefore, that they sometimes contain allusions to conditions which no longer prevailed at the time of Unas and his successors.'* A relic of an even more ancient culture is contained in a passage (Spells 273-4) that describes the dead king as a hunter who catches and devours the gods so that he may appropriate their qualities unto himself. When compiling the texts during Dynasty V, the priesthood used older religious and funerary spells, supplementing them with incantations of a later date to meet contemporary needs.

In his academic paper, 'The King and the Star-Religion in the Pyramid Texts', R O Faulkner, acknowledged expert on ancient Egyptian writing, pointed out that the funerary art forms from the Middle Kingdom onwards were contemporary interpretations of *'a very ancient stratum of stellar religion, in which the stars were regarded as gods, or as the souls of the blessed dead'*. Here we learn that there was a distinction between the sky (*pt*) as a natural element of daily life, and the 'Starry Sky' (*shdw*) where the King goes on death, as in *'May you* [the King] *go to those northern gods the circumpolar stars ... '*

In his conclusion, Faulkner's analysis of the Pyramid Texts shows two distinct strata. One, being concerned with the circumpolar stars and the northern sky, which appears as the abode of the gods and the illustrious royal dead, to which the King ascends on his journey from this world. The other is connected with the constellation of Orion and Sothis, the Morning Star and the Lone Star, with only three mentions of the moon.

It is noticeable that these two strata overlap very little and, while one deals with the ultimate abode of the dead King in the northern sky, the other, the Lone Star apart, appears to be concerned with those celestial bodies which mark the passage of time in the course of the year ... Orion is either a companion of the King, and is joined by him, making with Sothis a celestial trio; the King may thus be thought of as sharing in the responsibility for regulating times and seasons.

The association of the Morning Star with the dead King and the entourage of Re often displays conflicting details, but without doubt it refers to Phosphorus-Venus as seen at dawn. The Lone Star is the King himself, and Faulkner suggests this is Hesperus-Venus as seen just after sunset, since the Lone Star is spoken of as 'ascending from the eastern sky' and as a 'hawk seen in the evening traversing the sky'. As fragmented as these details are, it shows that the power of this archaic stellar-cult was still making itself felt, well into the Pyramid Age and beyond.

But why, we may ask ourselves, did the Egyptians choose those pyramidal shaped structures in the first place, and why the continuous references to the stars when everyone knows that the chief Egyptian god was the solar deity Atum-Re?

In *Rogue Asteroids and Doomsday Comets*, research astronomer at the Anglo-Australian Observatory, Duncan Steel, offered some further points to ponder which may alter the way we view the astronomer-priesthood of the Nile Valley. Apparently our Earth moves through a permanent cloud called *zodiacal dust*. This name gets its name because it gives rise to the *zodiacal light*, a diffuse glow in a huge triangular shape that follows the path of the sun across the sky. This natural phenomenon is best seen an hour or two after sunset or before dawn, in near-tropical latitudes.

Few people are fortunate enough to observe zodiacal light today because it is necessary to be well away from any light pollution to be able to distinguish it, but it was known to the ancient people of the Middle East as the 'false dawn' because it stretched far above the horizon, more than half way to the zenith. From an especially dark viewing site, it may even be possible to perceive a dim band reaching right across the sky along the ecliptic. *'This zodiacal band is due to dust that is exterior to the terrestrial orbit, while the zodiacal light proper (the pyramid in the sky) is due pre-dominantly to sunlight scattered from dust interior to our orbit.'*

Steel goes on to explain that when a large comet breaks up, an enormous amount of zodiacal dust will occur, making the zodiacal cloud and band much brighter than they appear today. *'In fact,'* he writes, *'they would look like the river that Re navigates his boat along each day, followed also at night by the newly bright comets in low-inclination orbits. At each end of the 'river' lies the triangular profile of the main zodiacal light, a pyramidal shape.'* Could this be the 'ladder' the dead King needed to ascend in order to climb his stairway to heaven?

Early written accounts of the sky speak of a phenomenon that historians *'primed by astronomers who assumed in error that what was seen* then *was the same as what we see now, have interpreted as being the Milky Way'*. The same records state that this 'Milky Way' was the path formerly taken by the Sun (that is, ecliptic) and that it was produced by comets. *'This is obviously* not *the Milky Way that we see now: what was being described was a super-intense zodiacal light and band.'*

Another important point is how the zodiacal light and band would appear as sunrise approached. According to Steel, the zodiacal band would come closer to being perpendicular to the horizon as the middle of the night passes and, as the pyramid of light begins to peek above the horizon hours before daybreak, it is still tilted far over. As time progresses, it straightens more and more, never quite reaching the perpendicular position. Then the whole sky would begin to brighten and redden in the northeast, until eventually the Sun would rise from the middle of the zodiacal cloud. This would have created a very strong impression on the Egyptian people, especially if that zodiacal light was much brighter 5,000 years ago than it is now.

Before *'inviting anthropologists and antiquarians to have their paroxysms and apoplectic attacks'*, Steel presses home his theory that the ancient Egyptians would also have seen a much more pronounced 'brightness enhancement' due to the huge amount of dust released at that period into the Taurid stream. *'Is there anything to link the ancient Egyptians with such calamitous events occurring in the sky?'* he asks. *'Well, one example, is from the Egyptian hieroglyphics; the symbols for thunder and meteorite are the same, and contain a star. It seems that the Egyptians associated meteors and meteorites with explosions above their heads, which is certainly indicative of a tumult taking place in the sky of a type different to our experiences today.'*

Finally, as even more food for thought, and one that will probably also upset the Atlanteans, he supports this theory by asking where else in the world were pyramids built? Those that immediately spring to our minds are Mexico (the Mayan pyramids are known to have had astronomical/calendrical motivations), East Asia, and the Babylonian and Assyrian ziggurats. And what these all have in common is their *latitude* – all near the Tropic of Cancer. *'From tropical latitudes the zodiacal light is most impressive and therefore we might anticipate finding buildings there that mimic its shape.'*

Nevertheless, although the stars played an integral part in Egyptian religion, we know that they did not adopt the astrological belief that the stars controlled human destiny until the Hellenistic period (330-30BC). Absorbing these later influences from Mesopotamian astral beliefs and Chaldean astrologers they quickly made up for lost time and immersed themselves in this new 'science'. According to S G F Brandon (in *Man, Myth & Magic*) these 'new age' Egyptians adopted the idea with enthusiasm and developed a form of astral religion or mystical philosophy that became widely influential in the world of Graeco-Roman culture. *'Star charts were elaborated, comprising 56 deities who presided over the various time units of the year ... the importance of horoscopes became so great that they were inscribed on the roofs of* [later] *tombs.'*

Despite the contemporary popularity of astrology, for thousands of years the human race lived without these illusions simply because it was inconceivable that the stars could have even the remotest link with *everyday* existence. Those sparkling beads of light were too remote from the familiar world of direct experience: they were the home of the gods. Divination, however, always played an important role in ancient times and those 'new age' astrologers often held prominent places within the higher echelons of society. As with all cultures, however, it was superstition that continued to keep the common people in check under the watchful eye of the priesthood.

The first known book of astrological lore with its pseudo-scientific overtones, *Tetrabiblos*, was written by Ptolemy around the 2nd century AD, in which he attributes all manner of influences to the planets in much the same way that modern astrology is consulted today. This star-lore was elaborated even further into the complex doctrine known as the *Corpus Hermetucum* (which also still exists), being attributed to Hermes Trismegistus, the Egyptian god Thoth/Tahuti himself, although it is now accepted that they were compiled by an unknown Christian scholar.

By the first century AD, the Babylonion zodiac at Dendera had been adopted and accepted as the 'Egyptian zodiac'. With the onset of Christianity, we can see why the myth was swiftly created that Jesus had delivered mankind from the domination of the stars ... and there is a great deal of reference to this in the writings of St Paul. Nevertheless, astrology survived through the Middle Ages and beyond to re-emerge as one of the more profitable aspects of the new New Ageism.

Written In The Stars

But let's turn the clock back to the beginning ... to those archetypal figures known as the 'Imperishable Ones' who personified the ever-visible circumpolar stars in the north of the sky. As we have discovered, archaeological evidence shows that for the pre-dynastic Egyptians (5500-3200BC), the religion of the time was stellar-based. It was from this point in history that the observations made by those early people of the Nile Valley noted the northern-most and southern-most turning points of the Sun at the solstices from which almost all of Egyptian astronomy and religion were ultimately derived.

In other words, even from the earliest period of history, the beliefs of the Egyptians *were* based on scientific observation, not primitive superstition, and as such, we can still identify with them today. *All* esoteric language is shot through with allegory and metaphor, sigils and correspondences, hieroglyphics and symbolism – and the Egyptian Mysteries are no exception – but we should not allow ourselves to forget that this astronomer-priesthood were at the scientific cutting-edge of their time. In fact, if we refer back to the quote from Carl Jung relating to the collective unconscious ...

> *In a pristine society such as Egypt's it should be possible to see it at work in a way quite different from the experience of later cultures. The collective unconscious is the fountain from which the archetypes flow. The collective unconscious in Egypt would, in this view, be especially powerful and as pristine a phenomenon as the society itself.*

... we see how the thread of scientific observation, influencing the magical symbology of religious and ritual magic archetypes, has endured for something like 6,000 years!

Here we have Nut, the celestial mother, portrayed as a naked female stretched across the sky with the sun shown entering her mouth, passing through her star-speckled body, and emerging from her birth canal. The faint outer arm of the Milky Way was perceived as the goddess, whose legs are formed by a bifurcation at the cross-shape of the constellation Cygnus with its principal star Deneb marking the birth canal exit; while the face is situated in the 'swirling star clouds' in the vicinity of Gemini. About 45 minutes after sunset at the Vernal Equinox, the head of Nut can be seen passing below the horizon face upwards with her mouth open at (or very close to) the position where the sun had set. Far-fetched ideas? Not at all ...

Ronald Wells, contributor to the academic paper 'Astronomy in Egypt' (*Astronomy Before the Telescope*) describes the final act of the drama as occurring 272 days later on the morning of the Winter Solstice, when the lower half the goddess is visible above the horizon for only a few hours. As the rosy-hued dawn spreads across the sky, Deneb intersects the horizon at exactly the spot where the sun rises … a phenomena only valid at the Winter Solstice, since the point of sunrise is further north on other dates. In other words, Re enters Nut at sunset on the Spring Equinox (at which time the goddess presumably conceives) and nine months later, she gives birth to him on the Winter Solstice

Perhaps the most remarkable aspect of these events, a convincing tie to actual astronomical observations, is that the number of days between the spring equinox and the winter solstice is the period of human gestation!' he concludes. 'The implied method of conception is oral, but that is not an unusual belief in a primitive society.

By the Old Kingdom (2686-2181BC) this stellar belief was confirmed by texts outlining the ruler's role in the Afterlife; here Pharaoh, represented by the Lone Star, devolves into the guide for the wise Imperishable Ones (the **ikhemu-sek**, literally 'the ones not knowing destruction') by the order of Atum. From those Old Kingdom texts we find one of the keys to the ancient stellar Mysteries. Here, it is revealed that the divinity of Pharaoh is not diminished by physical death; it is also recorded that Egypt will descend back into the chaotic waters of Nun should he be prevented from becoming one with the star-gods in the Afterlife. As if to emphasise this continuing or ancestral divinity, the deceased Pharaoh is referred to by the title 'god older than the oldest' – in true Mystery Tradition meaning that he becomes One with the Creator until the Divine King is reborn in his successor.

In historical terms, this can be seen as an attempt to amalgamate firmly entrenched stellar beliefs with the now dominant solar theology, and throughout remaining Egyptian history the Sun-god travels across the celestial ocean with the Imperishable Ones (including Pharaoh) in his barque. By the New Kingdom (1567-1085BC), however, the Imperishable Ones are merely 12 oar-carrying gods who are described as coming out of the primeval waters with Re. The rapid growth of the Osirian death-cult, however, saw them relegated to being merely referred to 'the followers of Osiris'.

The subsequent Hellenisation of Egyptian culture introduced a much more elaborate conceptualisation of the night sky as it developed and expanded the concept of the 'decans' – the 36 star-gods (constellations)

moving by barque across the firmament in 10-day cycles. Tomb paintings depicting the star-gods travelling across the ceiling reveal the images of the constellations, but present-day archaeologists and astronomers remain uncertain about identifying the Egyptian star groupings by any equivalent 'modern' names. The only major constellations that can be identified with any certainty are Orion with Sothis (Sirius), and Ursa Major (The Great Bear, or Plough) known as 'the four spirits of the north' who comprise the 'foreleg of Set'. Had we retained the Egyptian symbols for the constellations, we would today have a crocodile and the hippopotamus amongst the signs of the zodiac.

Virginia Lee Davis writing in *Archaeoastronomy* admits that the identification of ancient Egyptian constellations is a tantalising field of study.

> *On the one hand there is the almost embarrassing abundance of constellation pictures produced in the course of more than two millennia and beautifully preserved right down to the present day. On the other hand there is an almost complete dearth of reliable data on which to base attempts at identifying the pictured constellations. Presumably the Egyptians felt no lack, each one having learned the constellations from the cradle up by the simple expedient of having them pointed out to him.*

As an archaeologist, Davis is willing to trawl through the vast quantities of religious and mythological material in the hope of finding a few vague clues, but is no doubt hampered by an academic reluctance that prevents the cross-pollination of ideas between the applications of science, history, theology, philosophy and magic. The old Egyptian stellar-cult continued to form the basis of the ancient Mysteries, but just as every Egyptian child could have identified the stars themselves, only the higher astronomer-priesthood would have known the religio-magical significance of each of the constellations. Neither child nor priest, however, would have required them to be written in stone on the walls of the funerary monuments in order to understand their symbolism, but even committed Egyptologists seem to demonstrate a marked reluctance to credit these people with even a fundamental grasp of astrophysics.

Davis also cites the occasional reference in the Pyramid Texts of 'two skies', with frequent mention of a 'northern sky' and a 'southern sky' – but, she says, there is no mention of an eastern or western sky. *'There is also mention of 'two horizons' and frequent mention of 'eastern horizon' and 'western horizon'* (meaning the places of sunrise and sunset) *but no*

24

mention of northern horizon or southern horizon.' When dealing with mystical, religious and philosophical matters it is unwise to take the written word literally, since esoteric texts were never intended for the eyes or understanding of the layman.

We know that the Egyptians built the pyramids and aligned them with the stars ... they were obviously descended from generations of star-gazers, so why shouldn't they be aware of the movement of certain stars between the northern and southern hemispheres, just as modern astronomers are today. They may not have been able to explain the phenomena, but that does not mean they weren't aware of it, just as they were aware of the shifting position of the Milky Way in the heavens throughout the changing months of the year. The dual-headed god, Aker, was the guardian of the entrance and exit of the underworld; with one head facing east and the other west: and only places of mystical/magical significance would have been included in the Pyramid Texts.

Sir Norman Lockyer, one of the great Victorian astronomers, recorded his observations of this ancient science in *The Dawn of Astronomy*, first published in 1894.

The various apparent movements of the heavenly bodies which are produced by the rotation and the revolution of the earth, and the effects of precession, were familiar to the ancient Egyptians, however ignorant they may have been of their causes; they carefully studied what they saw, and attempted to put their knowledge together in the most convenient fashion, associating it with their strange imaginings and their system of worship.

In her Introduction to Christian Jacq's earlier edition of *Egyptian Magic*, Rosalie David stated that for the Egyptians, *magic was regarded as an exact science in its highest form*, its secrets revealed only to the highest orders of priesthood. This area of magic was used as a system of defence, and played an important role in the service of the State, protecting the country and its king. In reality, however, by the end of the Old Kingdom, Egypt's 'Golden Age' was over as the land was plunged into anarchy and chaos as revolution overturned the old established order.

From pre-dynastic times, right up until the collapse of the Old Kingdom, the king, was considered personally responsible for the wellbeing and stability of the Land and its people. He was the intermediary between gods and men, and his role in life was to ensure this equilibrium was maintained via the channels of daily prayers and offerings at the temple. If the king did not fulfil his daily obligations to the gods on behalf of his people, then there *was* the danger of plunging everything back into Chaos and darkness from which it had originally sprung. We also know from historical evidence that around the end of the Old Kingdom, this system did, in fact, break down.

Archaeologists argue over whether the cause for such social catastrophe was due to several long years of famine, or civil unrest against the established system of a failing monarchy, but recent excavations suggest that it could have been a combination of both. During work at the temple site of Mendes, in Lower Egypt, during 1999-2000, Professor Donald B Redford's team discovered under the Dynasty XVIII foundations, human remains dating to the second half of Dynasty VI.

> *Found sprawled where they had fallen ... were the remains, in whole or in part, of 20 human individuals of all ages and sexes. Some lay in piles: an old woman over an old man who in turn lay over a child; others lay singly: two adult males beside a slain pig. A young teen had fallen ... clutching a rodent of all things! Not a few had been dismembered as they lay. Following the slaughter (for such it surely was) came the destruction: parts of the mud-brick structure, which can only be the temple itself, had been demolished, and the debris allowed to fall on the bodies. Then someone had set fire to some combustibles and a conflagration had ensured, sending more fired and reddened brick cascading over the area ...'*
> [*The Akhenaten Temple Project Newsletter*, ed. Susan Redford]

The excavation revealed that a number of people had perished in the destruction – the team having recovered the remains of 20 – with many sprawled in groups, attempting to flee the temple, and in the aftermath no one returned to retrieve the corpses for burial. At other sites dating from the same period (Dynasty VI), excavations have uncovered mass graves, which indicate that people died, or were killed in large enough numbers that traditional burial was impossible. Whatever happened at the end of Dynasty VI, the Old Order that had lasted for so long was finally shattered by social revolution. This affected the whole governing system as the different classes threw off their burden of obligation and resorted to violence, bringing about a revolutionary upheaval that destroyed the ancient customs and traditional religious practice forever. Archaeological evidence indicates that the fury of the mob spared neither temples nor royal monuments; even the archives of government buildings, and tombs were not respected.

From the cemeteries of the great, blocks of stone were removed and used for the tombs of little men. As a result a whole world was rent asunder ... For more than a century, social and religious values declined until the country reverted to a primitive state not seen in the Nile Valley since pre-dynastic times. Those remnants of the old traditions, which remained after the radical upheaval, were combined and modified to form a new mode of social existence in the new order, but the soul of ancient Egypt never recovered completely from the shock of this decisive change. [*Egypt*, K Lange and M Hirmer]

This social upheaval, which destroyed the elitism of the Old Kingdom, needed to be brought back under control, and religion for the masses has always proved to have a uniting or calming effect on civic unrest. While the Sun-god remained the deity of the ruling family, the Theban priesthood had cornered the market with their own particular brand of evangelism; the propaganda machine geared into action, introducing the Cult of Osiris, which subsequent Greek historians faithfully recorded for posterity as if nothing else had ever existed.

What history *doesn't* tell us is what happened to the priesthood of the old stellar-cult following this revolutionary uprising? *If* the discoveries at the Temple of the Divine Cult of *Ba-neb-djed* ('Ram-Lord of Djedet') at Mendes are anything to go by, it is possible that many of the stellar-priesthood were butchered within the confines of their own temples. *If* the people believed the gods had deserted them, then someone would need to be held to account – and who more appropriate that the priests who had failed to serve them. *If* such massacres took place, then some of the priests (along with their families) would have been forced to flee the country, taking their vast stores of magico-religious knowledge with them.

Logic and historical precedence tells us that isolated pockets of Egyptian 'magi' would have survived, both inside and outside Egypt since it is impossible, either by legislation or genocide, to wipe a faith out of existence. There are subtle hints that the Mysteries still played an important part in Egyptian royal worship right up until Dynasty XIX, but this would have been a private affair, hidden from the scrutiny of the public and the lower echelons of the priesthood. Nevertheless, oral traditions can be incredibly tenacious, especially those that have been subjected to local variations and, in this manner, quite a considerable amount of stellar wisdom would have spread around the Mediterranean as the exiles moved further away from their native land – just as much later material would survive in the form of *Hermetic* texts.

To summarise: from a very early stage in their long history, the Egyptians were familiar with certain identifiable astronomical phenomena. As Christian Jacq observes in *Egyptian Magic:* 'We find ourselves faced with a sacred science which needs specialists trained for many years to grasp the most secret forces of the Universe …' Consider for a moment:

- They had calculated that the calendar consisted of 365 days [although did not take the necessity of the leap-year into account].

- They understood that precession forced the calendar out of alignment, resulting in the civil and astronomical calendars only coinciding every 1,460 years.

- There are a number of artefacts dating from the Old Kingdom that appear to have come from naturally occurring meteoric iron.

- From at least as early as the Middle Kingdom, they recognised five of the planets in our solar system.

- They used an early form of astrolabe to align the foundation of the pyramids and sun-temples with the cardinal points and constellations, with an error of less than half a degree.

- The early Greek credited them with formulating the zodiac despite the fact that the idea of astrology didn't reach Egypt until the Ptolemaic age and the famous 'Egyptian zodiac' at Dendera is of Babylonian origin.

- They plotted and charted the movement of stars and constellations.

- They believed we come from the stars and return to the stars when we die.

- They also believed that all elements of life, both animate and inanimate, were animated by a force or energy and that the spiritual and material were woven from the same substance.

But even if this 'sacred science' was of little interest (or use) to the usurping Osirian, or great Theban priesthoods, the ancient stellar-wisdom continued to flow along like a stream of unconscious thought throughout the remaining march of Egyptian history. And Osirian funerary rites still followed the tradition of painting the ceilings of tombs with stars and the image of the archaic star-goddess. In *Daily Life of the Egyptian Gods*, however, the authors offer a more tantalising glimpse of Egypt's concept of the heavens.

*The sky, both the portion that men could see and the portion that remained hidden from them, was incarnated by the body of a woman who took her place on high in the final stages of creation. This body, that of the goddess Nut, represented the limits of the domain Re travelled through every day. It made it possible to put the entire mechanism of the universe into place and established the framework of the organised world, of which it was an integral, concrete part. But Nut's body and the area delimited by it did not constitute the whole of existing space. Beyond it were regions the sun never reached. Unknown to the other gods, or even to the dead, **this peripheral zone was shrouded in eternal darkness: the sun never rose there. It would one day serve as the creator's ultimate refuge: he would return to it when the world came to an end ...***

*By day or by night, Nut offered a space for men to observe. Yet what they saw only hinted at all that was concealed from them. The heavenly bodies – no matter which ones were involved and no matter when one observed them – **were but the luminous images of a vaster whole one could only guess at. The more intense the light – and the sun's is intense – the more it hid, and the more effectively it prevented people from looking at it** ... men received all manner of things from the day sky; from the night sky, they had all manner of things to learn. The Sun had knowledge of all the space he travelled through; but he delegated the nocturnal space of knowledge to the god of the moon, Thoth.* [Author uses **bold** for added emphasis. MD]

29

The Atlantis Syndrome

Before the dawning of the science of Egyptology and the deciphering of the hieroglyphs, much of what passed for early authority on the subject of history and the religious beliefs of Egypt was taken from the Greek historian, Herodotus (480-425BC). Exiled from his homeland as a young man, he travelled widely in Egypt and in other parts of the Greek world, and relied much on what he was told by foreigners when writing *Book 2* of his *History*. As a result, the historical errors arose from the untrustworthiness of his sources, i.e. the contemporary Egyptian priesthood, who would no doubt have delighted in telling a visiting historian tall-tales about Egypt's great past.

By the time Herodotus visited Egypt, it was during what is referred to chronologically as Dynasty XXVII, the First Persian Period, and had been under Persian rule for almost a hundred years. His writings also reflect the later 'Greek propaganda' that was to colour views of the Persian dynasty, at a time when the 'Old Religion' of stellar worship was all but forgotten outside the realms of folklore and funerary customs. By then, most of the Egyptian deities had been assimilated with the Greek pantheon, and it is from Herodotus that many of the Graeco-Egyptian names of the gods, as we know them today, passed into the history books.

By reading Herodotus, we can see that nothing remained of the old religious beliefs of archaic Egypt and yet ... there must have been some 'magical truths' hidden in those tall stories that had filtered down to the Graeco-Roman world. Perhaps there is room here for a *personal* theory that Plato's concept of 'Atlantis' partly had its roots in the collapse of Egypt's Old Order: an age that had lasted for so long but was finally shattered, destroying established customs and traditional magico-religious practice in its wake.

When Plato (427-348BC) wrote about Atlantis in his *Timaeus* and the incomplete *Critias,* he was in old age and was also living through 'disillusioning times'. Taking the explanation for Plato's work from *The Atlantis Syndrome*, Paul Jordan writes that is was *'a basically rationalistic attempt to arrive at a system of absolute validity not only in scientific terms but also in the realms of politics, law, ethics and theology'*. In short, Plato was trying to come up with a universal philosophy for 'an ideal state in a far from perfect world', but first he had to grab the contemporary world's attention, and force it back from the brink of the chaos into which it was about to descend, by using shock tactics.

The basis for *Timaeus*, is an imaginary conversation between Socrates and his friends, which took place in 421BC, during an annual Athenian festival, in which Socrates advocates an ideal, self-sufficient state where everyone knows their place, and no one engages in trade, or piles up unnecessary wealth. A classic demonstration of good old-fashioned Athenian intellectual snobbery! Nevertheless, Plato realised that the Athenian establishment would not take kindly to being publicly denounced as being a corrupt, godless bunch, since it was only in 399BC that Socrates himself had been executed for 'introducing new deities and corrupting youth' following his public comments on the weaknesses of democratic governments.

Plato did what any good fiction writer of today would do, and that was to draw on familiar historical happenings of his world as a setting for the 'plot'. The great famine and social uprising during Egypt's Old Kingdom was probably still part of Mediterranean folklore and the principal character, *Critias*, tells of the origins of the Atlantis legend as coming from the priesthood of Egypt *'who opened his eyes to the long-forgotten history ...'* and no doubt to the fount of all wisdom and knowledge as well. Modern archaeology has revealed evidence of the destruction of a particular Minoan community on Santorini (the Greek name was Thera), when the volcano erupted and the whole island disappeared beneath the waves. The additional collapse of Cretan culture, at much the same time, no doubt also played its part in the creation of the Atlantis myth and the 'detailed' plan of Atlantis with its inner and outer cities and harbour, bears more than a passing resemblance to a passage in the *Odyssey* ... and Plato would have known his Homer.

The story tells of divine wrath against the luckless Atlanteans for their 'greedy pursuit of wealth and power for its own sake, and to the loss of their own virtue' and a whole range of ancient authors regarded Atlantis as a pure form of allegory **... which is what Plato had intended.** Paul Jordan sums it up as follows:

> *Atlantis started with Plato and in his hands it was never a super-civilisation of the sort conjectured by later authors; perhaps in strictly Greek* [philosophical] *terms it was no civilisation at all but rather a fatally luxurious elaboration of an essentially barbarian way of life, for all its inception by a god. At all events, it was no seminal civilisation: it wasn't the* fons et origo *of all later civilisations in the world, indeed Athens was its independent contemporary. Both Atlantis and old Athens were, for Plato, but episodes in the ever-ongoing cycle of catastrophes and renewals that he saw as the most rational and scientific interpretation to which the field of*

31

human experience could be subjected. For him, science and religion were quite bound up together, so that the natural catastrophes were at the same time eras in which the divine light was withdrawn from the world and the equally natural renewals were times when it returned ...

But what of the legendary 'wisdom' that survivors from Atlantis were supposed to have carried with them to the far flung corners of the earth? The author merely puts forward the suggestion that this *was* the old pre-dynastic stellar-wisdom, carried into exile by the surviving priesthood and their families of the Egyptian Old Kingdom, fleeing from banishment and massacre. Nevertheless ...

- It would explain why there are familiar refrains underlying the Inner Mysteries of the various Western Traditions.

- It would explain why historians and archaeologists periodically discover some dubious 'Egyptian' influence among early European artefacts.

- It would explain why some people are inexplicably drawn to the anthropomorphic deities of proto-dynastic Egypt, when in Western culture these images would normally be viewed as demonic.

- It would explain why the early Church was so keen to stamp out 'the domination of the stars', and why St Paul wrote condemning the practice of astrology at some length.

But people in the ancient world would often hark back to 'that which is never fully remembered, and yet never fully forgotten'. Lucretius, the great Roman philosophical poet lived at a time when the old Roman religion had lost its hold on the educated classes 'and a general scepticism prevailed; but the gloom and uncertainty of the times no doubt rendered people superstition and nervous.' In his *De Rerum Natura (On The Nature of Things)*, we find echoes of the classical Egyptian view of the cosmos, its dangers, and the fact that life itself emanated from deep space and subsequently returns to it, which was also prevalent among other earlier Greek philosophers such as Leucippus, Epicurus and Democritus.

Democritus (c460BC), hailed as the greatest of the Greek physical philosophers, had himself travelled extensively in Egypt and Asia in pursuit of learning, and lived to a great age. He settled in Egypt for seven years, during which time he studied the mathematical and physical systems of the ancient schools, although according to the entry in the *Encyclopaedia Britannica*, the extent to which he was influenced by the magi and the eastern astrologers is a matter for pure conjecture. He adopted and developed the earlier atomistic doctrine of Leucippus, believing that the atoms of which the universe is composed were similar in quality but differing in volume and form, moved about in space – and were variously grouped into bodies: but whereas the latter decay and perish, the atoms themselves are eternal. (***Nothing can arise out of nothing; nothing can be reduced to nothing***).

Despite access to the Egyptian Creation myths, Democritus rejected the notion of a deity being instrumental in the creation of the universe, but acknowledged the existence of a class of 'beings', of the same form as men, but grander and composed of even more subtle atoms: less liable to dissolution, but still mortal, that dwelled in the upper regions of air. According to Plutarch, Democritus recognised the One God in the form of a fiery sphere – the soul of the world – *the anima mundi* – and he attributed the popular belief in 'gods' to offer an explanation for extraordinary phenomena (thunder, lightning, earthquakes) as reference to superhuman agency.

Lucretius (99BC-55AD) believed that: *'After an invocation of Venus, the great creative force of nature, sets forth the atomic theory of Epicurus, which satisfactorily explains, and alone explains, the phenomena of the world. The atoms, infinite in number and eternal, endlessly falling through space by their own nature, colliding when they swerve a little from their path, form into masses, from which the universe by chance arrangement is built up.'* [*The Oxford Companion to Classical Literature*] Lucretius, however, held that: *'this universe and all that is in it act according to law, and there is no room in it for the gods and their interference. Popular religion and the terrors introduced by it have no foundation ... The soul, material in its nature, though composed of extremely rarefied elements, is mortal and dies with the body.'*

Two philosophers, one Greek and one Roman writing almost 400 years apart, and expounding similar theories to those pre-dynastic beliefs that existed in Egypt some 2,500 years earlier – that all life came from and returns to the stars. Alexandria housed the greatest library of the ancient world and contained texts from all over the known world, plus thousands of manuscripts from Egypt itself. Was it from this source that the ancient wisdom passed into the writings of later scholars? And was this the real reason for the library's destruction?

An Introduction to the Hermetica also suggests that Plato (or rather his teacher Socrates) also learnt much of what he put down in the *Timaeus* from Egyptian sources, and that both Plato and the later Christian writer who compiled the *Hermetica* drew on a common source – supposedly the secret teachings handed down by Egyptian Initiates. Did Democritus find evidence to support his atomistic theory in the Great Library, and what other great stellar secrets were destroyed by Roman arsonists?

The classic atomistic theory offered that: 'the endless variety of substances known to man can be explained if matter is assumed to be composed of small indivisible and indestructible particles – or atoms.' In all its various forms, however, the atomism of the ancient Greeks (and later the Romans) was a philosophic rather than a scientific doctrine, and although as a philosopher, Lucretius might not pay homage to the old gods, his *De Rerum Natura* left no doubts as to what he believed would someday happen to the planet: and it was not divine retribution:

And so some day,
The mighty ramparts of the mighty universe
Ringed round with hostile force,
Will yield and face decay and come crumbling to ruin.

In fact, a belief in some form of Armageddon is deep-rooted in most religions and cultures (both ancient and modern) just the same as most cultures have similar flood myths, often involving some object arriving from the sky with catastrophic consequences. In 1694, Sir Edmond Halley (he of comet fame) presented a lecture to the Royal Society of London, in which he expressed the view that the story of the biblical flood may have been a result of cometary impact. This suggestion was too much for the Church of the time, because his explanation of the flood threatened the concept of divine intervention, and so his ideas were quickly suppressed!

The Setian

With all these cosmic goings-on, it is little wonder that the ancients spoke of wondrous visions in the sky, moving across the heavens and causing widespread panic and consternation. With no light pollution to obscure the view, much more would have been seen of this inter-stellar activity. Comet Halley has re-appeared every 76 years for more than two millennia, periodically manifesting brighter than the planets with its highly distinctive tail and its comparatively swift motion when approaching the Earth. For the Egyptians, there was only one god responsible for all this highly volatile aerial activity: Set.

Posterity has attributed a demonic role to 'this most unloved of all the ancient Egyptian gods' but as we know, recorded history is always the province of the victor. As Alan Richardson wrote in his Introduction to *The Setian*:

> *The venom that came to be directed toward Set became so intense that any fair-minded researcher eventually pauses to ask whether any deity could be* that *bad – or whether in fact, something else was going on behind the scenes. Any serious study of archaic Egypt inevitably unearths fragments of worship from times when Set was the deity of choice for the common folk, long before the usurper Osiris came on the scene. They worshipped him, not because they feared his power, but perhaps because they understood the qualities of Night and Darkness better than we do today.*

As we discussed earlier, the 'body' of the goddess Nut did not constitute the whole of existing space. *Beyond* her starry form were regions that only hinted at all that was concealed from the early astronomer-priesthood. The distant heavenly bodies of deep space were merely the luminous images of a vaster whole, about which they could only speculate. This then, was the realm attributed to Set: the realm of spirit to where the dead returned after the correct funerary rites had been performed, and the soul of the king made its final journey in the company of the mighty psychopomp, the 'Son of Nut'.

Set's original role in the ancient Mysteries was (in the company of Horus the Elder) to escort the deceased king to take his place among his ancestors and, as we have seen from the Pyramid Texts, there *is* evidence of these earliest beliefs, which held that the soul returned to the stars after the death of the body. This belief harks back to an even remoter time when the indigenous Egyptians worshipped a stellar-goddess who, in dynastic times, became known as Nut; the origins of Setian belief can also be traced back to the Egyptian stellar or cosmic religion at the dawn of their civilisation. Again we remind ourselves that the *Berlin Papyrus 3024* expresses these Setian sentiments in referring to the Mysteries:

Brother, As long as you burn you belong to life.
You say you want ME with you in the Beyond!
Forget the Beyond!
When you bring your flesh to rest
And thus reach the Beyond,

In that stillness shall I alight on you;
Thus united we shall form the Abode.
For above is exalted by below
As is written in the Scriptures.

Just as the emerging Christian Church made a point of stamping out 'the domination of the stars', it was merely following the attempts of the Osirian priesthood who tried (and failed) to eliminate the Setian-stellar religion over 2,000 years earlier. Even after the collapse of the Old Ways at the end of the Pyramid Age, there was still nothing the Egyptians feared more than the descent into Chaos, that negative state and the opposite of Ma'at – the order of all things. Set was the god of Chaos, pure primordial energy that fuelled the Will of the individual as opposed to a society that held Ma'at (order and harmony) as sacrosanct. By demonising Set, the Osirian priesthood created their own 'imbalance', albeit a benign one: but good intentions were not enough if the disorder (which has been the ultimate fate of every subsequent civilisation), was to be avoided.

Despite all the 'bad press', however, Egyptologists are now beginning to look behind the myth and recognise that throughout the empire, Set remained a royal god and patron of the King. Hilary Wilson in *People of the Pharaohs* explains: 'The patronage of Horus and Set was an essential aspect of the overall duality of Egypt itself'. The Pyramid Texts include references to the role of the Two Lords, as in the hymn for 'awakening' the dead King: '…Cause the Two Lands to bow to this King even as they bow to Horus; cause the Two Lands to dread this King even as they dread Set.'… Set continued to be shown as a tutor of the King, especially in the arts of war.'

To quote the narrator from the film version of *The Lord of the Rings*: **'The world is changed. Much that once was, is lost, for none now live who remember it. History became legend, legend became myth and some things that should not have been forgotten were lost …'**

But, like the Ring in that fabulous fictional quest, some things can lie dormant for many centuries before bursting into life again, if only we know *how* to look. The widely travelled Strabo, writing in his 17-volume *Geographica*, says: 'All discussion respecting the gods requires an examination of ancient opinions, and of fables, since the ancients expressed enigmatically their physical notions concerning the nature of things, and always intermixed fable with their discoveries.'

In other words, even from classical times we were being warned against taking things literally when it comes to the interpretation of ancient texts. The Egyptians themselves, held that 'God is hidden, and no man knoweth his form', so why should we expect to pick up a collection of ancient esoteric writings and be handed the secrets of the Universe on a platter, without bothering to seek for the answers. For 15 years, scholar George St Clair (*Creation Records*, 1898) conducted a systematic study of Egyptian mythology and among the results he concluded that:

- The myths of Egypt were all related to one another, and were neither separate fables nor idle fantasies.

- They revealed an astro-religious system and told a true story of astronomical progress, calendar correction, and theological changes, from before the time of written histories.

- An era not far removed from the traditional Creation was an important era in history, but not the Beginning.

- They had a good deal of knowledge of astronomy; they discovered that the Earth was a globe; and they were acquainted with the precession of the equinoxes, though they did not know its cause.

- The magnificence of their temples bears witness to the seriousness of their piety, and the after-history of the world shows how deep were the impressions made so early by those priesthoods.

St Clair also realised that:

this Wisdom is so ancient that it passed out of knowledge 2,000 years ago [sic]; *the language was dead, the clue to the allegory was lost, and Plutarch protests against those who would seek to rationalise it ... The discovery of the key does not mean that all the doors can be unlocked at once by an unpractised hand.* [The] *task has been like that of rebuilding an overthrown structure, and showing that what seemed to be only a chance melody of stones was the ruin of a majestic temple. The proof is in the manifest design, when the parts are put together again ...*

37

We must also remember that in Egypt those early priests *were* astronomers, and that there were probably no astronomers who were not members of the priesthood. The study of the stars was unequivocally a priestly business and shows why it is impossible to disconnect Egyptian belief from astronomy. According to St Clair, we also have to accept that nearly everything in its early religious symbology appears to be mythical or mysterious, and embraces certain astronomical 'facts', in order to reproduce a harmony between terrestrial and celestial phenomena.

Although George St Clair's identification of the deities is often incorrect, or out of chronological sequence (his writing and knowledge were products of his time), his *Creation Records* offer us a template by which to pursue our quest of this ancient stellar wisdom.

Two things are required in order to unravel the Egyptian system of mythology, the first being a knowledge of the astronomical clues, and the second an acquaintance with the natural language of symbols ... The facts and ideas of the Egyptian astro-religious system are set forth by emblems or symbols [hieroglyphics], as for example when the returning year is indicated by a migratory bird, an annual visitant (i.e. the swallow); and the repetition of the cycles of time is represented as the renewal of the life of the phoenix (i.e. the blue heron). When the astronomical facts and phenomena are numerous and run into narrative, the symbolical relation extends itself into allegory. The mythology of Egypt is chiefly an allegory of the heavens and the calendar. The language of this allegory has long been lost, but it is recoverable ...

For those well-versed in the language [i.e. correspondences] of magic, it is easy to grasp how natural this language of symbols is, and how easy and obvious (in some instances) is the interpretation. George St Clair goes on:

When we find the god Amun ram-headed, we may suspect that he is connected with the ram-constellation, and that what is stated concerning Amun will be found true of Aries, if we know how to interpret it ... Among the sacred animals of the Egyptians was the scarabæus, a beetle common in the country. But the Egyptians did not worship the beetle itself, they only reverenced it as a symbol of the sun, or as being in some other way an emblem of time ...

By now, the seeker will have realised that the language of the old stellar Mysteries (like all Higher Magic) has always been made up of allegory, symbol and metaphor. Mystical truths that are concealed behind symbolic narrative; emblems that traditionally represent something else; and figures of speech by which a thing is spoken of as being that which it only resembles. By confining his (or her) studies to book-learning, the seeker cannot even begin to grasp the immense store of energy that is generated in this uncharted sphere of the cosmos.

What we also need to contemplate, is that *if* the old stellar priesthood of Egypt was forced to flee and live in exile, then the remnants of the Mysteries they took with them to foreign lands may been partially absorbed into the cultures that welcomed them, thereby preserving the 'key' that has been waiting for thousands of years to be rediscovered. And *if* we really wish to rediscover these ancient powers, then we must turn our attention to the stars.

Question:
But what exactly is this stellar wisdom? And what could a revivalist star-worship offer us in an age of computer technology, when a space probe is capable of examining Saturn's rings at close quarters? Why should we need to resurrect primitive beliefs, reminiscent of the worst kind of superstition and astrological mumbo-jumbo?

Answer:
To finally understand and embrace the true meaning of everlasting Life; a concept that drove the Egyptians to build the pyramids and seek to preserve their dead for eternity. The old stellar religion might have gone into the Shadows after the civil uprising at the end of the Pyramid Age, but modern science can help the modern seeker to subscribe to this knowledge where successive generations of the Egyptian priesthood failed.

"Set seems to have been a generic name applied to the northern (?circumpolar) constellations, perhaps because Set/Darkness, and these stars, being always visible in the night, may have typified it. The Thigh [Ursa Major] was the thigh of Set."

[*The Dawn of Astronomy*, Norman Lockyer]

According to Maspero, Set formed one of the divine dynasties at Annu, and the northern stars seem to have been worshipped there ... In short, in Lower Egypt the temples are pointed to rising stars near the north point of the horizon or setting north of west. In Upper Egypt, we deal chiefly with temples directed to stars rising in the south-east or setting low in the south-west ... Now with regard to the northern stars observed rising in high amplitudes, we found traces of their worship in times so remote that in all probability at Annu and Denderah a Ursae Majoris *was used before it became circumpolar.*

Part Two: Iron In The Soul
"Learn the secret that hath not yet been revealed."
Liber AL Vel Legis pt 2 v.2

So far all we have is a potted history of early astronomy and astrology, combining history, ancient beliefs and superstition with 16th century occultism and New Age mysticism – none of which can be regarded as having the least connection with science or astro-physics, and a relevance of ancient Egyptian beliefs in the 21st century!

Or can they?

Back in the late 1960s there were mixed feelings about the first lunar landing because it ostensibly debunked the mysterious influence the moon had held over mankind for thousands of years thereby 'reducing the goddess Diana to a lump of sterile clay'. Sceptic Owen S Rachleff in the *The Secrets of Superstitions*, wrote scathingly about those he termed as 'stargazers':

> *True, the Aquarian Age implies wonder and adventure and far-reaching exploration, but not the type of exploration that will destroy their myths and dreams. Don't tell them astrology is unscientific and out of step with astronomy ... Aquarius is a giver of dreams, a sustainer of illusions, not someone who strips away the veil of mystery and leaves them naked in the ice-cold climate of space.*

Agreed the lunar landing did strip away the 'dream-veil' but in doing so, science gave an even more tantalising view of the cosmos and to be frank, *serious* occultists are made of sterner stuff. Rather than destroying the illusion of mystery, science offered a much more enthralling view of the stars than the ancient astronomer-priesthoods could ever have imagined. Those more discerning occultists who were also students of

41

their own cultural history swiftly drew parallels between the ancient stellar wisdom and new astronomical discoveries. Rather than disproving the fragmented, esoteric teachings that had filtered down through the ages, it *confirmed* that the ancients had indeed, had their fingers on the cosmic pulse.

What the ancients *didn't* know, of course, was that the Universe began in a colossal explosion, in which energy, space, time and matter were created. With the aid of modern science, however, we can now trace the history of the Universe to within a minute fraction of a second after the Big Bang. We can also see the way the Universe expanded from its primeval origins, and how the material that emerged from this cosmic explosion, served to determine its ultimate future. The fact is inescapable: the beginning and the end of the Universe are inextricably intertwined ... **as the ancient Egyptians instinctively understood.**

In recent years, science has proved that instead of slowing down as was first thought, the universe is speeding up and that there is a vast energy field out in deepest space that is denser than all previous studies had indicated. Nearer to home (Earth), the Voyager space probes also showed that instead of just 'dull, crated rocks' there is still a considerable amount of volcanic activity and icy splendour on the many moons that circle the planets – not to mention the twenty-two new moons that were discovered in the process. The Hubble space telescope has since identified a previous unknown planet outside our own solar system, which astronomers think was only created 1,000 years ago – adding to the proof that the universe, of which we are a small insignificant part, is indeed a living, growing thing.

All this deep-space probing, however, also revealed other, more alarming things. In *The Last Three Minutes,* Professor Paul Davies wrote:

"The universe itself is subject to physical laws that impose upon it a life cycle of its own: birth, evolution, and – perhaps – death. Our own fate is entangled inextricably with the fate of the stars. Astronomical research points to a universe that has a limited life span. It came into existence at some finite time in the past, it is currently vibrant with activity, but it is inevitably degenerating towards a heat death at some stage in the future. Whatever we would like to believe, the stars cannot have been burning forever, because they would have long since run out of fuel. The fact that they are burning now implies that the universe must have come into existence at a finite time in the past."

42

We have to accept that there are certainly lots of nasty things that could happen to Earth, a puny object in a universe pervaded by violent forces ... but the secret of our success on planet Earth, according to Davies, is space. Lots of it. Our solar system is a tiny island of activity in an ocean of emptiness. The nearest star (after the Sun) lies more than four light years away – some twenty trillion miles – and all this space means that cosmic collisions are rare.

"The greatest threat to Earth is probably from our own backyard. Asteroids do not normally orbit close to Earth; they are largely confined to the belt between Mars and Jupiter. But the huge mass of Jupiter can disturb the asteroids' orbits, occasionally sending one of them plunging towards the Sun, and this menacing the Earth ... Comets pose another threat but rarely does a comet collide with Earth. Giant clouds of cosmic gas can drastically alter the solar wind and may affect the heat flow from the Sun. Other more sinister objects may lurk in the inky depths of space – rogue planets, neutron stars, brown dwarfs, black holes – all these and more could come upon us unseen, without warning, and wreak havoc within the solar system."

When the comet Swift-Tuttle was visible in 1993, there was a flurry of early calculations that suggested a collision was a distinct possibility in the year 2126. Since then, space agencies have revised their calculations and imparted the reassuring news that the comet will miss the Earth by two weeks! Sooner or later, however, Swift-Tuttle, or an object like it, will hit the Earth and "many of the myriad of 'astronomical interlopers' are capable of causing more damage than all the world's nuclear weapons put together". It is only a matter of time before a comet or asteroid collides with the Earth, causing the abrupt demise of mankind.

For the planet Earth, however, during its long life span, such events have been more or less routine, since cometary or asteroid impacts of this magnitude have occurred on average, every few million years. In fact, the mass of meteoric debris that strikes the Earth each year is estimated to be around 40,000 tons in the form of small (subgram) particles, not to mention the 160,000 tons per annum of 'massive bodies' in the form of infrequent asteroids and comets that enter the Earth's atmosphere. Cheerfully, Professor Davies carries on:

"Looking further afield, astronomers have observed entire galaxies in apparent collision. And there is some evidence, in the very rapid movement of certain stars, that the Milky Way may have already been disrupted by collisions with small nearby galaxies. These collisions,

however, do not necessarily spell disaster for their constituent stars. Galaxies are so sparely populated that they can merge into one another without individual stellar collisions."

Nevertheless, if a 500-meter asteroid crashed into the Earth in some remote region such as the Australian Outback, or the Sahara, it would devastate an area of about 160,000 square kilometres and cause substantial damage over a far greater region, according to research astronomer, Duncan Steel [*Rogue Asteroids & Doomsday Comets*]. He observes that the consequences of the same asteroid arriving a few hours earlier and perhaps landing in the Pacific Ocean New Zealand and Tahiti would be far worse, since the impact would generate an enormous *tsunami* – the huge ocean wave normally caused by earthquakes.

Japan has been the constant victim of these devastating *tsunamis* originating from earthquakes as far away as South America and travelling across the Pacific Ocean. The major damage resulting from the huge momentum being released as the waves reached the continental shelf at the edge of the Japanese coast. Other Pacific islands have also suffered from *tsunamis,* but due to the fact that most are the tips of sub-ocean volcanic peaks, the tsunami can flow around them, rather than break over them as happens when they encounter the continental shelf. The worst *tsunami* in recent history being Boxing Day 2004 when 275,000 people were killed in fourteen countries across two continents around the Indian Ocean, with the last two fatalities being swept out to sea in South Africa, more than twelve hours after the earthquake.

The threat of *tsunamis* caused by the impact of the hypothetical 500-meter asteroid would cause a tidal wave several kilometres in height. And impact between New Zealand and Tahiti would produce a tsunami some 200-300 metres high breaking on Japan and, as Duncan Steel observes, "heaven help New Zealand and Tahiti themselves."

Evidence that devastation of this magnitude has occurred before is suggested by the fact that although the large islands of Australia and New Guinea have been inhabited for the past 40,000 years, it was not until the last 5,000 that the small Pacific islands have been populated. "We might therefore speculate whether past impacts produced *tsunamis* that swept the pacific islands clear of humans in some earlier period," suggests Steel.

But it's not only asteroids and comets that should cause us concern. M31 is the only large galaxy apart from the Milky Way that can be seen with the naked eye, and the most distinct object in the universe visible without instruments. On a dark night M31 appears as a small, fuzzy blob of light but it will not always be so faint and distant because it is rushing towards us at a speed of 300,000 miles an hour. Today it lies 2.2 million light-years away but if it continues on its present course for the next three billion years, it will eventually collide with the Milky Way.

M31 is a 'cannibal' galaxy. It consists of two galaxies, which long ago devoured each other and, according to astronomers, our galaxy will be its next meal! A few hundred thousand years before this happens, the sky will bee filled with the vast brilliance of M31. Eventually two bands of light will arch overhead, like two Milky Ways. There will be few stellar collisions because the stars are so far apart, but the stars will be much more densely packed. So much so, in fact, that the night sky would be bright enough for us to read by.

The concept of a continuously expanding Universe is often beyond the comprehension of most people, especially those who misguidedly feel that mankind rules the Earth; or that their 'earthly gods' are omnipresent and omnipotent. And one particular detail that is extremely difficult to swallow (particularly from established religions' point of view) is that God's Earth and its inhabitants are *not* the centre of the Universe. We need to get to grip with the fact that space is elastic, and can bend or stretch, depending on the gravitational properties of the material in it ... and neither does the rate at which the Universe expands remain constant with time. This again, is due to the force of gravity, which acts between thee galaxies – and, indeed, between all forms of matter and energy in the universe, over which we have no control.

The Universe began in a colossal explosion, in which energy, space, time and matter were created – and with the aid of modern science and computer simulations, we can now trace the history of the Universe to within a minute fraction of a second after the Big Bang. We can also see the way the Universe expanded from its primeval origins; and how the material that emerged from this cosmic explosion, served to determine its ultimate future. The fact is inescapable: the beginning and the end of the Universe are inextricably intertwined.

Nearer to us, in terms of time and distance, on the night of 23-24th February 1987, high in the Andes, an off-duty astronomer taking a breath of fresh air, glanced up at the sky and noticed something unusual. On the edge of the nebulous patch of light known as the Large Magellanic Cloud was a star – a star that hadn't been there the night before. Astronomers around the world began watching the star (now named Supernova 1987A), and during subsequent months its behaviour was watched and recorded in meticulous detail.

Although the word *nova* means 'new' in Latin, Supernova 1987A was not the birth of a new star. It was *the death of an old one* with all the attendant cosmic fireworks to herald its passing. Only hours after its discovery, astronomers were able to identify which star, amongst the few billion contained in the Large Megellanic Cloud, was the one that had blown up. The stricken star was of a type known as a B3 blue super-giant, and its diameter was about forty times that of the Sun. It even had a name: Sanduleak 69 202.

The theory of exploding stars had been investigated during the 1950s but the impact of the visible demise of Sanduleak 69 202 gave a live performance of the 'ceaseless struggle with the forces of destruction' – or hell on a cosmic scales. All stars (including our own Sun) are simply balls of of gas held together by gravity. If gravity were the only force at work, they would instantly implode under their own immense weight and vanish within hours. The reason they don't is, as discussed in the first chapter, that the inward force of gravity is balanced by the outward force of the pressure of the compressed gas in the stellar interior. The interior of a star has an enormous pressure because it is so hot, and the energy it generates can sustain a star for billions of years, but when the fuel runs low, the star begins to lose its battle with gravity until it finally explodes. For a few days the star shines with the intensity of ten billion suns, only to fade away a few weeks later.

Our Sun is a typically low-mass star, steadily burning through its hydrogen fuel and turning its interior into helium. To prevent collapse, thee Sun must expand its nuclear activity outward, in search of fresh hydrogen – but meanwhile, the helium core gradually shrinks. As the aeons slip by, the Sun's appearance will imperceptibly alter as a result of these internal changes. It will swell in size, but its surface will cool, giving it a reddish hue. This trend will continue until the Sun turns into a red-giant star, perhaps five hundred times as big as it is now. Red giants are familiar to astronomers, and several bright stars such as Aldebaran (in Taurus), Betelgeuse (in Orion) and Arcturus (in Bootes), fall into this category: the red-giant phase marks the beginning of the end for a low-mass star.

Similarly, the Sun's planets will face a hard time some four billion years down the line: the Earth will become uninhabitable long before this, its oceans boiled away and its atmosphere stripped. As the Sun grows more distended, it will engulf Mercury, then Venus, and finally Earth within its fiery embrace and our planet will bee reduced to a cinder. It is our Sun's destiny to become a white-dwarf in the far distant future. Because the internal nuclear furnace will have shut down for good, there will be no reserves to replenish the slow leakage of hear radiation into the cool depths of space. Very slowly, the dwarf remnant of what was our might Sun will cool and dim, until it will fade out completely, merging quietly into the blackness of space.

Although a supernova spells death to the star, the explosion – like all natural cycles – *does* have a creative aspect to it: ***nothing can arise out of nothing; nothing can be reduced to nothing.***

Heavy elements beyond iron – such as gold, lead and uranium – are forged in that final and most intense of stellar furnaces. The enormous release of energy blasts these elements out into space to mingle with the detritus of countless other supernovas and, over the ensuing æons, these elements are scooped up into new generations of stars and planets.

Without the manufacture and dissemination of these elements, there could be no planets like the Earth. Life-giving carbon and oxygen, the gold in our banks, the lead sheeting on our roofs, the uranium fuel rods of our nuclear reactors – the iron in our blood, all owe their terrestrial presence to the death throes of stars that vanished well *before* our Sun existed. It is a humbling thought that the very stuff of our own bodies, here on Earth, is composed of the nuclear ash of long-dead stars … **as the ancient Egyptians instinctively understood.**

Marcus Chown describes this quite poetically but with plenty of good scientific data to back it up.

> *Every breath you take contains atoms forged in the blistering furnaces deep inside stars. Every flower you pick contains atoms blasted into space by stellar explosions that blazed brighter than a billion suns. Every book you read contains atoms blown across unimaginable gulfs of space and time by the winds between the stars ... If the atoms that make up the world around us could tell their stories, each and every one of them would sing a tale to dwarf the greatest epics of literature ... The iron in your blood, the calcium in your bones, the oxygen that fills your lungs each time you take a breath – all were baked in the fiery ovens deep within stars and blown out into space when those stars grew old, and perished. Every one of us is a memorial to long-dead stars. Every one of us was quite literally made in heaven ... For thousands of years, astrologers have been telling us that our lives are controlled by the stars. Well, they were right in spirit if not in detail. For science in the 20th century has revealed that we are far more intimately connected to events in the*

cosmos than anyone ever dared imagine. Each and every one of us is stardust made flesh ... '
[*The Magic Furnace*, Marcus Chown]

Heady stuff, but Chown isn't the only one to hammer home the fact that the atoms of 20th century science are the same as those referred to in the early atomistic theories of Democritus and Lucretius. When Lawrence Krauss formulated the idea for *Atom*, he chose to use an atom of oxygen, located in a drop of water, to tell the story ... *'because atoms, like people and dogs, and even cockroaches, have individual histories'.* This single atom could have been present in the cup of water taken by Ramesses II as he watched the construction of his mighty monuments. It could have been in a drop of sweat on Antony's brow as he waited in the marketplace for the arrival of Cleopatra, or the very first lap of floodwater to register on the original Nilometer. Or as Krauss would have it ... it could have been part of Julius Caesar's last breath.

At first this comes across as fanciful thinking, but imagine for a moment that the oxygen atoms we are breathing now are being continually redistributed again and again throughout the atmosphere on a time-frame of centuries *Nothing can arise out of nothing; nothing can be reduced to nothing*.

Remember that each oxygen atom in the breath we are taking at this very moment in time has had a unique history. Some histories are exotic, and others are not. For example: the ancient poetry of Amhairhin, a Druid poet who lived c400AD, shows how we are connected, each time we breathe in and out, to almost all the rest of life on Earth, today, and in the past. And before the Earth was formed, to the stars ... And by the same token, we are equally linked to the future ...

I am an estuary into the sea.

I am a wave of the ocean.
I am the sound of the sea.
I am a powerful ox.
    I am a hawk on a cliff.

I am a dewdrop in the sun.
I am a plant of beauty.
I am a boar for valour
    I am a salmon in a pool.

I am a lake in a plain.

I am the strength of art

A similar analogy was made by the renowned British astro-physicist, Sir Arthur Stanley Eddington: *'Take a cupful of liquid, label all the atoms in it so that you will recognise them again, and cast it into the sea; and let the atoms be diffused throughout all the oceans of the earth. Then draw out a cupful of sea-water anywhere; it will be found to contain some dozens of the labelled atoms.'* So, life begins with the process of star formation: we *are* made of stardust as the ancient Egyptian believed, but we still have to find the key to unlock the door of this ancient wisdom.

But if we are made of stardust, how did 'life' get here – or anywhere else for that matter. As John Gribbin wrote in *Stardust*: "Since the Earth, and everything on the Earth (including ourselves), is now seen as the natural by-product of the existence of stars and the Milky Way Galaxy in which we live, it is highly likely that other planets like the Earth, and other life forms like us, exist."

Gribbin also cites an old idea that has recently been revived and improved in the light of new astronomical knowledge, and a theory put forward by William Thomson back in 1871. Using an analogy of how life appears on a newly formed volcanic island, it was just a dozen years after Charles Darwin published his theory of evolution by natural selection: "We do not hesitate to assume that seed has been wasted through the air, or floated to it on a raft – we must regard it as probable in the highest degree that there are countless seed-bearing meteoric stones moving about through space. If at the present instant no life existed upon this Earth, one such stone falling upon it might, by what we blindly call natural causes, lead to it becoming covered with natural vegetation."

Eminent astronomers like Sir Fred Hoyle and his colleague Chandra Wickramasinghe also subscribed to the theory, albeit in a much advanced form, in view of the complex organic molecules discovered in the interstellar dust, containing 'structures indistinguishable from desiccated bacterial material'. "Could comets, that were formed in the early days of our planetary system, have harboured a sprinkling of viable microbes in warm watery pools at their centres," asked Professor Wickramasinghe in *Cosmic Dragons*, "and could life on Earth, once a dead planet, have been sparked by the fallout from a comet's tail, or even the collision with a comet?"

The theory of *panspermia* holds that the Earth was 'seeded' with life when celestial objects collided with Earth and while this idea had been discussed by the ancient Greek philosophers, the modernised theory did not gain much credence until the late 20th century. Recent experiments, however, prove that certain life forms can tolerate the intense doses of radiation, freezing temperate and vacuum pressures that a transplanetary journey through space would involve.

Bacteria are the most hardy of life forms and by creating endospores, which are tough and resilient protective coverings, bacteria enter a dormant state and can survive through all manner of trauma such as lack of nutrients and extreme temperatures. We also know that life = micro-organisms, can exist on Earth in the most inhospitable of places, where humans cannot. There are those that:

- Thrive in temperatures above boiling point in the oceanic thermal vents;

- Form entire ecologies present in the frozen wastes of thee Antarctic;

- Live in the Earth's crust some eight kilometres below the surface;

- Even thrive in nuclear reactors using enzymes to repair DNA damage.

As one scientific writer pointed out: "There is scarcely any set of conditions prevailing on Earth, no matter how extreme, that is incapable of harbouring some form of microbial life." If this is the case, then why shouldn't life, in some form or another, exist on some of the other 'inhospitable' planets in our solar system, and beyond?

As colossal as it is, a supernova explosion does not completely destroy a star. Although most of the material is dispersed by the cataclysm, the imploded core that triggered the event remains in place. It may form a ball of neutrons (the size of a small city) as a 'neutron star' or, if the force of gravity is so strong that it cannot resist further compression, in less than a milli-second it creates a black hole, and disappears into it.

It's a frightening thought that at present the Milky Way blazes with the light of a hundred billion stars, and *every one of them is doomed*. In ten billion years, most of what we see now will have faded from sight, snuffed out from a lack of fuel. But the Milky Way will still glow with starlight, for even as stars die, new ones are born to take their place. In the galaxy's spiral arms, such as the one in which our Sun is located, gas clouds become compressed, collapse under gravity, fragment, and produce a cascade of stellar births.

We also know that planets may form from the residual cloud of remnant gases and dust. "Stars have been observed condensing is this way," explains Professor Steel, "in one form of what astronomers call *nebulae*; when discussing the origin of the solar system, the cloud from which the Sun and planets are assumed to have formed is called the pre-solar nebula."

A glance at the constellation of Orion reveals the activity of such a stellar nursery. The fuzzy blob of light in the centre of Orion's sword is not a star but a nebula – a huge cloud of gas studded with bright young stars. Astronomers looking at this nebula have glimpsed what appears to be stars in the very first stages of formation, still surrounded by obscuring gas and dust. The Orion Nebula, which stretches 20 light-years across space, and which would take over 10,000 solar systems in a line to span it, is actually a mixture of bright and dark clouds, the most spectacular being the famous Horsehead Nebula.

The formation of new stars will continue in the spiral arms of our galaxy as long as there is enough gas. The gas content of the galaxy is partly primordial – material that has not yet aggregated into stars and partly gas that has been ejected from stars in supernovas, stellar winds, small explosive outbursts, and other processes. But not every concentration of gas and dust will form into stars. If there is sufficient material in a gas cloud to make it condense, its temperature will not rise to the critical level at which nuclear fusion begins.

Fully developed stars bear signs of the epoch in which they were born and the earliest – the first to be born after the Big Bang – condensed from the primal material: hydrogen with a proportion of helium Later generations formed from material that had been mixed with the remnants of exploded stars. Our Sun contains such material elements, which shows that it is not a first-generation star.

Obviously this recycling of matter cannot go on indefinitely. As the old stars die and collapse to become white dwarfs, neutron stars, or black holes, they will be unable to replenish the interstellar gases. Slowly the primordial material will become incorporated into stars, until it too, has become totally depleted. As these later-day stars pass through their life cycles and die, the galaxy will gradually grow dimmer but the fade-out will be a long and protracted one. Many billions of years will elapse before the smallest and youngest of the stars complete their nuclear burning and shrink into white dwarfs ... but with slow, agonising finality, a perpetual night *will* inevitably fall.

A similar fate awaits all the other galaxies scattered across the ever-widening chasms of space. The entire universe, currently aglow with the prolific energy of nuclear power, will eventually exhaust this valuable resource. The era of light will be over forever. For billions of years, stars shored themselves up against their own weight by nuclear burning but all the while gravity was waiting to claim them and no object illustrates the power of gravitational pull more graphically than a 'black hole'. Here, gravitation has triumphed totally, crushing a star to nothing, and leaving an imprint in the surrounding space-time in the form of an infinite time-warp.

The Last Three Minutes offers a spine-chilling theory because when astronomers peer at the heavens, they do not see the universe in its present state, displayed like an instantaneous snapshot of space. And because of the time that light takes to reach us from distant corners of the galaxy, we see any given object in space as it was when the light was first emitted. As Paul Davies so aptly describes it, the telescope is also a time-scope. The farther away the object is situated, the further back in time will be thee the image we see today.

> *"In effect, the astronomer's universe is a backward slice through time and space, known technically as the 'past light cone'. It follows that any physical influence coming at us at the speed of light comes entirely without warning. If catastrophe is heading our way up the past light cone, there will be no harbinger of doom. The first we will know about it will be when it hits us! To give a simple hypothetical example, if the sun were to blow up now, we would not be aware of the fact until about eight and a half minutes later, this being the time it takes for light to reach us from the sun. Similarly it is entirely possible that a nearby star has already blown up as a supernova – an event that might bathe the Earth in deadly radiation – but that we shall remain in blissful ignorance of the fact for a few more years yet while the bad news races across the galaxy at the speed of light. So although the universe may look quiet enough at the moment, we can't be sure that something really horrible hasn't already happened.!"*

There is, however, a reassuring scientific theory floating around which, like most, grows in popularity and is then dismissed, before re-emerging at some later stage, and that is the subject of the 'baby universes'. As Professor Davies freely admits, this 'may sound like the last word in fanciful speculation but the subject has been around for a

52

while'. The 'baby universe' theory works on the principle that a bubble of space balloons out from the 'mother universe' to form a 'child universe', connected to the mother universe by an umbilical 'wormhole'. From the viewpoint of the mother universe, the mouth of the wormhole would appear to be a black hole.

Colin Ronan, the former president of the British Astronomical Association and Fellow of the Royal Astronomical Society describes the phenomena: "A wormhole passing through higher dimensions could in theory link different regions of space-time. One mouth of the wormhole would be a black hole, into which matter and energy are drawn, while the other would be a white hole, a hypothetical entity from which matter and energy would pour out. The connecting region, the wormhole, would be unobservable from the outside universe."

As the black hole evaporates, the throat of the wormhole pinches off, disconnecting the baby universe, which then leads an independent existence as a universe in its own right. The new universe would create its own space, and not eat up any of ours. Ronan continues: "In principle it would be possible for matter passing through the wormhole to travel backwards in time, emerging at an earlier time than that at which it entered. It has also been suggested that ... a section of the interior of a wormhole could develop a cosmos in its own right. Thus every universe could spawn others, throughout eternity."

Professor Paul Davies goes on to speculate that our descendents may decide to go for the 'ultimate in emigration' and scramble through the umbilical wormhole into the universe next door before it pinches off. "The very possibility of baby universes opens up the prospect of genuine immortality – not just for our descendents but for universes too. Rather than thinking about the life and death of *the Universe*, we ought to be thinking about a family of universes multiplying *ad infinitum* ... If immortality is limited to having the same thoughts and experiences over and over again forever, it does seem truly pointless. However, if immortality is combined with progress, then we can imagine living in a state of perpetual novelty, always learning or doing something new and exciting."

The scientific theory of the 'parallel universe' has also been around for a long time – long before the advent of the popular television series, *Quantum Leap*. Some theories suggest that our Big Band was not the only one. Sir Martin Rees, former Royal Society Research Professor at Cambridge University and Astronomer Royal of Great Britain wrote in *Our Cosmic Habitat*: "Space inflates so fast that it opens up enough 'room' to trigger a perpetual succession of independent Big Bangs. This line of speculation dramatically enlarges our concept of reality – from a universe to a multiverse ..."

Sir Martin continues to explain that there are other conjectures that suggest a multiplicity of universes. For instance, whenever a black hole forms, processes deep inside it might trigger the creation of another universe into space separate form our own. "If that new universe were like ours, stars, galaxies, and black holes would form in it, and those black holes would in turn spawn another generation of universes, and so on, perhaps ad infinitum. Alternatively, it there were extra spatial dimension that were not tightly rolled up, we may be living in one of many separate universe embedded in a higher-dimensional space."

And here we should reflect for a moment that these theories are the views of serious, astrophysicists' minds, not the dreams of scientific fiction writers, although Sir Martin has the wisdom to add: "All these theories are tentative and should be prefaced by something akin to a health warning. But they give us tantalising glimpses of a dramatically enlarged cosmic perspective. The entire history of our universe could be just an episode, one facet, of the infinite multiverse."

While Professor Davies concludes: "None of these ideas amount to much more than wild conjecture, but the subject of cosmology is still a very young science ..."

Wrong!

"According to the orientation theory, the cult must follow the star; this must be held to as far as possible. But suppose the precessional movement causes the initial function of a star to become inoperative, must not the cult change? And if the same cult is conducted in connection with another star, will not the old name probably be retained? ... And, moreover, the antagonism of rival priesthoods has to be considered. It is extremely probable that the change of a Set temple at Denderah into a Theban-Hathor-Temple was only one example of a system generally adopted, at least in later times."

[*The Dawn of Astronomy,* J Norman Lockyer]

Part Three: The Company of Heaven
"Your holy place shall be untouched throughout the centuries."
Liber AL Vel Legis pt 3 v.34

"Every man and every woman is a star," wrote Aleister Crowley in 1929. *"What can we know about a star? By telescope, a faint phantasm of its optical value. By the spectroscope, a hint of its composition. By the telescope, and our mathematics, its course. In this last case we may legitimately argue from the knowing to the unknown; by our measure of the brief visible curve, we can calculate whence it has come and whither it will go ... Nothing can ever be created nor destroyed; and therefore the 'life' of any individual must be compared to that brief visible curve ... "*

Although Aleister Crowley believed that magic was the alchemical product of science and art, there was an extremely valid reason why he continued to use what might be viewed as the outdated symbols of sorcery and superstition, as Kenneth Grant explained in *Hecate's Fountain;* which echoes George St Clair's observations outlined in Part Three, and the doctrine of Jung's collective unconscious contained in Part One.

It may be asked, why then do we not abandon the ancient symbols in favour of the formulae of nuclear physics and quantum mechanics? The answer is that the occultist understands that contact with these energies may be established more completely through symbols so ancient that they have had time to bury themselves in the vast storehouse of the racial subconsciousness. To such symbols the Forces respond swiftly and with incalculable fullness, whereas the pseudo-symbols manufactured in the laboratory possess no link with elements in the psyche to which they can appeal. The twisting and turning tunnels explored laboriously by science lead, only too often, away from the goal. The intellectual formulæ and symbols of mathematics have been evolved too recently to serve as direct conduits. For the Old Ones, such lines of communication are dead. The magician, therefore, uses the more direct paths which long ages have mapped out in the shadowlands of the subconsciousness.

The mistake that is often made in assimilating modern magic with Egypt's ancient past, however, is that too many outside (or alien) influences are allowed to creep into the equation. Egypt's stellar-cult, as much as it may have influenced *subsequent* thinking down through the centuries, was not influenced by anything other than the home-spun philosophy of the indigenous gods of the early Nile people, with all its attendant symbolism. From that very early period, the astronomer-priesthood 'not only understood astronomical science so well that they recognised the precession of the equinoxes, but also that they founded every aspect of their civilisation upon a star-orientated, religio-mystic culture derived from such knowledge' [*The Land of the Fallen Star Gods*]. But let us return the baton to George St Clair for a moment:

The basis of the Egyptian Religion was Astronomy and the Calendar; the Divine Order in the heavens suggesting the rule for the life of man ... the men who framed this system had ceased to be savages and had attained to considerable knowledge in observational astronomy. They may have received an inheritance of custom and fancy from savage ancestors, and continued to use the language and ideas of it to some extent, but a higher revelation had come to them through the study of the stars. Hence the early astronomers became priests, and the religion of mankind was lifted to a higher platform than that of mere animism.

We may search for evidence of Egypt's stellar-cult in the writings of later civilisations, but this will always be a drastically diluted affair. One the other hand, it is unwise to view Egypt as the 'fount of all wisdom', and harbour a belief that subsequent or parallel cultures were magically or scientifically inferior. As we now realise, the social, religious and magical elements of Egyptian life were inextricably interwoven, and therefore it is impossible to view any aspect of one without the others. But, by the time the indigenous stellar-cult had been wholly integrated within the developing solar-cult during the pyramid-building era, Egypt itself was on the brink of social and religious revolution. The stellar-priesthood went into the shadows ...
... but this did not necessarily mean that the cult disappeared

completely, since there *is* evidence of it persisting, albeit as part of the Inner Mysteries, right up until the advent of the Ramesside family of Dynasty XIX (1293-1185BC).

In *The Setian*, Billie Walker-John reveals how, hundreds of years after the end of the Pyramid Age, the Ramesside dynasty brought about a 'Setian revival' following the ascent of Seti I to the throne. The family are believed to have been descendents of a Set priest from an area where this indigenous god had long been worshipped: Seti I's birth-name means 'He of the god Set' and he retained his Set-name throughout his reign. If Seti I were the only king to show Setian leanings, the Setian revival could be dismissed as wishful thinking … but this was not the case.

If his father's references to the ancient Mysteries were veiled, Ramesses II was much more up front about his family's association with Egypt's oldest god. It was Ramesses the Great who brought Set worship out into the open and paid homage to his own ancestors who had preserved the ancient Mysteries of the Set-Horus psychopompos, as we can see from the famous statue in the Cairo Museum. It also confirms that the worship of Set was still an important and integral part of the Mysteries, which spanned over three thousand years of continuous loyalty from an 'inner' or underground priesthood. This priesthood kept those Mysteries alive despite civil unrest, religious upheaval, invading armies, foreign rule and the adverse publicity of having their god turned into a reviled assassin by a rival cult.

The main difficulty in trying to tie all these 'stellar strands of 'Khemeticism' together as one coherent whole, is the conflicting disciplines of history, science, theology, philosophy and magic.

History is concerned with that which can be proved via the discovery of ancient artefacts and writings, and is often interpreted quite literally, rarely taking into account that ancient esoteric beliefs (exactly the same as modern ones) relied heavily on allegory and metaphor, which were the main methods used in both the magical thinking process and its outward expression. As Alexandre Piankoff, a well-known translator of Egyptian texts wrote:

> *… the approach to the study of Egyptian religion has passed without transition from one extreme to another.*

For the early Egyptologists, this religion was highly mystical and mysterious ... then came a sudden reaction; scholars lost all interest in the religion as such and viewed the religious texts merely as source material for their philological-historical research.

Science, on the other hand, regularly discards one theory in favour of a better one and by using approved 'scientific methods' of radiocarbon dating and DNA testing, boundaries are pushed further and further back in tracing the origins of the earliest Egyptian cultures. But science and history have always made uneasy bedfellows as the debate about the *geological* dating of the Sphinx and its surrounding mortuary temples will testify. But as Eliphas Levi wrote: '***without faith, science leads to doubt; without science, faith leads to superstition ...***'

Needless to say, **Theology** [faith] is *always* a minefield, whether ancient *or* modern, since incoming beliefs, more than often than not, absorb or obliterate any existing ones. The original religion of the early Egyptians (i.e. the stellar-cult) is as far removed from the solar-beliefs of the later dynasties, as the latter are from contemporary Islam and Christianity. The modern view of the Egyptian gods is that they all fit snugly into a one single, internally coherent and self-contained pantheon, without taking into account the mighty deities of the pre-dynastic era, who were marginalised and trivialised by the incoming priesthoods (with the exception of those pertaining to the Inner Mysteries). Egyptian magico-religious psychology is indeed complicated, and our present-day enumeration of 'body, soul and spirit' is quite insufficient as parallel concept.

According to the entry in the *British Museum Dictionary of Ancient Egypt*, the Egyptians considered that each individual person was made up of five distinct spiritual parts, separate from the physical body: the *ba*, the *ka*, the *ren*, the *shwt* and the *akh*.

The *ba* has similarities with our concept of 'personality'. In other words, it comprised all those non-physical attributes that made one human being unique, although the concept of *ba* also referred to a power, which could be extended to gods as well as inanimate objects. In order for the physical bodies of the deceased to survive in the afterlife, they had to be reunited with the *ba* every night. Far from corresponding to the modern western concept of a 'spirit', the *ba* was closely related to the physical body, to the extent that it too was considered to have physical needs for such pleasures as food, drink and sexual activity.

The *ka* is an almost untranslatable term used by the Egyptians to describe the creative Life-force of each individual, whether human or divine, and was considered to be the essential ingredient that differentiated a living person from a dead one. It came into existence at the same moment that the individual was born; when the individual died, the *ka* continued to live, so long as it was provided with sustenance in the form of prayers, offerings and remembrance.

Egyptians set a great store by the naming of people and objects, and the name or *ren* was regarded as an essential element of every human individual. The *ren* was regarded as a living part of each human being that had to be assigned immediately after birth, otherwise it was felt that the individual would not properly come into existence. The symbolic importance of the *ren* also meant that the removal of personal names from monuments was considered to be the equivalent to the destruction of the very memory and existence of the person to whom the name referred as revealed in the example given in Part One: *'To speak the Name of the dead is to make them live again. It restoreth the breath of Life to he who hath vanished.'*

The shadow, or *shwt*, was also regarded as an essential element of every human being, and was considered necessary to protect its owner from harm. Funerary texts describe the shadow as an entity imbued with power and capable of moving at great speed, but the Egyptian word for shadow (*shwt*) also had the connotations of 'shade' and 'protection'.

The *akh* was the fifth principal element that was considered necessary to make up a complete personality. The *akh* was believed to be the form in which the blessed dead inhabited Otherworld, and also the result of the successful reunion of the *ba* with its *ka*. Once the *akh* had been created by this reunion, it was regarded as enduring and unchanging for eternity.

As discussed in Part One, a broad overview of the religious history of Egypt will tell us that there were several pantheons, all of them very confusingly cross-related, which carefully concealed the enduring

Inner Mysteries. The fact that many of the gods had half a dozen alter egos, all with different animal heads or crowns, or other headgear and apparel to match, is in itself a source of endless confusion to the uninitiated. For all the multiplicity of gods and goddesses in the pantheon, however, the regard for Atum-Re was consistent throughout the long history of the Nile Valley. For the Egyptian, he was that 'Unseen' omnipresent Life-force in every microscopic fragment of the cosmos, with the Sun being the visible expression of his Being made manifest.

I am the Creator of what hath come into being and I myself came into being under the form of the god, Khepera in primeval time and formed myself out of primeval matter ... My name is ... who is the essence of primeval matter ... I appeared under the form of multitudes of things from the beginning. Nothing existed at that time and it was I who made whatever was made ... I made all the forms under which I appeared out of the god-soul which I raised up out of Nu, out of a state of inertness. [Egyptian prayer]

When it comes to **Philosophy**, that 'pursuit of wisdom and knowledge: investigation of the nature of being; knowledge of the causes and laws of all things; the principles underlying any department of knowledge', we find little in terms of written texts when it comes to ancient Egypt. Philosophy is bound up in what we know, tempered with what we hypothesise, blended with what we would like to believe makes up an ideal society. Much of what we 'know' comes from other philosophical writers and according to Schwaller de Lubicz in *Sacred Science*, and Jane B Seller in *Death of the Gods in Ancient Egypt*, the Egyptian astronomer-priesthood *was* fully aware of the phenomena of the 25,920 year cycle of the precession of the equinoxes, even if they didn't understand the root cause.

And it is here that we can slide into the realms of fantasy (i.e. the Atlantean theory) if we pay too much attention to contemporary hypothesists, or to the classical historians who swallowed these tall tales. For example: Herodotus opined that whether the origin of the Zodiac is Aryan or Egyptian, it is still of immense antiquity. Simplicius (6th century AD) writes that he had always heard that the Egyptians had kept astronomical observations and records for the last 630,000 years ... Diogenes Laertius carried back the astronomical calculations of the Egyptians to 48,863 years before Alexander the

Great. Martianus Capella corroborated the same by telling posterity that the Egyptians had secretly studied astronomy for over 40,000 years before they imparted their knowledge to the world ... Diodorus Siculus (1st century BC) was told by the Egyptian priests that the Gods and Heroes had ruled over Egypt for slightly less than 18,000 years, while mortals had ruled for just under 5,000 years!

Magic, of course, has always been an 'occult' (i.e. hidden), science and it takes an experienced magician to tease some semblance of order out from all the tangled skeins of history, science, theology and philosophy. The Egyptians believed in everything in the universe following a single, repetitive pattern ...

> *It was this, inherently, which underlay the principle of hierarchy and the need for it in maintaining perfect harmony throughout the cosmos ... It was because of their understanding of the divine origin of everything on Earth and of its hierarchically organised place in the scheme of things, that science and art – the very foundations of all objective culture – originally came to exist and be practised in Egypt, always with prior dedication to a particular divinity ... The ancient Egyptians did nothing without it having an esoteric significance, and this must also apply to their architecture. Each aspect of proportion, acoustics, light and darkness, number and style of columns tells us something about the nature of the deity and the way in which it was to be approached and/or worshipped.*
> [*Land of the Fallen Star Gods*, J S Gordon]

Much of what the ancient Egyptians perceived as having magico-religious significance appears to have been what was appearing in the heavens at the time of recording. For example, among the natural cosmic phenomena that affect the weather patterns here on Earth are the regular cycles of sunspot activity that peak every eleventh year, and which were first recorded by Chinese astronomers well over 2,000 years ago. The solar winds caused by the eruption of 'flares' associated with sunspot activity, distort the magnetic fields of the Sun and the Earth, often playing havoc with modern-day, earth-bound technology and computers.

Unlike the magnetic field on Earth, where the lines run tidily from one pole to the other, the Sun's 11-year cycle begins with this pattern. But because the electrically charged gases at the Sun's equator flow faster than at the poles, the magnetic field crossing the Sun's middle is pulled out of shape. Some of these contorting field lines break through the Sun's surface producing *'hundreds of magnetic field lines which criss-cross the surface like a haphazard jumble of overlapping croquet hoops ... responsible for sunspots, prominences, flares and coronal mass ejections ...'* (*Encyclopaedia of the Universe*). And, for the Egyptians, all this solar activity was, of course, the province of Aten-Re.

Similarly, the 19-year period is also a crucial one. About every 19 years (18.64 years, to be exact), the sun-moon eclipses in the same point of the sky. The Chaldeans, who called it Saros and believed that its magic powers could cause the end of the world, knew of this phenomenon. We know that the combined gravitational pull of the sun and moon causes widespread disturbances in bodies of oceanic water, even accounting for climatic changes over the centuries. A study by hydraulic engineer, E. Paris-Teynac, also revealed a similar pattern for several large rivers, and especially the Nile. If the Chaldeans had recorded the fact that terrestrial life was controlled by astral phenomena, then the Egyptians too, would have made similar observations.

> *Data on the tides of the Nile are available as far back as four thousand years. The pharaoh, worshipped as the 'master of the growth of the waters', attached a great importance to exactly how much water there would be in the river each year, for it brought wealth and nourishment to his people ...*
> [*The Cosmic Clocks*, Michel Gauquelin]

Some strange facts about rivers emerge from these records. The great Egyptian river has followed clear rhythmic variations that approximate certain astronomical cycles and Paris-Teynac identified an 11-year variation that seems to be tied to the sun-spot cycle. More importantly, he showed that these 18-year periods, roughly corresponded to the Saros, which reflects the sun-moon eclipse intervals. In ancient Khem, the moon's influence was evident everywhere, continues Gauqueli:

It's waxing was called 'the opening of Horus' eye'. When the eye of the hawk-god was completely open, the moon was full. The twenty-eight-day lunar cycle was compared to a staircase with fourteen steps: first one ascended the staircase to the 'fullness of the eye', then one went down it until the eye closed ... Lunar eclipses were considered to be evil omens presaging sad events. Often the moon itself was seen as dangerous. Its crescent was sometimes seen as a knife, 'a golden sickle in the starry field'. An Egyptian manuscript asks: 'Isn't the moon a knife? It can therefore punish those who are guilty'.

The shapes and movements of the stars also gave rise to numerous myths and rituals. The sky was seen as causing the beneficial growth of the Nile because each year the waters increased when the brilliant star Sirius rose at the same time as the Sun. Not surprisingly, this suggested that the floods were due to the alliance between the propitious actions of the Sun and Sirius – an alliance that occurred only once a year. It was the time when the black soil of Khem spread across the Valley, and why the New Year was celebrated on the date that Sirius rose with the sun. According to E. Zinner, in *The Stars Above Us*, the Egyptians believed that the:

> *fixed stars were lamps, suspended from the vault, or carried by other gods. The planets sailed in their own boats along canals originating in the Milky Way, the celestial twin of the Nile. Towards the fifteenth of each month, the moon god was attacked by a ferocious sow, and devoured in a fortnight of agony; the he was reborn again. Sometimes the sow swallowed him whole, causing a lunar eclipse; sometimes a serpent swallowed the sun, causing a solar eclipse.*

'When human prevision fails, it is God's will that is being carried out,' says a text of Dynasty V. The people of Egypt didn't have the slightest idea *why* their world grew colder when the stellar cycle brought Orion rising in the east at twilight ... or *why* the world grew warmer again when Lyra rose at dusk, and Orion was no longer visible. As John V Cambell points out in *Analog,* 'When the world is one vast collection of mysteries, the business of a wise man is to establish some sound, reliable correlations, letting the question of why go until he has more information.'

Another celestial phenomena recently discussed in scientific circles are the storm-related 'red sprites' – upper atmospheric optical phenomena associated with thunderstorms. Although only barely detectable with the naked eye, the sprites are massive luminous flashes that appear directly above an active thunderstorm and are coincident with cloud-to-ground, or inter-cloud lightning strikes. To see them requires visual access to the region above the storm, unobstructed by intervening clouds and although rare, it seems likely that they have been a part of thunderstorms that have occurred over millions of years. Red-tinged 'sprites' rarely appear singly, usually occurring in clusters of two, three or more and would most certainly have been identified with Set and his followers, if these 'storm devils' were viewed from a distance across the vast reaches of the desert.

As we have observed, the Egyptian priesthood was familiar with all manner of natural occurrences in the heavens, which proved to them that all things came from, were influenced by, or caused by those powers that dwelt beyond the stars. To repeat, for example, that difference of 0.014173 days per annum between the sidereal year (according to the stars) and the tropical year (according to the seasons); that slippage of close to 14 days per millennium that is termed the *precession of the equinoxes*.

Duncan Steel's calculations concerning precession are based on the meteor showers of the Taurid and Leonid streams. 'The rate of precession of the Leonid stream is virtually identical to the precession of the equinoxes, both being 14 days per millennium, meaning that a thousand years ago the Leonid meteor storms would be expected to have been occurring near mid-October rather than mid-November, and this is borne out by historical records.' When he applied the appropriate precession rates for the Taurids, he found that back in 3000BC they would have peaked in mid-July – 110 days earlier than they do today with the activity starting around mid summer. That is 22 days earlier per millennium.

Find a clear dark site one night and let your eyes become well adjusted to the low light levels. Then, by looking randomly across the sky, you may expect to see up to 10 meteors (or shooting stars) an hour. In fact, most people are asleep during the best time for viewing meteors (during the last hour or two before dawn), when the count rate is two or three times higher than in the late evening. 'On certain nights of the year a larger number of meteors will be seen in what is called a meteor shower. Most such showers occur annually on the dates that the Earth passes through a meteoride stream and each shower is usually distinguished by the constellation from which it appears to come. Because it takes about a week to pass through the stream, showers will continue to show pronounced activity for some days,' he writes in *Rogue Asteroids and Doomsday Comets*.

The question we must again ask ourselves, of course, is *how* could the ancient Egyptian priesthood come to possess such knowledge?

Even on the surface, it would suggest that they must have perfected highly sophisticated levels of scientific astronomical evaluation, in order to be able to recognise and *make long-term comparisons* of this cyclical phenomena and astronomical activity. But these long-term comparisons would often require the studied observations across hundreds of years to establish recognised patterns, and men were not as long-lived as they are today. This means that the phenomena must have been carefully watched and recorded across several generations in, for example, the plotting and predicting the return of a comet. Neither is it far-fetched to assume they would be familiar with the pattern of 'cause and effect', even if they did not understand the precise nature of the 'cause' itself.

This ancient stellar knowledge would, of course, only be known to select members of the priesthood and probably not even understood by the king himself, despite holding the rank of the highest High Priest. What is even more astounding, is that this stellar knowledge may probably be the surviving remnants from *zep tepi* – the 'First Time' of the Nile civilisation whose origins are lost beneath the proverbial sands of Time.

This was also the time of the Egyptian **Urshu**, that mysterious race of mystical beings that haunt the periphery of every culture, and all Adepts are familiar with the 'First Time' – the universal Golden Age during which the waters of the Abyss receded, the primordial darkness was banished, and humanity, emerging into the light, was brought the gifts of civilisation by these 'Watchers' or 'Light-bearers', who acted as intermediaries between the gods and men.

Needless to say, modern Egyptologists dismiss this 'First Time' as nothing more than myth, but the 'Building Texts' from the Temple of Edfu, appear to refer to a 'mythical temple that came into existence at the beginning of the world' (*The Mythical Origin of the Egyptian Temple* – E. A. E. Reymond) and are synonymous with the First Time, or Early Primeval Age. The texts record that the 'Seven Sages', the 'Builder Gods', the 'Lords of Light', the 'Senior Ones' brought light, i.e. knowledge, to the people – and the similarities between the Lords of Light of Edfu and the ***shemsu hor*** of the later Heliopolitan period, are so similar that they are probably all descriptions of the same shadowy brotherhood.

The central idea behind early Egyptian beliefs, is that the gods would literally (if properly invoked at the correct time) descend from the stars and waken the god-nature in the priest, or that the god would manifest through the consciousness of the individual. Again this is where fantasy can often take over with the suggestion that the 'appearance and disappearance of these seasonally returning hierarchies of hugely intelligent, spiritual or divine beings' [*Liber Ægyptius*] can manifest to contemporary humans. Modern thinking, however, rarely gets beyond the concept that if these beings come to Earth and take a phenomenal form (perhaps sometimes akin to our own), surely they must travel in some form of spacecraft.

The answer is an emphatic 'No!'

The traditions of the ancient Egyptian priesthood give us the answer to that question in the recognition of the soul-bodies (the ***akh*** and ***ba***), which have for so long been regarded as almost, if not entirely mythical entities, then to be so ethereal as to have no real existence in our physical world. It is here, where we find the lengthy esoteric training of the Adept's mindset, that allows them to embrace the idea of interaction with those discarnate entities, or extra-terrestrial intelligences. Beings who can best be likened to a spirit version of the Bodhisattvas of Madhyamaka Buddhism, who can move between different planes, or levels of consciousness, in order to bring guidance or protection to those who are able to make the mystical connection. This doctrine has filtered through to the present day in the concept of 'the Great White Brotherhood' of the Western ritual magical traditions, which Helena Blavatsky described as 'boneless, formless, spiritual essences called the Self-born ...'

Whatever these ethereal beings are, for a more tangible example we need to turn first to Aleister Crowley and examine the most famous of his writings: *Liber Al Vel Legis*, or *The Book of the Law*. This beautiful prose poem is possibly his greatest achievement and, purported to have been dictated to him by what he identified as his 'Holy Guardian Angel', is reminiscent of the exquisitely beautiful eroticism of *The Song of Solomon* from the Old Testament. Compiled in three separate parts, each one honouring a different Egyptian deity – Nuit [Nut]; Hadit [Set] and Ra-Hoor-Khuit [an amalgam of the different aspects of the ancient falcon-god-child usually identified with Horus] – although the choice of Egyptian names is pure arbitrary, and it should not imply that this philosophy is confined to Egypt. Nevertheless, Crowley's subsequent Thelemic teaching honours the oldest deities in the Khemetic pantheon.

Nuit, Nu or Nut, 'Our Lady of the Starry Heavens'

Invoke me under my stars!
Love is the law, love under will.

Goddess of the night sky, frequently depicted by the Egyptians in the form of a woman arched over the earth, her body strewn with stars. This representation of the all-embracing, infinite goddess power is of vital importance in the Thelemic teachings.

Hadit, her son/consort: The Chaldean form of Set.

I am the flame that burns in every heart of man,
And in the core of every star.

Hadit/Set represents the infinitely small yet supremely potent point which, in union with Nuit, generates the manifest Universe (Ra-Hoor-Khuit) ... Set was the first and oldest of the gods and of supreme importance in Thelemic doctrine, being not only the name of the primal creative spirit but also embodying the essential formula of sexual magick.

Ra-Hoor-Khuit, the child, Lord of the Eastern Horizon, Hoor-paar-Kraat.

Nu is your refuge as Hadit your light;
and I am the strength, force, vigour, of your arms

In magical terms he stands for the projection of energy which begets the 'child' formulated from the combined wills of Nuit and Hadit ... Horus, the Crowned and Conquering Child, Lord of the New Aeon, and the perfect manifestation of the magical Will in the form of the Universe. This is the magical/mystical offspring of the dual aspects of primordial and stellar power.

From this we can immediately understand why Crowley was (and still is) accused of devil-worship. By identifying Hadit/Set as the principal deity in his new Thelemic philosophy, he was allegedly honouring evil over good. Both the Crowley and Grant explanations could be dismissed as crackpot occultist theory except that these primitive forms in the ancient Egyptian pantheon are confirmed on an academic level by dozens of the world's leading Egyptologists, including Professor E. O James, who wrote in *The Ancient Gods:*

> *It would seem that Set was the god most widely worshipped among the indigenous population ... in prehistoric and early dynastic times ... Set was a Storm-god and a Rain-god originally personifying the sky and weather, and when Osiris was equated with the life-giving waters of the Inundation (the Nile), he had to be suppressed as a serious rival of the Osirian cultos ... in spite of his great antiquity and status ...*

With his inimitable honesty, Crowley wasn't afraid to admit in later years that much of *The Book of the Law* was still incomprehensible to him. He worked tirelessly in his attempts to interpret its meaning, but decided he was too close to the subject and, in the end, entrusted the task to his friend, Louis Wilkinson, who wrote:

> *In some one phrase or other of* The Book *there is direct message for every human being. The best way for the layman to approach this* Book *is to regard it as a letter written directly to himself. Even though he may not be able to understand some parts of the letter; he is sure to find other parts that are unmistakably addressed, in an intimately personal sense, to him.*
>
> *[The Law Is For All, Louis Wilkinson]*

Needless to say, Crowley's detractors claim that he made up *The Book* himself and passed it off as divine writing, but this does not account for the differences in the use of language. Who, or whatever Aiwass was, English was not his mother-tongue, but it *was* one that Crowley excelled in. *If* Crowley had invented *The Book,* his monumental ego would never have allowed him to publish such bad grammar and syntax – and if he hadn't believed it to be a genuine mystical document, he could never have resisted the urge to tinker with it. *The Book of the Law* was dictated in Cairo between 8th-10th April 1904.

> *The Author called himself Aiwass, and claimed to be 'the minister of Hoor-paar-kraat'; that is, a messenger from the forces ruling this earth at present. How could he prove that he was in fact a being of a kind superior to any of the human race, and so entitled to speak with authority? Evidently he must show Know-ledge and Power such as no man has ever known to possess. He showed his Knowledge chiefly by the use of cipher or cryptogram in certain passages to set forth recondite facts, including some that no human being could possibly be aware of them; thus, the proof of his claim exists in the manuscript itself.*
>
> *[Confessions, Aleister Crowley]*

Following the Cairo revelation, Crowley had the manuscript typed out, but took no further trouble to follow it up. Even admitting in *Confessions* that he deeply resented *The Book of the Law*, being bitterly opposed to its principles on almost every point of morality. *'The third chapter seemed to me gratuitously atrocious.'* Not only that, the real horror for a man who had been brought up under a strict magical conditioning, which forbade any publishing of even the least part of the 'secret knowledge', was that he was now being instructed to make public the 'Secret Wisdom of the Ages'. Up to that point, Crowley had been 'absurdly scrupulous' with regard to the secrets entrusted to him and was fully aware of the serious repercussions that had resulted by apparently trivial indiscretions on the part of others who had been less discrete.

Far from being proud of being chosen as the channel for such revelation, he admits to being reluctant and afraid. He found himself in the most invidious of positions. He was bound by oath to the most solemn of obligations and would never have dreamt of attempting to dodge his responsibilities, but it took a long time before Crowley accepted that the 'Masters' or 'Lords of Initiation' had other plans for him:

> *They had ordained that I should pass through every kind of hardship at the hands of nature, suffer all sorrow and shame that life can inflict. Their messenger must be tested by every ordeal – not by those that he himself might choose ... The Masters test every link in turn, infallibility and inexorably; it is up to you to temper your steel to stand the strain; for one flaw means failure and you have to forget it all afresh in the fires of fate, retrieve in a new incarnation the lost opportunity of the old. I had got to learn that all roads lead to Rome. It is proper, more, it is prudent, more yet, it is educative, for the aspirant to pursue all possible Ways to Wisdom. Thus he broadens the base of his Pyramid, thus he diminishes the probability of missing the method which happens to suit him best, thus he insures against the obsession that the goat-rack of his own success is the One Highway. [Confessions]*

Crowley's method of resisting the pressure to publish the typescript of *The Book of the Law* was to kick it around until he lost it but the 'Masters' had other ideas. With hindsight he realised there was a powerful message contained within its pages but that the gods deliberately kept him away from coming to any great personal conclusions. In short, he was embarrassed by the whole thing and repeatedly found excuses for postponing the publication.

For many years the typescript languished in the attic of his Scottish home at Bolskine and, despite his deliberate carelessness and the conviction that secrecy was necessary to a magical document, that publication would destroy its importance, it would not go away. Crowley both hated and feared *The Book* and tried desperately to escape from its influence; at one stage, convincing himself that the typescript had been well and truly lost. In a diary entry for 28th June 1909, he records the accidental finding of an old portfolio in the loft that contained the missing typescript

It is interesting to note that although much of Crowley's subsequent Thelemic philosophy is firmly rooted in stellar wisdom it may come as a surprise to hear him state that astronomy was a subject about which he knew nothing. "In spite of innumerable nights spent under the stars, I can recognise few constellations except the Great Bear and Orion," he wrote, but could still continue to draw on stellar analogies within the framework of his own teaching Order, *Astrum Argentinum* or Silver Star.

Not all extra-terrestrial intelligences that come through to Earth, however, should be considered benevolent. This form of discarnate entity is what a magical practitioner (regardless of Tradition) calls upon, or communicates with, for mystical/magical purposes. They are what others may refer to as deities or gods, demons or angels – they are what are summoned to the Quarters to protect the magician, invoked into the magician in order to channel magical energy, or to act as a 'Holy Guardian Angel'. As Bob Clay-Egerton wrote on the subject:

> What we should never lose sight of is the fact that these energies/entities can be helpful or harmful, and should be treated with the greatest respect and caution. Remember these are cosmic energies on a very lowly level but they are far more powerful than we can ever imagine and as such can destroy us if treated in a cavalier manner. Keep in mind that once summoned, the entity requires your energy on which to feed (i.e. recharge its batteries) and if you do not keep it under firm control, or forget to close down properly, it may continue to feed/grow until it manifests into something unpleasant and difficult to shift. This is not as rare as we would like to think!
>
> Whatever we wish to call these 'powers' they do have the necessary link to the abilities and attributes that the magician strives for in the hopes of finding all he seeks. If the invocation is gone about in the right manner, there is no reason why this cannot be achieved – but remember that they are not interested in your development, only their own. Only by encountering these varying aspects can the magician learn to differentiate between the positive/negative, active/passive beings that exist out on the other planes. Be careful with your preparations and protections, because for every one that will help, guide and give advice, there are the

same number who will hinder, deceive and even destroy you, if they get the opportunity.

Again, we could view these instructions as further evidence of crackpot New Age fantasy if it were not for the fact that in 1992, NASA launched a major space project to search for extra-terrestrial intelligent life – namely the SETI programme: Search for Extraterrestrial Intelligence. In his book, *Are We Alone?*, Professor Paul Davies reflects on how little contemporary thought has been given to the far-reaching implications of SETI on earthly philosophical issues, which stands in stark contrast to the speculations of earlier generations.

> *Contrary to popular belief, the possibility of extra-terrestrials was often debated, and the ramifications analysed, in previous ages ... and the impact that the discovery of alien life forms would imply for our science, religion and the beliefs about mankind.*

The concept that we may not be alone in the Universe is not a new one, since the idea of the 'plurality of inhabited worlds' dates back to the very dawn of rational thought and scientific enquiry. Despite that speculation about extraterrestrial 'fact' rested almost entirely on philosophical debate, in the 4th century BC the Greek philosopher Epicurus wrote to Herodotus:

> There are infinite worlds both like and unlike this world of ours. For the atoms being infinite in number ... are borne on far out into space. For those atoms which are of such nature that a world could be created by them or made by them have not been used up on either one world or a limited number of worlds ... so that there nowhere exists an obstacle to the infinite number of worlds ... We must believe that in all worlds there are living creatures and plants and other things we see in this world.

Justification for this belief in other worlds was closely associated with the philosophy of atomism and as Professor Davies points out:

> *There is a tendency to regard SETI as a space-age activity. In fact, as we have seen, belief in, and the*

search for, extra-terrestrial beings stretch back into antiquity. Today a separation is usually made between belief in extraterrestrial life forms and belief in supernatural or religious entities – i.e. between aliens and angels. Yet it was not always thus. For most of human history the 'heavens' were literally that: the domain of the gods. Beings who inhabited the realm beyond the Earth were normally regarded as supernatural. In spite of the fact that ET is now firmly in the domain of science, or at least science fiction, the religious dimension of SETI still lies just beneath the surface. Many people draw comfort from the belief that advanced beings in the sky are watching over us and may some day intervene in our affairs to save us from human folly.

Even the eminent astronomer Sir Fred Hoyle maintained that life extends throughout the Universe and "hints at the existence of advanced beings out there who have contrived to create in our cosmic neighbourhood the rather special physical conditions needed for carbon-based life. These alien beings fulfil a function similar to that of Plato's Demiurge ... a much more powerful 'super-intelligence' who directs these acts of intelligent design from the timeless advantage point of the infinite future." While Professor Davies warms to this powerful theme of alien beings acting as a conduit to the Ultimate.

The attraction seems to be that by contacting superior beings in the sky, humans will be given access to privileged knowledge, and that the resulting broadening of our horizons will in some sense being us a step closer to God. The search for alien beings can thus be seen as part of a long-standing religious quest as well as a scientific project. This should not surprise us ... As we have seen, it is only in this century [20th] that discussion of extraterrestrial beings has taken place in a context where a clear separation has been made between the scientific and religious aspects of the topic. But this separation is really only skin-deep.

In view of these comments from such eminent astro-scientists, is it mere co-incidence that the project – the Search for Extraterrestrial Intelligence – should be better known worldwide by its acronym of SETI? Has this universal, collective unconscious, been influenced by the long-dead Seti I, whose birth-name means 'He of the god Set', and who brought about the 'Setian revival' some 1,000 years after the old stellar worship went into the shadows, finally triumphed over obscurity? Can this 'super-intelligence' be the core of the old Khemetic star-gods, the 'Imperishable Ones ... who grow not weary'? Is *this* the 'privileged knowledge' that enabled the people of the Nile Valley to construct their pyramids and temples on such a monumental scale? **Was the ancient Egyptian astronomer-priesthood already plugged into the Divine?**

We have tentatively picked up the key to this ancient Wisdom, and even though *our* unpractised hand cannot yet unlock its secrets we have to remind ourselves that for the Egyptians:

- The study of the stars was unequivocally a priestly business;

- There were probably no astronomers who were not members of the priesthood;

- It is impossible to disconnect the Egyptian religion from astronomy;

- In order to unravel the system of mythology, knowledge of the astronomical clues is essential;

- The facts and ideas of the Egyptian astro-religious system are represented by emblems or symbols [hieroglyphs];

- The mythology of Khem is chiefly an allegory of the heavens and the calendar.

The next question, of course, will inevitably lead us to the brain-teaser of where do these ethereal beings reside if they are not hurtling around the cosmos in hi-tec spacecraft? Perhaps it is time to make a quantum leap of our own imagination and explore the possible associations of the parallel or multiple Universe, the string (or M-) theory, and the *practical* Qabalah of the Western Mystery Tradition. Marcus Chown, as cosmology consultant for *New Scientist*, wrote:

> *The idea that our Universe could, without our knowledge, be superimposed on another, 'mirror' universe with its own light and matter and even stars and plants and animal life is an amazing concept. This idea that there exists a multiplicity of universes is not new. The most striking evidence that there is a multiverse comes from the fundamental laws which control the Universe. A very peculiar thing about these laws is that they appear to be 'fine-tuned' so that human beings, or at least living things, can exist.*

The notion that the Universe has four dimensions – three of space and one of time – has become a familiar scientific 'fact', but modern cosmologists suggest that the Universe may possess more dimensions than this. The string (or super-string) theory views the fundamental building blocks of all matter as ultra-tiny pieces of 'string' vibrating in a space-time of *ten* dimensions, and unifying all the forces of nature, including gravity. According to super-string theory, fundamental particles resemble tiny strings or loops that 'sweep out a two-dimensional surface in space-time and which can be likened to a film on a soap bubble'. According to Colin Ronan in *The Natural History of the Universe*: "Super-string theory awaits confirmation. It is too soon to make sweeping judgements about it, but it holds the possibility that it is step towards the most fundamental basic of physics: a TOE, or theory of everything."

A few years after its initial explosion on to the theoretical physics scene, the super-string theory seemed to have stagnated. By the early 1990s there were a number of different versions of the theory and no one knew which one was correct. Then a US physicist, Ed Witten, proposed a solution that suggested the fundamental entities were membranes rather than strings and it became known as the membrane theory, or M-theory for short. Many in the field of physics liked to think of the 'M' as standing for Magic, Mystery or Mother, and since the study of the stars was unequivocally a priestly business it really would have been the cosmic-mother of all theories! Witten was able to unify the different versions of string theory into M-theory by requiring yet another dimension. Thus, M-theory is an 11-dimensional theory. "It also has the advantage over the older super-string theories of allowing a more natural merging of gravity with the other three forces."

The 11-dimensions also fits more snugly into the theory or philosophy of the practical Qabalah (as opposed to the wholly Jewish theological philosophy), although this is *not, and has never been,* a part of traditional Khemetic teaching. Nevertheless, this system, probably more than any other mystical philosophy, has had a profound effect on Western occultism. Like most forms of mysticism it describes the levels of consciousness and being between man and Godhead, but it is not for this reason that it has become the basis of modern magic. The Qabalah employs a complex symbol called the Tree of Life as its central motif, and it is because this Tree is such a pragmatic framework on which to base rituals and meditations that the Qabalah is relevant today, observed Neville Drury and Gregory Tillett in *The Occult Sourcebook.*

In Qabalistic terms, the whole of the manifested Universe originated in Ain Soph, the hidden and infinite God-Energy that is without qualities or attributes ... similar to how the early Egyptians saw their own Creator-God as shown by *Osiris and the Egyptian Resurrection,* Vol I., E A Wallis Budge:

"Alone, without a second
One, the maker of all things,
the Spirit, the hidden spirit, the maker of spirits.
He existed in the beginning, when nothing else was.
What is he created after he came into being.
Father of beginnings, eternal, infinite, ever-lasting.
Hidden one, no man knoweth his form,
or can search out his likeness
he is hidden to gods and men,
and is a mystery to his creatures.
No man knoweth how to know him;
his name is a mystery and is hidden.
His names are innumerable.
He is the truth, he liveth on truth, hi is the king of truth.
His is life, through him man liveth; he gave life to man,
He breathed life into his nostrils.
He is the father and mother,

the father of fathers,
the mother of mothers.
He begetteth, but was not begotten;
he bringeth forth, but was not brought forth;
he begat himself and gave birth to himself.
He created, but was not created,
he made his own form and body.
He himself is existence;
He neither increaseth nor diminished.
He made the universe,
The world, what was, what is, and what shall be ... "

The Tree describes a type of 'crystallisation process' by which the *Infinite* gradually becomes *Finite*, the latter being the world as we see it all around us, with intermediary stages of mind or being, of energy or consciousness. The Ain Soph thus reveals aspects of its divinity to man and on the Tree of Life these are represented symbolically by ten major stages called *sephiroth* ... or 11 if we count Daath, the 'hidden' sphere. In modern magical usage, the *sephiroth* are best regarded as levels of consciousness, or different levels of being, both on the front and the reverse side of the Tree. Within ritual, the priest-magician begins at his present level of 'earth consciousness' and tries to retrace the sacred steps back to Godhead. In the writings of Iamblichus we find that:

> *The Egyptian priests were accustomed to exhibit simulacra of the gods in circles and globes as symbols of the uniform principle of Life. Hermes Trismegistus compared Divinity to a circle, and the sublime description will be remembered, that its centre is everywhere and the circumference nowhere. The Pythagoreans regarded the circle as sacred and considered it as the symbol of the highest spiritual truth. It also represents very aptly all human progress, which is never in straight lines, but in circles returning on themselves as if advancing in ascending spirals, or retrograding in vortices tending downward.*

Study of the Qabalistic Tree soon reveals that each of the *sephirahs'* levels of consciousness plays an important harmonising role in conjunction with that of its neighbours. Some of the *sephirah* have distinct personal attributes – the Father, Mother, Son and Daughter, etc., – while others are represented by more abstract forms. The re-occurring triad of paths and circles also represent the 'trinity' of fulfilment and sacred wisdom. In practical Qabalistic usage, the priest-magician takes account of the different 'gods' and 'goddesses' assigned to the individual *sephirah*, and endeavours to compare and correlate them in terms of the attributes, correspondences, sacred qualities and aspirations that they personify.

> *He considers the gods to be symbols of what he himself may become, and regards their mythology as a type of symbolic energy process deep in the spiritual areas of his mind. This is what Jung was implying in his theory of the Archetypes of the Collective Unconsciousness, but for the magician it is a pragmatic reality. He knows the gods are inherent in his mind and he devises rituals and meditations as aides for encountering them.*
>
> *[The Occult Sourcebook]*

As we have seen, all these symbols are so ancient that they are buried deep in the 'vast storehouse of the racial subconsciousness', responding swiftly and with incalculable fullness, along the more direct paths, which ages before have mapped out in the 'shadowlands of the subconsciousness'. Not only that, throughout the history of religion the 'company of gods' were repeatedly three in number, often formed by the local deity and two gods who were associated with him and who shared the focus of worship *with* him. In later times, two of the Triad were gods, one young one old, and the third a goddess who was, naturally, the female counterpart of the older god. The conception of the Egyptian Triad (Trinity) is probably as old as the belief in the gods themselves.

So, even in the most simplistic of terms, we can see that the Qabalistic Tree of Life could be used as a template for the whole Universe, in that the pillars, paths and *sephiroth* – and even the concept of the 'reverse side of the Tree' – correspond to the scientific theories of multiple and parallel universes, black holes, worm holes, cosmic membranes and vibrating strings. Of course, the Egyptians of the ancient Khemetic beliefs had none of this 'advanced' scientific theory, but to repeat a refrain – they recorded their concept of Life as coming from beyond the stars, and returning to the realms of the Imperishable Ones after death.

Unfortunately, because of Aleister Crowley's infamous reputation – much of it promulgated by himself – any reference to him as a prophet of stellar wisdom will be met with incredulity and the likelihood of downright hostility from some quarters. If we trawl through his voluminous writings, however, we find that the 'star' is a re-occurring theme. Esoteric author Robert Anton Wilson considered Crowley to be:

> *One of the most original thinkers of this era – right up there with such titans as Einstein and Joyce. Indeed, what Einstein did for physics and Joyce for the novel (and Picasso for painting, and Pound for poetry, and Wright for architecture), Crowley did for the mystic tradition. He swept aside all 19th century barnacles and incrustations, redefined every concept, and created something that is totally contemporary with our existence as 20th century persons ... Crowley was always true to that inner 'governor' – that hidden star in every human psyche – and followed it without flinching.*

Much of Crowley's writings were concerned with the Great Work: the transformation of man in the quest for self-discovery. This 'quest' holds that:

> *...man has far vaster potentiality for know-ledge, and hence power over his fate, than he ordinarily dreams of as possible ... that it is possible to know – in a way that is completely different from the mere accumulation of facts – man's essential nature and his true relationship to the creative force behind the universe, and wherein his fulfilment lies – that is what it is he values most highly when the meaning of life is clearly seen.*
>
> [*Eye in the Triangle*, Israel Regardie]

The first steps towards the Great Work are, as every magical practitioner knows, 'To obtain the Knowledge and Conversation of the Holy Guardian Angel', or experience of the mystical enlightenment in both vision and the waking state. And as Israel Regardie observes:

It must be an occurrence of the greatest significance in the treading of the Path because it appears always and everywhere as unconditional. It is an experience which defies definition, as well in its elementary flashes as in its most advanced transports. No code of thought, philosophy or religion, no logical process can bind or limit it. It always represents, spiritually, a marked attainment, a liberation from the perplexities and turmoils of life, and from nearly every psychic complication.

At this point we need to ask ourselves:
What exactly *is* a Holy Guardian Angel?

and

Does *everyone* have this guiding spirit watching over them?

In truth, the answer to the second question is 'No!' Superstition and the establishment religions would like everyone to bask in the religious certainty that there was a personal guardian angel watching over each and every one of us from birth to the grave, but in reality the answer is not so simple. These 'guardians' may watch over mankind in order to single out the 'promising students' in terms of spiritual development, but as each individual succumbs to the lure of earthly pursuits and material pleasures, so the guardians withdraw to concentrate their energies on those who stay the course.

This particular kind of cosmic bonding was *never* an option for all. It was the growing power of the incoming priesthoods that overthrew the early priest-astronomers, and who promised eternal and everlasting life to the common man. It might have been Karl Marx who coined the phrase that religion was the opium of the people, but he was not the first to have realised this – the concept was already being exploited by the Osirian priesthood as early as Dynasty VI. The elitist Old Order had been swept away and, in the place of direct communication with the cosmic entities, there was an ancient equivalent of happy-clappy evangelism that promised everyone would be welcomed into the embrace of the gods in the Afterlife.

As we have seen, however, the central idea behind early Egyptian belief was that the 'god' would descend from the stars and waken the god-nature in the priest, or that the god would manifest through the consciousness of the individual. Here the divine spirit is brought down into the priest-magician and as a result, 'familiar objects take on a divine radiance illuminated by an internal spiritual light'.

In *The Eye in the Triangle*, Regardie describes this process in these words: "All we can say honestly and simply is that the awakening comes. There is no certain method, no stereotyped set of stimuli or patterns, no standard set of responses. But when it is there, when it does come, the individual is never the same. It is rather like being brought to the Light, in the ritualistic sense, except that this is no ritual. It occurs in the most natural, and, in one sense, the most unsought way." But this descent into the Mysteries does not confer automatic insight into the Will of the Divine.

> *These are the experiences and events which occur to every aspirant when initiation forces the realisation upon him, through the activation of the latent contents of his own psyche, that 'all is sorrow'. In fact, the existential criterion or hall-marks of successful initiation is the occurrence of these or similar experiences.*

In other words, the more enlightened the seeker becomes, the more he (or she) comes to realise that:

> *...the whole universe, under the stimulation of the magical elements ... seems to tumble like a pack of cards crazily about one's feet. The significance of all this is to point to a higher type of consciousness, the beginning of a spiritual rebirth. It acts as a self-evolved link between the higher Self at peace in its supernal place, and the human soul, bound by its fall to the world of illusion, fear and anxiety. But until that self-awareness and acquired knowledge are tuned to higher and initiated goals, sorrow and anxiety are the inevitable results.*

Here we find that direct contact with the Divine spirit following Initiation does *not* bring an inner peace and contentment ... in fact, the reverse is true. The Initiate is overwhelmed by a sense of futility and desolation; the 'innocence' of the pre-initiatory state cannot be regained, and the way ahead is uncertain and dangerous.

These were the lofty heights of Crowley's own magical experience and experimentation, and why he could preach to his followers: 'I say to each man and woman, 'You are unique and sovereign, the centre of the universe ... Every man and every woman is a star!' You, being man, are therefore a star. The soul of a star is what we call genius. You are a genius.'

And strangely enough, it is within Aleister Crowley's own Thelemic philosophy we find that elusive amalgamation of history, science, theology, philosophy and magic. 'The land of Khem is my spiritual fatherland,' he wrote, ' ... my gods were those of Egypt,' thereby linking the remote historical past with the scientific future's belief in and search for praeter-human intelligences [SETI]; and encompassing the receiving of knowledge derived from the investigation of nature through the senses and intellect. The bringer of *The Book of the Law*, Aiwass, claimed to be 'a messenger of the Lord of the Universe' and was revealing a method by which men may arrive independently at the direct consciousness of the universal Truth and 'enter into communication directly on their own initiative and responsibility with the type of intelligence which informs it, and solve all their personal religious problems'.

When Crowley writes about religion, however, he is not referring to the doctrines of the established faiths when he goes out to prove the existence of 'god'. "The existence of true religion pre-supposes that of some discarnate intelligence, whether we call him God or anything else. And this is exactly what no religion had ever proved scientifically ... But there is no a priori reason for doubting the existence of such beings. We have long been acquainted with many discarnate forces ... Especially in the last few years science has been chiefly occupied with the reactions, not merely of things which cannot be directly perceived by sense, but of forces which do not possess being at all in the old sense of the word."

So here, in the magical writings of a 20th century magus, we find reflected the observations of the ancient world in placing their gods in the realms beyond the stars, but with whom *both* could make direct contact by harnessing the power of the senses and intellect. And here is the right place to repeat an earlier extract, which observes that, however much we might like to deny it, evidence of god – *or what is left of Him/Her/It* – *is* out there. This may not be the benevolent, divine presence of the religious textbooks, but current exploration produces a more reasonable argument for the existence of God from the *scientist's* point of view. By facing up to the future destruction of the planet by natural forces, and the rebirth of new stars, rather than confirming the *non-existence* of God, science actually proclaims long and loud that there is proof of everlasting, regenerating life ...

But what do we mean by 'what is left of God'? In his novel, *The Survivors*, Simon Raven has one of his characters put forth the theory that God had actually destroyed himself. It is, of course, pure fiction but it raises a few points to ponder if we are of a mind to do so; if we allow ourselves to travel backwards in time, just as the this character had done and the subsequent conversation in which a friend describes his vision to another:

> In his dream-vision he'd been catapulted back in time to witness what had happened before space and time began ... where there was Nothing. Not even emptiness, for there was not yet any form of space to be empty ... But how, he'd asked himself, had existence sprung from this nothingness. Because there was total nullity, nothing whatever could have been born in it or emerged from it. He had seen the explosion, and now he was seeing the nullity that had preceded it, and out of which, 'it' must have come.
>
> What he'd seen, he convinces himself was God's death. *'For there could only be one explanation ... The nullity which preceded the universe only commenced when there was a universe to precede. The explosion which was the birth of the universe had created nullity in retrospect. Before the universe began there must have been something, which we may call God. But God, in creating the universe, had destroyed himself – he had become the universe, and so left a blank, a nullity, where he himself had once been.'*
>
> His companion, obviously a sceptic, observes cynically that if he'd been privileged enough to travel back that far in time to where the Universe began, he

must have encountered God, or whatever there had been there before God existed. *'No. In becoming the universe God abdicated. He destroyed himself as God. He turned what he had been, his true self, into nullity and thereby forfeited the Godlike qualities which pertained to him. The universe which he had become is also his grave. He has no control in it, or over it. God, as God, is dead.'*

The companion persists in humouring his friend by asking why had God in effect, committed suicide. *'The only person who could answer that question,'* came the reply, *'would be the true God who no longer exists to answer it. It is conceivable that he got bored with his own perfection.'*

[*The Survivors* from the 'Alms for Oblivion' series, Simon Raven]

Heady stuff and pure speculative fiction ... but there are more than a few atoms of truth in that speculation. What if the Big Bang, as well as being the birth of the Universe as we know it, was also the death of its Creator in the true spirit of the original Sacrificial/Dying God? And what if the atoms of his corpse, catapulted across time and space gave form to those discarnate, or extraterrestrial intelligences that both science and magicians believe to exist? We might accept that God is very much dead, but we must also consider the possibility that the atoms of his 'wisdom' as well as his corporeal body were blasted across the cosmos in much the same way as the debris from an exploding supernova. To return again to Eliphas Levi:

> *Without faith, science leads to doubt; without science, faith leads to superstition. Uniting them brings certainty, but in so doing they must never be confused with each other ... The science of the Qabalah makes doubt, as regards religion, impossible, for it alone reconciles reason with faith by showing that universal dogma, at bottom is always and everywhere the same, though formulated differently in certain times and places, is the purest expression of the aspirations of the human mind, enlightened by a necessary faith.*

By now, it should be apparent that the stellar path is the path of the individual and reached only after long years of magical journeying. It may often mean walking away from the group confines of a particular Tradition, while always remaining true to one's own roots regardless of how far we may travel ... still part of it, but no longer belonging. And if we wish to take our quest further into the uncharted, esoteric regions of the cosmos, it will be necessary to rid ourselves of the altruistic ethos of modern pagan thinking and reflect upon Aleister Crowley's own brand of stellar wisdom. "In a galaxy each star has its own magnitude, characteristics and direction, and the celestial harmony is best maintained by its attending to its own business. Nothing can be more subversive of that harmony than if a number of stars set up in a uniform standard of conduct insisted on everyone aiming at the same goal, going at the same pace, and so on. Even a single star, by refusing to do its own Will, by restricting itself in any way, would immediately produce disorder."

In other words: the Will of Set as opposed to the Order of Ma'at. For as we have seen, Set was the god of Chaos, pure primordial energy that fuelled the Will of the individual, as opposed to that of Ma'at (order and harmony). Unequivocally, the seeker needs to be able to differentiate between the need for social order and the freedom of the individual, for there is nothing altruistic about the pursuit of mystical enlightenment.

What is needed to turn the key is the right mindset, and this means adopting a completely different concept in terms of philosophy and morality. But as our sympathetic scholar, George St Clair, observed, the discovery of the key does not mean that 'all the doors can be unlocked at once by an unpractised hand'. Neither does it take much of a flight of fancy to make the link between the ancient stellar gods of Khem; those known as the Great Old Ones, who control the destiny of this planet (and many other celestial realms), radiating their influence through the stars; and the SETI quest for extraterrestrial intelligence in deepest space.

The mystic in pursuit of these celestial contacts will, at some stage in his life, be unexpectedly offered the opportunity to undergo a magical or mystical ordeal: the main test being the recognition that the incident is of paramount importance. Crowley wrote:

> *I announced that since 'Every man and every woman is*
> *a star', each of us is defined and determined by a set of*

co-ordinates, has a true will proper and necessary, the dynamic expression of that nature. The conclusion from these premises is that the sole and whole duty of each of us is, having discovered the purpose for which he or she is fitted, to devote every energy to its accomplishment.

It should also be obvious by now, that the religious doctrines of the world-dominant monotheistic religions would be more than anxious to suppress any philosophy that exalted the Will of the individual as opposed the social obligation of order and harmony ... and excluded the vast majority of its followers. Needless to say, this does not mean that the magician should ride roughshod over the rest of humanity, but it does mean that he (or she) has an obligation to discover their own true Will and act in harmony with it to the best of his (or her) ability – in other words: *'Do What Thou Wilt Shall Be The Whole Of The Law.'*

It also explains the measures such opposing theologies will take to invalidate any suggestion that there are elements of their faith that are not normally revealed to the man or woman in the street. In fact, as far back as the end of the Pyramid Age, this promise has been used to strengthen the hold of the new religious establishments of the time, so can we even begin to imagine public reaction if it were given out officially that everlasting life was *not* for everyone?

Much of the problem of embracing new philosophies lies in the fact that most theologians (of any faith) are some 100 years behind the times with their visions of God. If they were to be more open and honest about the vast, glaring chasms between contemporary religious teaching and scientific advancement, people might show more respect, but for most, the theologians are still pre-occupied with the question of obedience, suffering and self-sacrifice, which enlightened seekers see as undermining present society. Crowley, of course, had something to say on the subject that should make everyone sit up and think before they consider themselves right for the stellar Path.

We have a sentimental idea of self-sacrifice ... it is the sacrifice of the strong to the weak. This is wholly against the principles of evolution. Any nation which does this systematically on a sufficiently large scale, simply destroys itself. The sacrifice is in vain; the weak are not even saved. We should not protect the weak and

86

the vicious from the results of their inferiority. By doing so, we perpetuate the elements of dissolution in our own social body. We should rather aid nature by subjecting every newcomer to the most rigorous tests of his [or her] fitness to deal with his environment. The human race grew in stature and intelligence as long as the individual prowess achieved security, so that the strongest and cleverest people were able to reproduce their kind in the best conditions. But when security became general through the operation of altruism the most degenerate of the people were often the offspring of the strongest.

Obviously, scientist and theologian Dr David Wilkinson does not share this view, but he does believe that the importance of the expanding Universe has yet been recognised by the theological community. "If the universe keeps on increasing its acceleration rate, then it will eventually lose energy, everything will cool down, there will be no life, no light, no warmth. That poses a number of theological questions. For example, why did God create a universe which was destined to futility? What does this tell us about God's purposes for the future? If the universe is winding down, and is a lost cause, what's the point of it all? A transformation of the cosmos is going on. The creation of a new heaven and a new earth is not simply the result of the evolution of this universe, but a sovereign act of God. Some people have thought that God can destroy the earth and then create a new earth in the midst of this cosmos. I think the cosmos is telling us that view is much too limited, much too anthropomorphic."

But, however Dr Wilkinson chooses to word it, it is obvious that the Earth is going to run out of steam and, even if science had made the journey possible, it would not be physically viable to transport every man, woman and child on the planet to the new 'Earth'. Even here, behind the words of comfort, the message is veiled, but clear: the Path is not for everyone!

Again, the difference between science, theology and mysticism is that the priest-magician is always willing to risk his (or her) life and sanity in pushing the boundaries of the mystical experience in pursuit of 'truth'. In order to understand something of the process and ethos of mystical Initiation, we have to bear in mind that the aim is to help produce a spiritually self-conscious and self-sufficient individual. In order to achieve this, the individual has to be a well-equipped 'all-rounder', not just someone with highly developed 'occult' powers.

In recent years, so much has been made of the issue of Initiation into the Mysteries that people tend to forget about the very necessary and very extended prior training, the latter in itself being no guarantee of success for the individual. Successful accomplishment of mystical advancement, however, offers a chance to walk between the worlds and attain, in esoteric terms – 'conversation with the Holy Guardian Angel'.

Once the Initiate has stepped through the portal, there is no going back and it alters the perspective on almost everything that we once held to be of worth and consequence. Even family and friends assume a lesser degree of importance when compared with the quest upon which we have embarked. This is why the first steeps on the Path should never bee taken lightly or without due thought about the consequences. We must accept that those we care about cannot lay claim to 'everlasting life' whether it be a Christian or pagan Afterlife, and that we may never again cross paths with those we've considered to be our soul-mates. There can be no re-tracing of our steps once we have stepped through the Gate.

The stellar Path is not for the faint-hearted. Nevertheless, if we fail to grasp the importance or appreciate the opportunity at its full value, we will have missed the supreme chance of our spiritual life and the gateway (or Stargate) to another world will be shut to us, at best for this lifetime, at worst – forever.

Part Four: *Liber Ægyptius*
"Let my servants be few and secret."
Liber AL Vel Legis pt1 v.10

It should now be apparent to the genuine seeker that the stellar wisdom of ancient Egyptian disciplines was never intended for those outside the inner sanctum of the temple. And from archaeological sources we can glean several plausible reasons why the Nile Valley was plunged into civil unrest at the end of the Pyramid Age. Despite hundreds of years of stability and prosperity, and from the advantage point of hindsight, we can see how a magically *inferior* priesthood might be willing to sanction the destruction and even murder of the old stellar priesthood, on whom they could apportion blame for the misfortunes of the State.

Liber Ægyptius, the *Book of Egyptian Magic*, offers only a tantalising glimpse into the fiery brilliance of the distant past, just as it can only suggest what lies behind the star-spangled veil of the future. The old stellar wisdom has been inert for too long for it to suddenly burst upon the consciousness like a supernova. To quote Crowley: "In all systems of religion is to be found a system of Initiation, which may be defined as the process by which a man comes to learn that unknown Crown. Though none can communicate either the knowledge or the power to achieve this, which we may call the Great Work, it is yet possible for initiates to guide others."

These first guided steps, therefore, come in the form of a series of pathworkings that differ each time the seeker performs them.

Stellar, Solar and Lunar Pathworkings

It is important that a full and accurate account of each exercise is recorded in a Magical Journal for comparison. There is sometimes confusion over the term 'pathworking' because often this is mistakenly referred to as 'visualisation'. There is a difference between the two applications but here visualisation is the relaxed and controlled state that is *the lead-in* to pathworking proper. Most magical practitioners will be familiar with the moon/earth tides and so we begin by exploring the natural lunar energies.

The Lunar Pathworking

Choose the phase of the moon when your *personal* magical energy is at its strongest. Check on the time of moon-rise, and unless you are going to work on the dark phase, you should try to ensure that the moon is visible throughout your pathworking. For this first, simple exercise we are going to bathe in moonlight and let its rejuvenating powers wash over us, and because this is a very individual exercise there are no instructions other than to go with the flow. For all moon phases, sit in the moonbeams, watch them as they glow all over and around you like shimmering silvery mercury. You can pick handfuls up and watch it stream through your fingers like fine sand or silvery water. **How does that make you feel?**

If you are using the dark phase, simply gaze up into the dark sky above, and allow yourself to drift out into the comforting darkness; visualise yourself slipping deeper and deeper into the void. There is no danger here and you can return whenever you wish. Let yourself drift out into the softness, where it feels like sinking into beautiful velvet or the softness of unseen feathers. It is gentle, soft and welcoming.

How do you feel in this black, silent world?
Record the results in your Magical Journal.

The Solar Pathworking

We may not, however, be as familiar with solar energies, since most magical practitioners channel their activities under the cover of darkness. By contrast, the Egyptian priesthood performed their devotions during the hours of daylight: at dawn, noon and dusk – see the *Book of Days*.

Try this as a *daytime* pathworking by sitting in a patch of strong sunlight either outdoors or indoors. Make yourself comfortable and concentrate on a candle flame burning in a shaft of direct sunlight, which will give a completely different effect to that which we usually experience in a darkened room. You are working with the element of fire through the sunlight and flame.

Imagine that you are being drawn gently into the candle flame. Feel the warmth as you pass into the centre of the flame. Allow your being to dance in the flame; you are one with it. If you feel your eyelids drooping let them close but keep your mind focussed within the candle flame. See what happens ... maybe nothing will, but this is a form of lucid dreaming that can often produce some interesting results. If the working can be performed around the time of one of the solstices or equinoxes, then so much the better. Sunday would be a good day to try this, as it is traditionally the day of the Sun.

Record the results in your Magical Journal.

The Stellar Pathworking

Before embarking on the stellar pathworking, spend some time studying the placement of the circumpolar stars in any beginners' guide to astronomy. Over time, we *must* become familiar with the stars – and not with an astrologer's eye – but from an astronomer's perspective.

This exercise should be performed outdoors on a clear night before or just after the dark of the moon. [If you cannot perform this outdoors, sit at an open window with the interior lights switched off.] Your eyes will need 20 minutes to adjust to night vision so use the time to make yourself comfortable. Ensure that you are wearing something warm if you are doing this in winter. As you will need to spend some time with your head tilted back, it is a good idea to spend this waiting time arranging cushions or setting a reclining chair so that you can gaze at the heavens in comfort.

To begin, you will need to identify two star constellations; **Ursa Major** (the Plough) and **Cassiopia** (with its 'W' formation). These are known as circumpolar stars as they perpetually revolve around the **Pole Star** (Polaris), and can be seen as symbolising the male and female cosmic energies. They are both easy to identify.

After 20 minutes, look up into the sky again, and you will be surprised how many more stars you can see now that your eyes have made the adjustment. Watch Cassiopia and Ursa Major in their slow heavenly dance and think about the energies of male and female weaving their magical dance across the night skies. Let your eyes be drawn towards the brightest star that you can see and concentrate all your effort into reaching out to this star with your mind. Let the charm '*listen and glisten*' run repetitively through your mind over and over again the whole time …
See what happens … Record the results in your Magical Journal.

These elementary exercises are useful tools in that they focus and draw the seeker's attention away from the stereotypical planetary influences, and out into deep-space. Do not attempt to work them one after the other, but spread them over the course of a month to get the best from your efforts. The results will *always* vary, but the end-product will be a greater understanding as the journey deepens.

Despite claims to the contrary, the origins of the constellation patterns are not known with any certainty. Both the ancient Chinese and Egyptians drew up fanciful sky maps (as we know, two of the Egyptian constellations, for example, were the Crocodile and the Hippopotamus). The template followed today, however, is based on that of the ancient Greeks, and all of the 48 constellations given by Ptolemy in his book the *Almagest*, written about 150AD, are still in use. Ptolemy's list contains most of the important constellations visible from the latitude of Alexandria in Egypt. Among them are the two Bears, Cygnus, Herculus, Hydra and Aquila, as well as the 12 zodiacal groups. There are also some small, obscure constellations, such as Equuleus (the Foal) and Sagitta (the Arrow), which are surprisingly faint and, one would have thought, too ill-defined to be included in that original 48.

It has been said that the night sky is a mythological picture book, although none of the original Egyptian myths have been preserved in the telling. But it is interesting that an early reference in the Pyramid Texts identifies Sopdu, an early hawk-god who personified the eastern frontier of Egypt, as a star who was born from the union of the Orion (*Sah*) and the Dog Star (*Sopdet*). He later became associated with the more important hawk-god Horus, and the Triad of Sopdet (Sirius), Sah (Orion) and Sopdu was later paralleled by the divine family of Isis, Osiris and Horus.

As we have already discussed, the Greeks – despite creating the 'modern' star-maps – actually accredited the Egyptians with recognising the existence of the *movement* of the stars. Thales, who lived in the 6th century BC, was the first of the Greek philosophers to bring back to Greece the knowledge and records of the Babylonians and Egyptians, and put forward theories that lay somewhere between the 'mythologies of the past and future scientific discoveries'. But it was Ptolemy of Alexandria who drew together centuries of Babylonian observations of the motions of the planets to support his theory of an Earth-centred universe and it was his system that ruled the world of astronomy for nearly 1,500 years.

Perhaps it is not surprising that Egyptian 'mythology' failed to play a major role in these theories since, by that time, there was little preserved of the ancient religion, and the Greeks had already associated most of the old Egyptian gods with their own home-grown myths and legends. Despite trying to explain why natural events occurred without reference to supernatural causes, the Greeks appear to have little concept of the stellar energies of deep space that played such an important part within the Egyptian Mysteries.

Perhaps because the Graeco-Roman Mystery traditions tended to be chthonic rather than cosmic, they were dismissive of the strange anthropomorphic gods of a distant and long-dead civilisation. In addition, apart from the various creation-myths, there is very little by way of folklore preserved in the literature of Egypt. According to the entry in *The British Museum Dictionary of Ancient Egypt*, the Middle Kingdom was particularly characterised by the introduction of 'fictional' literature, all of which *purport* to be historical accounts, although many of the details of the narrative indicate that they were fantasies designed to entertain rather than record actual events. The Greeks probably considered them unworthy of consideration and, as a result, the modern astronomical references are devoid of any link to an older Egypt.

The Imperishable Ones

Before attempting to travel out into the cosmos, however, the seeker needs to return to the concept of the 'Imperishable Ones' – the circumpolar stars that provided the fundamental basis for the archaic religion. These are the stars that never set, but seem to circle around the celestial Pole or North Star, which in our time is Polaris in the constellation of Ursa Minor. This star is easily located by taking a straight line from the stars Merak and Dubhe in Ursa Major to the last star (Polaris) in the Little Bear's tail. Once you have got used to locating the Pole Star, use it as a focus for the stellar pathworking.

Polaris, however, has not always been the Pole Star. When the pyramids were being built around 4,800 years ago, during the Old Kingdom, the north-pole star was Thuban – Alpha Draconis in the constellation of Draco. Thuban was at its closest to the pole in 2830BC and there have been many academic discussions about the celestial pole and the alignment of the pyramids. Despite having no outstandingly bright stars, Draco sprawls across the sky and is the largest of all the constellations, occupying over 1,000 square degrees of the sky. Thuban, today, is only the eighth brightest star in Draco and can barely be seen with the naked eye in an unpolluted night sky, but it is not surprising that this large, rambling star-grouping was identified with Nut, the 'Mother of Set'.

Similarly, those seven stars of Ursa Major cannot be mistaken and the sacrificial offering – the 'thigh' – is easily identified from the zodiacal ceiling in the Temple of Hathor at Dendera. These are the seven stars that have long been associated with Set. Almost opposite Ursa Major is the distinctive constellation of Cassiopeia, which corresponds to the figure of the hippopotamus – Tauret, goddess of childbirth.

These four constellations: Ursa Major, Ursa Minor, Draco and Cassiopeia contain the principal stars with which the Egyptians identified as being the 'Stars That Grow Not Weary'. Or the place to where the king journeyed after death; to be reborn and returned to earth as an embodiment of the living god. Without the aid of telescopes, it *is* possible to watch and study these brilliant specks of light, which will eventually become the focus for future pathworkings and the first step on the stellar path.

In his extensive writings, Aleister Crowley has provided us with examples of his own pathworkings in order that we may try for ourselves, those first tentative steps in linking magically and intellectually with the universal energies so hungrily sought by men of science and faith from the beginning of time. In his own *Confessions,* he gives an insight into a meditation technique used for the purpose of projecting the Will.

The 'Star-Sponge' Vision

> *I lost consciousness of everything but a universal space in which were innumerable bright points, and I realised this as a physical representation of the universe ... I concentrated on this vision, with the result that the void space which had been the principal element of it diminished in importance; space appeared to be ablaze, yet the radiant points were not confused ...*

This vision led to an identification of the individual blazing points of the stars, and he perceived that each star was connected by a ray of light with its neighbour, and that certain stars were of greater magnitude and brilliancy than the rest ... The next step is to attempt to combine the previous stellar pathworking with the 'Star-SpongeVision' and see what kind of reaction can be obtained by focussing on Polaris ... *'listen and glisten'* ... Does the star glow bigger and brighter? Does it draw you toward it? Or does it cast you deeper into space on one of its rays of light?

All we are doing is opening up our minds to the power of cosmic forces. What is important to realise, is that this is only very elementary pathworking and, no matter how intense, illuminating or frightening the imagery, **these are merely the steps of a relatively humble beginner.**

We cannot, however, afford to *over*-estimate the effects of this simple psychic probing, simply because we could be laying ourselves wide open to attack from extra-terrestrial intelligences before we are ready to cope with them. And be warned, there *are* dangerous energies at large out there for the uninitiated. No matter how profound the experience, nor how intensely charged we *believe* ourselves to have become, we are not yet ready to claim the title of Master of the Universe!

The opening and closing verses of Crowley's famous poem, *One Star in Sight* becomes an allegory for the metaphysical transformation of the seeker. At the start of the journey the seeker's head and feet are held fast, imprisoned in ignorance of what lies beyond the veil.

Thy feet in mire, thine head in murk,
O man, how piteous thy plight,
The doubts that daunt, the ills that irk,
Thou hast nor wit nor will to fight –
How hope in heart, or worth in work?
No star in sight!

Few have the 'wit nor will' to challenge this state of ignorance or push the boundaries of Knowing and, as a result, most will remain fettered by spiritual doubt and uncertainty. But along with Knowledge and Wisdom, comes Understanding.

To man I come, the number of
A man my number, Lion of Light;
I am The Beast whose Law is Love.
Love under Will, his royal right –
Behold within, and not above,
One star in sight

Before we can 'behold within', there are many paths to travel and other worlds to explore. To repeat Crowley's words: "Though none can communicate either the knowledge or the power to achieve this, which we may call the Great Work, it is yet possible for initiates to guide others."

This guiding towards the rediscovery of the old stellar wisdom can only be in the form of general pathworking and visualisation, simply because each person's journey will take a different route. Some methods will appear as easy as following stepping stones across a stream, while others will plunge the seeker into the Abyss. Added to this, we still have no way of knowing how the earliest Egyptians acquired their knowledge of other worlds, but it is safe to assume that certain members of the priesthood would have closely studied every movement of those stars on which their beliefs were focused. Needless to say, that ancient night sky with its vast panorama stretched out across the open desert, would have offered a far greater stellar vista than our own present-day polluted sky-scape.

Three poems by Walter de la Mare refer to the stars that are visible from the northern hemisphere. The first extract from *Stars*, helps to identify those that make up the formation of Orion – the constellation that played such an important part in Egyptian beliefs. Look for Orion around the Winter Solstice ... and follow the instructions ...

If to the heavens you lift your eyes
When Winter reigns o'er our Northern skies,
And snow-cloud none the zenith mars,
As Yule-tide midnight these your stars:
Low in the South see bleak-blazing Sirius;
Above him hang Betelgeuse, Procyon wan;
Wild-eyed to the West of him, Rigel and Bellatrix,
And rudd-red Aldebaran journeying on ..

Similarly, *The Ride-by-Nights* can easily be adapted for a simple visualisation once you've deciphered the cryptic clues in the poem for the real names of the constellations: choose a clear, moonless night around the Winter Solstice to locate where they are. Now visualise yourself zooming through the night like a shooting star ... beneath Charlie's Wane (the Plough or Ursa Major) and under the Dragon's Feet (Draco). The air is cold and crisp and thousands of stars hurtle past, as you wheel and turn in a helter-skelter ride along the Milky Way. Imagine yourself soaring among the twinkling beads of light and between the legs of the Chair (Cassiopeia) and out past Leo. The unmistakeable form of Orion, with Sirius following behind, looms large ahead but you accelerate and fly between the legs of the Hunter before heading back home.

This is a simple exercise that can be repeated whenever there is a clear, moonless night ... and may just lead to a revealing pathworking, despite the fact that the imagery is one of British witchcraft, rather than the Egyptian Mystery Tradition!

The third poem, *The Wanderers*, focuses the mind on the planets, even though the Egyptians were not aware of the two furthest – Uranus and Neptune.

And through these sweet fields go,
Wand'ers mid the stars
Venus, Mercury, Uranus, Neptune,
Saturn, Jupiter, Mars.

Nevertheless, as we have seen earlier in this book, those planets with which the Egyptians were familiar were assigned to the various gods:

Horus 'who limits the two lands' – Jupiter
Horus of the Horizon – Mars;

Sebegu (a god associated with Set) – Mercury
Horus 'bull of the sky' – Saturn
Re or Osiris with Venus ('the one who crosses' or 'god of the morning').

Around 1590BC an anonymous Egyptian scribe wrote: *'Do you not know that Egypt is a copy of heaven and the temple of the whole world?'* Today, our 'temple' reaches out into space and, like all true seekers of the Mysteries, we need to understand the perils of the Path that draws us ever onward. In the 21st century we are no longer reliant on blind faith simply because we now have a wider view of the cosmos, and a greater belief in Source of all life, as a continuing and self-perpetuating concept. Visualise the rebirth of another world ...

> From out of nowhere, through the swirling fog, a world the size of the Earth's Moon looms into view. Its surface is glowing with lakes of bubbling lava, and a torrent of impacting meteorites sends white-hot rock spraying high up into its wispy jacket of sulphur-green clouds. The bombardment is relentless and stone by stone, rock by rock, boulder by boulder, the growing planet absorbs anything that dares stray into its path. Originally, just one of a huge army of rocks circling an embryonic Sun, this world has grown large. It has swallowed up countless smaller rivals. Others, which narrowly escaped its draw, it threw off course and sent to a fiery death in the heart of the Sun. The odds of this young planet surviving are slight – at any moment it could be torn apart in a cataclysmic collision with another large ball of rock. There are scores of others like it in this young Solar System, and only a handful will make it. Yet somehow it does survive. In 100 million years it will grow large enough to hang on to a thick layer of gas and cloud. Its surface, now hot enough to melt rock, will cool to a temperature where water will condense into oceans and, one day, it will develop life ...
> [Extract from *The Planets*, McNab & Younger]

By using the 'birth of a planet' sequence above, create your own pathworking in order to visit other worlds. To put your 'journeying' into perspective, bear in mind that unlike Ptolemy's theory of an Earth-centred universe, we now know that our Earth is situated in a remote backwater of the Milky Way galaxy. In fact, the Earth is on the middle arm of three great spirals – known as the Orion arm. Taking this as our cue, we now are going back even further than the birth of the planet, because the Stellar Path is all about pushing the boundaries. ... By now our own galaxy was already billions of years old and full of stars, and using the following as a basis for visualisation, see where this journey takes you ...

> From the centre of our galaxy, a massive cloud was gently drifting through space As this cloud floats between the distant star fields, being pulled first this way then that by gravitational tugs of other stars, pockets of gas in the cloud started to collapse inwards on themselves. As these imploding pockets reached a critical density, their cores heated up and ignited: stars were born. If we could watch the process of aeons speeded up into minutes, we might see small points of light flickering into life as stellar neighbourhoods sprang up throughout the cloud. Most of the smaller lights might glow steadily for several tens of seconds before slowly burning themselves out. But as the rash of stars spread throughout the cloud, a few of the lights – the largest and brightest – would flare for just a few brief seconds before disappearing. These are giant stars that burn for just a fraction of the lifetimes of their smaller, steadier siblings ... Deep in the twinkling parent cloud another light flickered on – it was our Sun.
>
> [Extract from *The Planets*, McNab & Younger]

The Realm of Chaos
Chaos: the shape of matter before it was reduced to order

If we want to work with *real* chaos energy, then it is necessary to have some idea of those naturally occurring phenomena that happen in space and yet have serious repercussions here on Earth. The solar pathworking given at the beginning of this section, is an exploratory exercise but if the more experienced practitioner wishes to work with *real* solar forces, then a basic scientific understanding of the type of energy manifesting in the form of solar winds and sun-spots – first discovered by the Chinese 2,000 years ago – is essential.

Sun Spots
The Sun is so brilliant that it can damage the eye within seconds and so we should *never* look at it directly through a telescope or binoculars, nor stare at it with the naked eye. If we *were* able to view the Sun direct, it would be possible to see small dark spots, just a few hundred kilometres across, where strong magnetic fields emerge through the Sun's surface. Some last for just a few hours, while others grow quite large, perhaps 10 times the size of the Earth, and last for months.

The number of sun-spots wax and wane over an 11-year period, in what is generally referred to as the 'sun-spot cycle'. In addition to the sun-spots, the cycle also produces a host of other activity on and above the Sun's surface. The *Encyclopaedia of the Universe* informs us that: "Among the more violent events associated with active regions, where the magnetic field is twisted and complex, are flares, in which a huge amount of energy is released – the equivalent of 10 billion one-megaton bombs in a large one … creating shock waves and producing strong bursts of radio emission."

Another manifestation of this type of solar activity is where 10 billion tonnes of hot gas are ejected into interplanetary space, pulling with it elements of the coronal magnetic field. As we should now expect: Earth is not isolated from these violent events – the storms of energetic particles shot out by the Sun often wash the near-Earth environment, affecting power lines and communications, generating auroral displays in the ionosphere around the north and south poles, and damaging sensitive equipment on spacecraft.

Solar winds
Close to the maximum of the sun-spot cycle, a steady flow of atomic particles of ionized gas streams out from the Sun in all directions. This activity is estimated to carry off 50 million million tonnes of material per year and the material flowing away from the Sun, at a few hundred kilometres per second, produces the solar wind. The intensity of solar wind is enhanced during solar storms but the average velocity as it passes the Earth is 300-400 kilometres per second! These wind-speed variations buffet the Earth's magnetic field and can produce storms in the Earth's magnetosphere, and are responsible for the Aurora Borealis, or Northern Lights.

However, a burst of radiation on 20th January 2005 accompanied a huge solar flare tripped radiation monitors worldwide and scrambled detectors on spacecraft, marking the 'largest solar radiation signal *on the ground* in nearly 50 years'. Normally, it takes two or more hours for a dangerous shower of positively charged protons to reach maximum intensity at Earth after a solar flare, and between one and four days for ejected solar material to arrive. But the particles from this vast flare peaked about 15 minutes after the first signs. So the next time you hear a chaos magician talking about butterfly wings flapping on the other side of the planet, just take a leaf out of *Crocodile Dundee's* book and think to yourself: *'Nah! THAT'S Chaos!'*

Needless to say, no one in their right mind would ever attempt to harness such uncontrollable power but it does serve as an example of bringing the might of the cosmos right to our doorstep. It also acts as a lesson in understanding that *'learning does not consist of knowing what we must or can do, but also of knowing what we could do and perhaps should not do'.* [Umberto Eco]

North Wind Meditation

As a workable substitute, a highly experienced member of the Temple of Khem's priesthood, following a guided exercise in working with elemental quarters, wrote the following meditation. Perhaps the results were produced because the spiritual or magical focus of Egyptian working is geared towards the North (i.e. the Imperishable Ones), or simply because North is always regarded in esoteric terms as the 'Place of Power', but this came through as extremely powerful imagery:

> The first wind that seemed to capture my attention was the North Wind. Before me stretched a vast expanse of dark space lit by the cold blue/white twinkling of the stellar bodies. The scene was cold and void and I loved every aspect of it, because I knew that somewhere out there was a mighty power waiting to be called and welcomed back to these realms. Between the archaic galaxies, a chill wind started to blow towards the circle and me. It's icy sharpness cut the surface of the skin like a thousand minute fine needle-points. There was a sensation of knowledge and enormous power, but also of destruction, darkness, fear and chaos. It was as if the Great Old Ones who created humanity had decided to return and see how their work was progressing. I experienced a total lack of sentiment, as we usually know it, and in its place was a feeling of the end of all time when false forms are cast off and you stand face to face with eternity. Perhaps when death itself has died.

Slowly I tried to channel the North Wind down from its lofty regions to the Earth plane, and gain mundane knowledge of it. The home of this wind on Earth is the high snowy mountain passes, or the tumbled chaos of the icefields of the Arctic or Antarctic. When working with this wind I was intolerant to people and noise, and longed for the freedom and solitude of those isolated places. I was reminded of the peoples of the Andes and Tibet as well as the Eskimos. My parting experience of this wind was that it was a wind of freedom and transformation that offered much to those who were committed to learning and service to magic. To me a good title for this wind is the Elder Wind because it brings change.

This pathworking is not, of course, without its risks and should not be undertaken merely for the thrill of the experience. And yet it is just another small step towards making that 'giant leap for mankind' in terms of a spiritual quest.

Batrachophrenoboocosmomachia

By contrast, in *The Complete Astrological Writings*, Crowley detailed a series of highly complicated exercises aimed at improving the capabilities of the seeker's mind. The final one being an extremely complex planetary pathworking that would take many years to master, involving the building up of the solar system within the mind's eye. Beginning with the Earth and the Moon, keeping in mind the relative sizes of, and the distance between, the planet and its satellite, the seeker will then add in turn Venus, Mars, Mercury and the Sun. At this stage it may be advisable to change the viewpoint to the centre of the Sun, since this makes it easier to add the Asteroids, Jupiter, Saturn, Uranus and Neptune.

The utmost attention to detail is now necessary, as the picture is highly complex, apart from the difficulty of appreciating relative size and distance ... Let this picture be practised month after month until it is absolutely perfect.   Once the exercise has been mastered, the practitioner should ... recommence the picture, starting from the Sun, and adding the planets one by one, each with its own proper motion, until he has an image perfect in all respects of the Solar System as it

101

actually exists. Let him particularly note that unless the apparent size is approximate to the real, his practise is wasted. Let him then add a comet to the picture; he may find, perhaps, that the path of this comet may assist him to expand the sphere of his mental vision until it includes a star. And thus, gathering one star after another, let his contemplation become vast as the heaven, in space and time ever aspiring to the perception of the Body of Nuit ...

The Urshu – Lords of Light

The *Urshu*, the old Great Ones of *zep tepi* – Egypt's 'First Time' – also have parallels in other esoteric cultures in the form of the Watchers, or Light Bearers – great cosmic beings who acted as intermediaries between gods and men, and played an important role in developing human affairs. The concept of these celestial beings appears to have originated in the Middle East, and entered the Western ritual magic tradition via the legend of the *Grigori*, or Watchers.

These were the Hebrew 'fallen-angels' or Ben Elohim, who mated with human women and taught them the magical arts, and from whom all esoteric traditions and occult knowledge are said to have sprung. This would not be the first 'idea' to have been hijacked by subsequent Middle Eastern cultures to add credence to their own burgeoning religious doctrine. Just as the Urshu became identified with the Ben Elohim, so the notion of the 'holy family' passed into Christian tradition, having already metamorphosed once within Egyptian history, from the early Triad of Sopdet (Sirius), Sahu (Orion) and Sopdu to the later divine family of Isis, Osiris and Horus.

In the book *Liber Ægyptius*, the suggestion was made that the Urshu decamped following the destruction of the stellar priesthood; repulsed by the excesses of mankind when they witnessed first-hand its capacity for self-destruction. Their continued presence as shadowy beings on the periphery of human consciousness has only added to the growing belief in guardians, angels and fairies within esoteric circles. When Crowley encountered Aiwass in that hotel room in Cairo, it was not a visitation by a 'good fairy' ... the Guardians are no longer kindly disposed towards humankind *en masse*. And we only have to read *The Book of the Law* to understand that there is even a certain amount of hostility towards those who remain impervious to the warnings.

Now let it be understood that I am a god of War and Vengeance ... I will give you a war-engine. With it ye shall smite the peoples; and none shall stand before you ... let blood flow to my name. Trample down the Heathen ...

Even up to his death in 1947, Crowley still found parts of *The Book* distasteful. This supposedly heralding in of the New Aeon in Part III of *Liber AL* proclaims *'an end to the humanitarian mawkishness that is destroying the human race by the deliberate artificial protection of the unfit'*. Are we to understand from such words, that no favours are to be expected from these extra-terrestrial intelligences that inhabit the 'world between worlds', seeking out receptive channels for their teachings? And, as if to endorse such musings, perhaps we should recall the results of the ToK priest's meditation, where he 'experienced a total lack of sentiment' when he encountered the old Great Ones.

For next stage of preparation, we need to reflect on the meaning behind the oldest religious writings in the world. "The texts can be understood through knowledge of the ancient Egyptian mythology and symbolism, which explain the origin, function and qualities of the natural laws,' writes Dr Ramses Seleem. "Someone who reads the texts without comprehension of the mythology and symbolism is like a deaf person trying to listen to the music of Mozart ... The Egyptian sages, through the mythology, mapped the path of eternity in detail ..." As we know, the Egyptian New Year was marked by the helical rising of Sopdet (the Dog Star, or Sirius). In the early Egyptian myth, it says that the newborn child, Sopdu, fathered by Sahu (Orion) came forth from the thighs of Sopdet. In death, the deceased then rises as a 'Sahu', or as a spiritual body, waiting to be reborn.

Star Thrall

Orion has been recognised as a distinctive group of stars for thousands of years. The Chaldeans knew it as Tammuz, named after the month in which the familiar belt of stars first rose before sunrise. The Syrians called it Al Jabbar, the Giant, and to the Greeks it was Orion, the great hunter. For the Egyptians it was Sahu.

Faulkner's analysis of the Pyramid Texts shows two distinct strata. One, the circumpolar stars and the northern sky, which appear as the abode of the gods and the illustrious royal dead; the other with the constellation of Orion and Sothis. *'Orion is either a companion of the King, and is joined by him, making with Sothis a celestial trio; the King may thus be thought of as sharing in the responsibility for regulating times and seasons.'* As fragmented as these details are, the power of the archaic stellar-cult was still making itself felt, if not wholly understood, well into the Pyramid Age and beyond. By this time, the Osirian cult was already transposed onto the earlier Sahu (*S3h*) – Sopdet (*Spdt*) – Sopdu (*Spdw*) Triad, the latter disappearing almost entirely. In Faulkner's 1969 translation of the Pyramid Texts, Osiris has already *become* Orion in the funerary texts.

Pyramid Texts

In Utterance 216 [151], for example, the king is represented as a star fading at dawn with the other stars:

Orion is swallowed up by the Netherworld,
Pure and living in the horizon.
Sothis is swallowed up by the Netherworld
Pure and living in the horizon.

In Utterance 218 [186] the king is identified with Osiris (Sahu):

In your name of Dweller in Orion, with a season in the sky and
a season on earth.

In Utterances 273-4 [408] ...

For the King is a god,
Older than the oldest.
Thousands serve him,
Hundreds offer to him,
There is given to him a warrant as Great Power
By Orion, father of the gods.

In Utterance 412 [723], a 'resurrection' text:

You shall reach the sky as Orion, your soul shall be as effective as
Sothis [Sopdet] ...

In Utterance 442 [819-21] the dead king becomes a star:

Behold, he has come as Orion, behold, Osiris [the king] *has come as Orion ... O King, the sky [Sopdet] conceives you with Orion [Sahu], the dawn-light bears you with Orion ... You will regularly ascend with Orion from the eastern region of the sky, you will regularly descend with Orion into the western region of the sky, your third is Sothis pure of thrones, and it is she who will guide you both on the goodly roads which are in the sky in the Fields of Rushes.*

In Utterances 466 [882-83] the king is again referred to as a star:

O King, you are this great star, the companion of Orion, who traverses the sky with Orion ... The sky has borne you with Orion ...

In Utterance 471 [[924] there is the 'ferryman' text:

I have come that I may glorify Orion ...

In Utterance 582 [1561] there is the 'ascension' text:

May Orion give me his hand, for Sothis has taken my hand ...

In Utterance 625 [1763] – As last:

I have ascended among the [Great Ones]; *I have gone up the ladder with my foot on Orion and my arm uplifted ...*

Even though the Osirian-cult has superseded the old stellar-cult of early times, it can still be seen how the ancient Mysteries were preserved within the doctrine of the new Egyptian religious beliefs.

Coffin Texts

These later funerary texts take their name from the fact that they were inscribed in ink on the inside walls of the wooden coffins during the Middle Kingdom. By this time, the Old Ways would have been forgotten, 'for there are none that now live who remember it'. The 'Spells' were added to and amended; and repeated by rote since the old priesthood had long since departed.

The Spells lack the mystery and majesty of the Pyramid Texts, and were probably 'dumbed-down' in order to appeal to the lower classes, who now had access to everlasting life. For example, Spell 44 [188] has faint echoes of the earlier texts, although there is the suggestion that the Spell no longer refers to the person of the king, but to anyone who could afford the funerary rites, as archaeological discoveries have shown:

May [Name] *be encircled by Orion, by Sothis and by the Morning Star, may they set you within the arms of your mother Nut ...*

Spell 227 [263] also reflects some of the old mystery ...

I am Orion who treads his Two Lands, who navigates in front of the stars of the sky on the belly of my mother Nut ...

As does Spell 236 [304]:

I ascend to the sky with Orion, I receive food-offerings with the Great Ones, my abode is at the high portals of the Entourage of Re ...

The Egyptians obviously retained the concept of the dead going to 'heaven', i.e. the abode of the stars, but this appears to be a purely collective religious belief, rather than a magico-religious one where the king assumes his moral obligation to transcend death to be reborn again as protector of his people and the State. The differences between the Pyramid Texts and the Coffin Texts can be seen as the demarcation of religion and the Mysteries, leaving what can best be identified as an 'Osirian death-cult' in the public domain.

Book of the Dead

Or to give the texts the correct name: 'The Chapters of Coming-Forth by Day', refers to the later collections of religious and magical texts, dating mostly from c1500-250 BC. The texts from this period are dominated by Osirian references, with only vague, infrequent mention of the original stellar-related beliefs. For example:

... may I see the Sektet boat of the sacred Sahu [Orion] *passing forth over the sky ...*

... triumphant are the fingers of Orion ...
... to Osiris-Orion (Sah) ...
Thou risest up like Sah (Orion) ...

We still have casual, fleeting glimpses of the old religion that had its roots in the belief in, or knowledge of, the unseen powers of the Universe, and knowing the order and the structure of things – i.e. the concept of Ma'at. The importance of the Mysteries, and knowledge that all things in the Universe are dependent on each other, however, appears to have been lost. This understanding is not, however, exclusive to the ancient Egyptians.

Reflected in many sacred systems of knowledge is the idea that the world is a mystery and yet, at the same time, operates according to strict, ordered relationships. Some questions can never be answered with a single answer and others can be answered simply by observing various cycles day after day, year after year ...
[*The Sacred: Ways of Knowledge, Sources of Life*]

But to return to the obvious link between the star-grouping of Orion and Sirius, and the ancient Mysteries. In January 2003, a claim was made by Dr Michael Rappenglueck, renowned for his pioneering work locating star charts painted on the walls of prehistoric caves, that the oldest image of a star pattern had been recognised as the constellation of Orion. Carved on an ivory tablet, *some 32,500 years ago*, this tiny sliver of mammoth tusk shows a carving of a man-like figure with arms and legs outstretched in the same pose as the stars of Orion.

It was found in a cave in the Ach Valley in Germany and the proportions of the man correspond to the pattern of stars that comprise Orion, despite the fact that these stars were in slightly different positions 32,000 years ago. Astronomical confirmation of the archaeological dating came from a computer reconstruction, which found evidence that Orion appeared completely above the natural horizon of the cave between 32,000 and 33,500 years ago! "The appendix between the legs would show a phallic star creature, in line with ancient ideas that Orion may be responsible for the celestial insemination of Earth, and for cosmic fertility."

Orion is the most striking of all the constellations and has had a special significance for many cultures throughout history, throughout the world. Perhaps this is where we should begin our search for ancient knowledge: in the stellar nursery of the Orion Nebula. Easily visible to the naked eye, as the central object in the 'sword' of Orion, this is a region of ongoing star formation. But … and it really *does* depend very much on how you like your magical energies served. If you *are* satisfied with that plain, wholesome fare with few surprises; if you prefer a satisfying but unchanging (and unchallenging) recipe in your ritual; or if adventure plays no part in your quest, then stellar magic certainly isn't for you.

On the other hand, if you *can* look beyond the picturesque seasonal life-death-rebirth cycle of planet Earth and out towards the stellar nurseries of deep space, then you might confront your Holy Guardian Angel on his own turf! As we have seen, the pursuit of stellar wisdom is, literally, as old as time. It has its roots in all the ancient creation myths – those primordial, indigenous forces – and to come full circle, *The Atum-Re Revival,* ends where it all began: with those Khemetic stellar beliefs of ancient Egypt:

> *The Path to Immortality is hard and only a few find it. The rest await the Great Day when the wheels of the universe shall be stopped and the immortal 'Sparks' shall escape from the sheaths of substance. Woe unto those who wait, for they must return again, unconscious and unknowing, to the seed ground of the stars, and (there) await a new beginning.*
>
> [From the *Divine Pymander of Hermes Trimegistus*]

Recommended further reading

Are We Alone? Paul Davies (Penguin)
Astronomy Before the Telescope, ed by Christopher Walker (BMP)
Atom, Lawrence M Krauss (Little, Brown)
Confessions, Aleister Crowley (Arkana)
The Cosmic Clocks, Michel Gauquelin (Paladin)
Cosmic Dragons, Chandra Wickramasinghe (Souvenir)
Creation Records, George St Clair (David Nutt)
Daily Life of the Egyptian Gods,
           Dimitri Meeks & Christine Favard-Meeks (Murray)
The Egyptian Revival, Dr James Stevens Curl (Allen & Unwin)
Egypt's Legacy, Michael Rice (Routledge)
Egypt's Making, Michael Rice (Routledge)
The Last Three Minutes, Paul Davies (Phoenix)
The Law Is For All, Louis Wilkinson (New Falcon)
The Magic Furnace, Marcus Chown (Cape)
Our Cosmic Habitat, Martin Rees (Weidenfeld & Nicholson)
Rogue Asteroids and Doomsday Comets, Duncan Steel (Wiley)
The Secret Lore of Egypt: Its Impact on the West, Erick Hornung
                                 (Cornell UP)
The Setian, Billie Walker-John (ignotus)
The Universe Next Door, Marcus Chown (Headline)

Starchild II

Lights of the Veil

And the people, hearkening,
Saw the Veil above them,
And the darkness deepen'd,
And the Lights gleamed pale.
Ah! the lamps numberless,
The mystical jewels of God,
The luminous, wonderful,
Beautiful Lights of the Veil!

From the *The Book of the Vision of Orm*,
Robert Buchanan

CONTENTS:

Introduction

Part One: Living Sapphires

Part Two: Burning Tapers of the Sky

Part Three: Golden Fruit Upon a Tree

Part Four: Mistress of Melancholy

Part Five: Viral Mythology

Summary: Star-Fall

Introduction

Astrotheology is the study of the astronomical origins of religion; how gods, goddesses, and demons are personifications of astronomical phenomena such as lunar eclipses, planetary alignments, and apparent interactions of planetary bodies with stars. The actual term *astro-theology* first appeared in a book by William Derham: *Astro-theology: or, A demonstration of the being and attributes of God, from a survey of the heavens* (1714) based on the author's observations by means of a telescope. Derham thought that the stars were openings in the firmament through which he thought he saw the Empyrean Heaven – the place in the highest heaven, which in ancient cosmologies was believed to be occupied by the Element of Fire, or the realm of Pure Light – i.e. Kether.

In *Starchild I: A Re-discovery of Stellar Wisdom*, we discovered how the ancient Egyptians viewed the stars, and how the roots of Western magic and mysticism are still linked to stellar energy. Stellar wisdom is, literally, as old as Time with its beginnings in the ancient creation myths; the primordial, indigenous forces that were later deemed demonic by those who were unable to comprehend their Mysteries. Stellar magic really does reach from the inner chthonic planes of the Earth to the outer limits of Space.

We also find that respected science writers like Marcus Chown, cosmology consultant for *New Scientist* magazine with a first class degree in physics and a Masters in astrophysics, can explain how every particle that makes up this world of ours originated in *The Magic Furnace* somewhere in outer space. "The iron in our blood, the calcium in our bones, the oxygen in our very breath – all were forged in blistering furnaces deep inside stars, and blown into space when those stars exploded and died." This is an on-going cosmic drama that began some 15 billion years ago and as Chown points out, we are directly connected to that most 'dramatic and awe-inspiring of cosmic events' – everyone of us is stardust made flesh.

Even Chet Raymo, professor of physics and astronomy, revealed that he has the soul of a poet in making a personal pilgrimage 'into the darkness and silence of the night sky in quest of a human meaning'. This pilgrimage is one that each of us must make alone, into this realm of stars and galaxies, to the limits of the Universe, to the boundaries of Time and Space where the mind and heart encounter the ultimate Mystery – the known unknowable. "It is," he writes, "a pilgrimage in quest of *The Soul of the Night*."

We are not talking about philosophical analogies of 20th century theology that 'figuratively align the three Abrahamic faiths' with astrological symbolism, or connect the 'solar allegory and the life of Christ, thereby cleverly rendering obsolete the cosmologies of the ancient Near East'. Our search takes us on a re-discovery of the earliest form of religion that fuelled the faith to construct the Pyramids and the vast Neolithic monuments of the British Isles, all of which were constructed in alignment with the stars.

Melusine Draco
Ireland 2016

Part One: Living Sapphires

"Now glowed the firmament With living sapphires;
Hesperus, that led The starry host, rode brightest,
Till the Moon, Rising in clouded majesty, at length
Apparent queen, unveild he peerless lihht,
And o'er the dasrk her silver mantle threw."
John Milton

Our ancient stellar beliefs *are* carved in stone – from the prehistoric monuments of Northern Europe to the mighty pyramids and temples of ancient Egypt, the stars are the earliest focus of mankind's faith in his gods. In those early days, the stars were much brighter than they are now. In fact, many of those listed by the astronomer Ptolemy in his 13-volume *Almagest* - published around150AD and taken from the catalogue of stars originally compiled by the astronomer Hipparchus of Bithynia (c135BC) - are no longer visible to the naked eye. While other constellations that appear on the Dendera zodiac from the temple of Hathor, dating from the Greco-Roman period, can no longer be identified.   Similarly, the famous 'precession of the equinoxes' has also muddied the celestial waters. Because the positioning of many ancient monuments was originally aligned with the constellations at the time they were constructed, these sight-lines have altered drastically due to the equinoxes slowly changing position in relation to those particular heavenly bodies. Over a 26,000 year precession period this effect is negligibly small for casual observations, but it is important for precise measurements in relation to astro-theology and astro-archaeology.

Stellar belief is the faith of the ancient world, with Babylon, Assyria and Egypt incorporating star-worship into the official pantheon of their respective religions. The Chaldeans came to be seen as 'the prototypical astrologers and star-worshippers' by the Greeks; while the Greek concept of astrology grew out of late-Egyptian and other Near Eastern practices of astrolatry. Even Mithraism, an austere military-mystery religion incorporated many aspects of the arcane stellar lore derived from Hellenistic astrology.

There is still clear evidence of stellar alignment in Egyptian temples such as that at Elephantine, which was oriented towards the star Sothis (Sirius) whose heliacal rising heralded the annual flooding of the Nile. The 11th Dynasty mud-brick temple built by Sankhkare Mentuhotep on top of a peak known as Thoth Hill (Thebes) was on a slightly different orientation from the earlier stone temple built on the same site in archaic times. Modern research reveals that the later temple was aligned towards the heliacal rising of Sothis; in the archaic period the same star would have appeared just over two degrees further south in the eastern sky – exactly the difference visible in the orientation of the earlier building. According to *The Complete Temples of Egypt*, rather than simply following the physical orientation of the earlier sacred structure, the Middle Kingdom architects had carefully adjusted the temple's orientation in order to align the new building precisely once more with Sothis – which was often equated with Horus, the patron deity of the temple.

As we have already seen, the complex alignment of the pyramids at Giza also reveals that architects had paid careful attention to the stars and their course across the heavens [*Starchild I*]. The narrow shafts in the King's and Queen's Chambers in the Great Pyramid reveal the stellar alignments of all four shafts in the epoch of c2500BC. The northern shaft in the Queen's Chamber was aimed at Kochab [Beta Ursa Minor] in the constellation of the Little Bear. The southern shaft was aimed at Sothis [Alpha Sirius] in the constellation of Canis Major. In the King's Chamber, the northern shaft was angled towards the ancient Pole Star, Thuban [Alpha Draconis] in the constellation of Draco. The southern shaft, focused on Al Nitak [Zeta Orionis], the brightest and lowest of the three stars in Orion's Belt. There is also speculation that the three stars in Orion's Belt correspond to the faulty diagonal line of the Giza pyramid group. The first two stars [Al Nitak and Al Nilam] are in direct alignment, like the first and second pyramids, and the third star [Mintaka] is off-set to the east of the axis formed by the other two.

In his book, *Before the Pyramids*, engineer-scientist, Christopher Knight also observes that the Neolithic henges at Thornborough in England, which actually pre-date the pyramids, are also earthly representations of the stars in Orion's belt. The Thornborough henges are an unusual monument complex that includes the three aligned henges that give the site its name, in addition to a cursus, burial grounds and settlements. The monument is thought to have been part of a Neolithic and Bronze Age 'ceremonial landscape' comparable with Salisbury Plain and Cranborne Chase, dating from between 3500 and 2500BC. Newgrange in Ireland, a masterpiece of megalithic architecture, is aligned with the rising sun so that its light floods the chamber at the Winter Solstice as part of an Irish ritual landscape. And whatever religious, mystical or spiritual elements were central to Stonehenge (*Stonehenge Decoded*), its design includes a 'celestial observatory function, which might have allowed prediction of eclipse, solstice, equinox and other celestial events important to a contemporary religion'.

It is only in recent years that scientists have accepted so-called primitive societies were in possession of cosmic knowledge that enabled them to build huge monuments with such precision that 21st-century engineers would be hard-pressed to copy. Yet it is here we have irrefutable evidence that the stars inspired primitive man to create these wonders; a magical-mystical-religious belief that moved mountains of stone and earth to honour the gods of their time.

So where did it go?

Why did it fail?

And, more importantly, *where did it come from*?

Seen during Northern Hemisphere winters (or Southern Hemisphere summers), the stars seem brighter. Why? Partly because during those winter evenings our bit of the night sky is facing into the spiral arm of the galaxy to which our Sun belongs; during the summer months, the night sky is facing *toward* the center of the Milky Way galaxy. The exact centre of the Milky Way isn't visible because it's obscured by galactic dust, but during those Northern Hemisphere summer months (Southern Hemisphere winter months), we're looking toward the combined light of billions upon billions of stars. In northern winters, we're looking the opposite way – into the outer galaxy and into its spiral arm in which our sun is located. Here there are some gigantic stars that are relatively close to us, although we are seeing fewer stars on winter evenings, as we look across the Milky Way, towards Deep Space. And it's one reason why this part of the sky has a sharper and clearer quality; we are seeing fewer stars, surrounded by the inky depths of space beyond our galaxy's boundaries.

Now imagine a night sky visible thousands of years ago when there was no light pollution and many stars that are invisible today, could be seen with the naked eye. Those ancient astronomer-priesthoods must have spent decades accumulating information, since stellar movement occurs on an annual cycle, unlike lunar and solar phases. For them, the starry night sky was the abode of their gods and the monuments they erected

119

across the globe are a testament to this age-old belief. Here on Earth they replicated what they saw in the heavens as the gods journeyed across the celestial landscape, followed by weird and wonderful creatures in their train, as they disappeared into the darkness of the Netherworld.

Most of us are familiar with the stellar-religious influences in early-Dynastic Egypt and the other Near East civilisations, and the megalithic monuments of Northern Europe but archaeological evidence confirms that a belief in the star-gods circled the world. Research astronomer Duncan Steel even offers a valid explanation for the ancient pattern of pyramid building in the natural phenomena known as 'zodiacal light' – a diffuse triangular glow in the dawn sky that follows the path of the sun. Rarely seen today because of light pollution, nevertheless the ancient people of the Middle East knew it as the 'false dawn' because it stretched far above the horizon in the form of a gigantic pyramid.

Steel adds: "To support this theory we have to ask where else in the world were pyramids built? Those that spring to mind are Mexico (and the Mayan pyramids are known to have had astronomical/calendrical motivations), East Asia, and the Babylonian and Assyrian ziggurats. What all these have in common, despite their dates of construction, is their latitude – all near the Tropic of Cancer. From tropical latitudes the zodiacal light is most impressive ... especially if it were much brighter 5,000 years ago than it is now."

Ethnologist Stansbury Hagar recorded back in the 1920s that many, and perhaps all of the Mayan cities of Central America were planned to reflect on Earth the supposed design of the heavens and that in four places - Uxmal, Chichen Itza, Yaxchilan and Palenque - an almost complete zodiacal sequence can be clearly recognized - and sequences of varying extent are seen in many other places, including the temples and stele of Copan and Quirigua. Some cities - Palenque, Uaxactun, and Utatlan - have alignments with the three main stars in Orion's Belt, while others, like Tikal, were aligned with the Pleiades.

In the south-western USA, the historic Pueblos people also preserve an astronomical tradition that goes back to prehistoric times, still mirroring the ways of their ancestors. Michael Zeilik, writing in *Archaeastrology*, says: "In addition to establishing a ritual calendar, the Sun Priest also used solar observations to establish a planting calendar, which, at Hopi, runs from roughly the middle of April to the summer solstice ... Assuming a reasonable continuity of these practices back to prehistoric time ... I will therefore assume that Anasazi sun watchers kept ritual and planting calendars, had to anticipate important ceremonial dates, and were required to predict the solstices to within a day or two of the actual date."

At Chaco Canyon the Solar Marker with its spiral carving concealed behind three stone slabs reveals how this was achieved.

The mysterious 'Nazca Lines' were created by the South American Nazca culture between 400-650AD and contrary to the popular belief that the lines and figures can only be seen from the air, they *are* visible from the top of the surrounding foothills. Archaeologists, ethnologists, and anthropologists have studied the ancient culture to try to determine the purpose of the lines and figures, and most appear to favour the theory that the lines were intended to act as a kind of observatory, to point to the places on the distant horizon where the sun and other celestial bodies rose or set at the solstices, with many of the figures possibly representing constellations. Although experts in archaeoastronomy refuted these explanations, many prehistoric cultures in the Americas and elsewhere did construct earthworks that combined such astronomical sighting with their religious cosmology.

It has also been suggested that there is correlation between the temples around Angkor Thom in Cambodia and the constellation of Draco. On the ground, the location of Angkor Thom matches the location of the ecliptic north pole in the sky with West Mebon, East Mebon and Ta Som having the same spatial relationship to Angkor Thom that Deneb, Thuban and Kochab have to the ecliptic north pole. When Draco is in alignment with the Angkor temples, it is below Polaris and below the horizon; during its nightly rotation around the celestial North Pole, when Draco is above Polaris and visible from Angkor, it is upside down in relation to the Angkor temples. Satellite images reveal the possibility of temple ruins to the northeast of Angkor Thom in the correct relative position and distance to represent Polaris.

A study of classical Greek literature also supports contemporary research that points to intentional orientation of temples in alignment with celestial phenomenon, with two important temples of Apollo suggesting to modern historians that the ancient Greeks saw the Aurora Borealis; and that it was a rare and special event, remarkable enough to be associated with particular gods and the construction of temples of unusual orientation. This orientation of buildings in the ancient world has been attributed to the observance of celestial bodies, although astronomical alignment may have been only one among several factors that determined the siting of their religious buildings.

A preliminary survey of eleven temples in the ruins of Pompeii have also found evidence that at least nine were aligned with the rising of particular stars, or with the position of the sun or moon on days of cultural significance. Pompeii had been a Greek and Phoenician port of call for hundreds of years before it fell under Roman rule in 80BC. Buried under volcanic ash from Vesuvius's major eruption in 79AD, Pompeii's well-preserved ruins are famed for the insight they provide into Roman life. The research agency *Astro-Archaeology Surveys* is interested in the way this insight contradicts known Roman texts that state all sacred sites should face west, but not all of Pompeii's temples do – perhaps because temples in coastal towns were built according to other religious principles of their cosmopolitan inhabitants.

More astronomical sleuthing at the Carmona necropolis in Seville has revealed the cultic past life of a Roman tomb, which researchers now believe was once used as a Mithraic temple, positioned to line up with the constellations and guide the sun's rays through its window at the equinoxes. Researchers have long debated what this structure was used for and archaeologists from the University of Pablo de Olavide now propose that it served as a place of worship for devotees of Mithraism, the powerful military cult that thrived during the Roman Empire.

Perhaps the most evocative of all, however, is the speculation that the hauntingly beautiful paintings in the Lascaux cave complex may incorporate prehistoric star charts. Based on her extensive survey of other prehistoric cave painting sites in the region, French researcher Chantal Jègues-Wolkiewiez suggested that the gallery of images in the 'Great Hall' represents an extensive star map and that certain key points on major figures in the group correspond to stars in the main constellations as they appeared in the Palaeolithic era. The magnificent painting of a bull near the entrance of the Lascaux cave complex has at its shoulder what appears to be a map of the Pleiades, the constellation also known as the Seven Sisters. Inside the bull painting, there are also indications of spots that may be a representation of other stars found in that region of sky: today, this region forms part of the constellation of Taurus the bull!

Needless to say, experts will argue forever over the interpretation and application of knowledge belonging to ancient civilisations that inexplicably appear to have an understanding of particular cosmic disciplines long before the birth of science. Erich von Daniken of *Chariot of the Gods* fame, even managed to develop a theory that the cultural advancements of primitive peoples were given to them by early astronauts, who appeared from the sky like gods! What modern day scientists refuse to accept is that for the people of the ancient world, religious beliefs were inextricably linked with magical-mystical practice that included communion with the gods - and this element of magico-mysticism was much more powerful then, than it is today.

There is, however, a well-known observation in esoteric circles that these things are never fully forgotten, nor fully remembered, because we all carry a grain of that knowledge in our own psyche. It may lie dormant for years until some brief line in an obscure book – like *Honey From Stone* or *The Soul of the Night* by Chet Raymo – echoes a magical truth and another portal opens up in our subconscious and allows light to stream in. That's why it's not surprising this sudden flash of inspiration, this uplifting by knowledge, in spiritual fraternities is referred to as enlightenment.

The Zodiac: Carved in Stone

The British Museum in London is home to a collection of cuneiform tablets that date back to around 2100BC. The *Mulapin Cuneiform Tablets of Babylon* reveal that the Chaldeans were well aware of the movements of the planets through the circle of the Zodiac, not to mention the procession of the Equinoxes and many other celestial phenomena associated with the heavens.

The Chaldeans of Mesopotamia were also known for great achievements in many scientific fields; some of which, having such an impact that many are still in use today. The concept of 1 hour equalling 60 minutes was implemented by the Chaldeans over 3,000 years ago, together with the 'time system' of days, months and year - as well as the creation of lunar and solar calendars. The Chaldeans reached the conclusions that the Sun, Moon and Earth, plus the other known five planets were all part of one system: a fact that took the rest of the world 2,000 years to agree upon. The Chaldeans also achieved tremendous strides in the sciences of algebra, geometry, and astronomy – and invented the Zodiacal system.

At this early date, however, the Zodiac was not used to cast personal horoscopes but probably as some form of celestial calendar linked to the cosmogony or the creation of the universe, and the emergence of the human race. The Chaldean priests used the twelve 'Signs of the Zodiac' to teach people the possibility of personal spiritual liberation and transformation along similar lines of the mystical Qabbalah in later times. That priesthood was referred to simply as the 'Chaldeans' after the name of their people – a name that became synonymous with magic, augury and astrology throughout the ancient world.

Unlike the East Semitic peoples whose ancestors had been established in Mesopotamia since the beginning of time, the Chaldeans were certainly not an indigenous people, but migrants from the south of the region, and had played no part in the previous 3,000 years of Mesopotamian civilisation and history. They seem to have appeared in the region sometime between 940-860BC, a century or so after other 'new' Semitic peoples arrived in Babylonia - but bringing with them a whole new system of learning. Yet by the time of Cicero in the 2nd century BC, Chaldea appears to have completely disappeared even as a societal term for Babylonian astronomers and astrologers; Cicero refers to 'Babylonian astrologers' rather than Chaldean astrologers but credits them with being privy to all sorts of obscure, arcane and occult knowledge. Horace also refers to 'Babylonian horoscopes' rather than Chaldean. Democritus claims to have become acquainted with a particular Chaldean magi who was said to have been taught by one of the magi accompanying Xerxes on his military expeditions.

'The Zodiac' is the expression used to describe the circle of twelve divisions of celestial longitude that are centred upon the path of the sun. The term 'zodiac' deriving from the Latin *zōdiacus*, which in its turn comes from the Greek *zōdiakos kuklos,* meaning 'circle of animals'. The original being created to calculate a passing of time using the movement of the stars for a farming-calendar tradition, and although the ancient Egyptians had knowledge of these twelve divisions, they did not adopt the twelve classic signs that were created by the Babylonians; the Egyptians absorbed them much later during the Ptolemaic period.

The classical map of the sky, with its forty-eight constellations, was derived from at least two different traditions. One, comprising of the twelve signs of the zodiac, which developed over 3,000 years in Mesopotamia in their religious or ritual tradition; the second, which appears to date from 2,800BC, probably from the Mediterranean region, was devised for the navigators of ships. This second tradition included huge bears and serpents which marked the celestial pole and equator, as well as some of the large southern 'marine' constellations.

According to Assyriologist and historian of science, Francesca Rochberg, there has been a great deal of speculation as to the origin of these constellations. "Until recently it has usually been assumed that they evolved from the fancies of primitive imaginations, but research now suggests that they were designed as a pictorial scientific coordinate system. A coordinate system is a set of imaginary lines for measuring positions, like the lines of latitude and longitude for determining locations on the earth. The constellations perform a similar function, but they employ pictures, which make it easy to identify stars without need of instruments. Moreover, this evidence points to a time and place that they originated: about 2700BC at about 36° north latitude. ... in Sumeria."

The Sumerians called the twelve major zodiacal constellations the 'Shiny herd', which was made up as follows:

Heavenly Bull (Taurus)

124

Twins (Gemini)
Pincers, Tongs (Cancer)
Lion (Leo)
Her father was Sin (Virgo)
Heavenly Fate (Libra)
Which claws and cuts (Scorpio)
Defender (Sagittarius)
Goat-fish (Capricorn)
Lord of the waters (Aquarius)
Fishes (Pisces)
Field dweller (Aries)

Having established that astrology originated in Sumeria, Francesca Rochberg speculates on whether this represents the *true* origins of the zodiac. "It is known that Babylonian astrology developed within the context of divination. A collection of 32 tablets with inscribed liver models, dating from about 1,875BC, are the oldest known detailed texts of Babylonian divination, and these demonstrate the same interpretational format as that employed in celestial omen analysis ...

"The discovery of an observatory in Metsamor, Armenia, predating the Babylonian kingdom by almost 2,000 years has changed our perception of events as the observatory at Metsamor apparently contains the first recorded example of dividing the year into 12 sections. Using an early form of geometry, the inhabitants of Metsamor were able to create both a calendar and envision the curve of the earth. The discovery of the astronomical 'observatory' at Metsamor and the presence of engravings which have been speculatively called 'zodiac creatures' has given credence to the assertion that the ancient figures of the constellations were probably created by ancient peoples living in the Euphrates valley and near Mount Ararat in eastern Anatolia and Armenia." The observatory and temple complexes consisted of seven sanctuaries with Neolithic stone circles dating back to c.5000BC.

The Egyptian Zodiac
The Dendera Zodiac is a map of the stars showing the twelve constellations of the zodiacal band forming thirty-six decans of ten days each, and the planets. These decans are groups of first-magnitude stars that were used in the ancient Egyptian calendar, based on lunar cycles of around thirty-days and on the heliacal rising of the star Sothis [Sirius]. The celestial arch is represented by a disc held up by four pillars of the sky in the form of women, between which are inserted falcon-headed spirits. On the first ring thirty-six spirits symbolize the 360 days of the

Egyptian year. The Egyptian zodiac recognized many of the same basic constellations, but they were imagined as being different shapes to the ones familiar today. For instance, the 'Big Dipper' was seen as the foreleg of an ox, while a crocodile and hippopotamus make up the figures shown on the Dendura zodiac dating from the late Ptolemaic dynasty.

The Hindu Zodiac:
The names of the Hindu zodiac and corresponding Greek signs sound very different, but it has been long recognised that their symbols are identical. For example, *dhanu* means 'bow' and corresponds to Sagittarius, the Archer; and *kumbha* means 'water-pitcher' and corresponds to Aquarius, the Water-carrier. The corresponding signs have been interpreted as the results of an early interchange of cultural influences, but there is clear evidence of trading between the Sumerian and Babylonian cultures and the Indus Valley millennia before the Greeks were ever in Asia - and the Sumerians have a record of astrological symbols that dated back to c.2,000BC. There are also several references to the zodiac in the *Rig Veda* and *Mahabharata*, both of which are ancient texts which predate any Greek influence in Asia.

The Chinese Zodiac:
Most Westerners are familiar with the Chinese animal zodiac, or **sheng xiao,** a rotating cycle of 12 years, with each year being represented by an animal and its reputed attributes. Astronomically speaking, the 'Chinese Zodiac' can be interpreted as a way of dividing the 'Jupiter Year because it takes twelve years for Jupiter to complete one orbit of the sun. To further complicate matters the Chinese calendar counts years in cycles of sixty years and each year consists of two parts. The first is the celestial stem being one of the five elements: Water, Fire, Wood, Metal and Earth which are the primary forces affecting the Universe. The second is the terrestrial branch represented by one of the twelve animal [zodiac] signs. The equation becomes five multiplied by twelve, equalling sixty - or one cycle in the Chinese calendar.

The legend of the origin of the Chinese zodiac says that the Buddha once invited all the animals in creation to join him; most ignored his call and those that did go to him were included in the Zodiac calendar. They were, in order of arrival: the Rat, Ox, Tiger, Rabbit (or Hare/Cat), Dragon, Snake, Horse, Goat, Monkey, Rooster, Dog and Pig (or Wild Boar). It is known from pottery artefacts that the animals of the zodiac were popular in the Tang Dynasty (618-907AD), but they were also seen much earlier from artefacts from the Warring States Period (475-221BC).

The late date suggests that the Chinese adopted the Indo-European concept of the zodiac and incorporated it into their own belief system.

The Mayan Zodiac

The so-called Mayan Zodiac is a system of calendars used in pre-Columbian Mesoamerica, and is still used in many modern communities in the Guatemalan highlands, Veracruz, Oaxaca and Chiapas, Mexico, having been in common use throughout the region dating back to at least the 5th century BC. It also shares many aspects with calendars used by other earlier Mesoamerican civilizations, such as the Zapotec and Olmec, and contemporary or later communities such as the Mixtec and Aztec calendars. According to Mayan custom, the god Itzamna is often credited with introducing the calendar system to the people, along with writing and other aspects of Mayan culture. The Mayan calendar consists of several cycles of different lengths including one that measured the 365-day solar year and another that details of the lunar phases that are ruled over by the nine Lords of the Night. There are also less-prevalent or poorly understood cycles, combinations and calendar progressions associated with different groups of deities, animals, and other significant concepts, which have been interpreted in modern times as a form of zodiac.

The Aztec Zodiac

The Aztec calendar system shares the basic structure of calendars from throughout ancient Mesoamerica. The calendar consisted of a 365-day calendar cycle called *xiuhpohualli* (year count) and a 260-day ritual cycle called *tonalpohualli* (day count). The *xiuhpohualli* is considered to be the agricultural calendar, since it is based on the sun, and the *tonalpohualli* is considered to be the sacred calendar. It is believed that the Aztec calendric cycle may have begun at some point in the distant past with the first appearance of the Pleiades (*Tianquiztli*) asterism in the east immediately before the dawn light. Due to the precession of the Earth's axis, however, it fell out of sync to a more constant reference point such as a solstice or equinox, as early Spanish chroniclers recorded it being celebrated in proximity with the Spring Equinox.

From these ancient systems, we can clearly see that the original calendars were archaic methods for marking time – both secular and sacred. They were not methods designed for divination, astrological or otherwise but the symbols are one of the earliest forms of writing. Pictography uses sets of pictures as a form of script and the Sumerians created the earliest known pictogram around 3200BC. They used a script known as cuneiform, which combined pictograms and phonograms (signs representing sounds). The pictograms in the cuneiform formed recognisable symbols: for instance, a picture of a cow's head represented a cow; a triangle next to a mountain represented a foreign woman. It was only much later that these symbols were used for astrological readings of an individual's past and future.

Astrology: Written in Blood

Even in ancient times there were many who considered astrologers as charlatans, although many powerful rulers had a permanent astrologer assigned to their court, who often held sway over the affairs of state. The Babylonians appeared to have developed the first organised system of astrology, dating from around the 2nd millennium BC. By the 16th century BC the extensive employment of omen-based astrology has been traced in the compilation of the *Enuma Anu Enlil*, a reference work consisting of seventy cuneiform tablets comprising 7,000 celestial omens. At this stage of its development, Babylonian astrology was a mundane affair, concerned with the prediction of weather and political matters; and prior to the 7th-century BC the practitioners' understanding of astronomy remained rudimentary.

By the 4th-century, however, their mathematical methods had progressed enough to calculate future planetary positions with reasonable accuracy, at which point extensive ephemerides began to appear and astrology developed within the context of divination. That collection of thirty-two tablets of inscribed 'liver models', dating from about 1875BC, are the oldest known detailed texts of Babylonian prediction, mirroring the same interpretational format as former celestial-omen analysis. Blemishes and marks found on the liver of the sacrificial animal were interpreted as symbolic signs that presented messages from the gods to the king and astrology was still linked to augury for the purposes of divination.

The gods were also believed to reveal themselves in the celestial images of the planets or stars with whom they were associated. Evil celestial omens attached to any particular planet were therefore seen as indications of dissatisfaction or disturbance of the god whom that planet represented. Such indications were met with attempts to appease the god and find manageable ways by which that god's communication could be understood. Mundane astrology is known to be one of the oldest branches of the art, and it was only with the gradual emergence of horoscope casting in the 6th-century BC, that astrology developed the techniques and practice of natal astrology, which was linked to an individual's birth date.

Although highly skilled in the science of astronomy, the Egyptians were late comers in adding astrology to their vast knowledge of magical and arcane wisdom. The Persian conquest of Egypt in 525BC would no doubt have brought numerous Near Eastern influences in its wake; and after the occupation by Alexander the Great in 332BC, Egypt came under Greek rule and influence. The city of Alexandria's scholars were prolific writers, and it was in Ptolemaic Alexandria that Babylonian astrology was mixed with the Egyptian tradition of 'decanic astrology' to create horoscopic astrology.

Decanic astrology combined the Babylonian zodiac with its system of planetary exaltations, the triple significance of the signs and the importance of eclipses. Along with this it incorporated the Egyptian concept of dividing the zodiac into thirty-six decans of ten degrees each, with an emphasis on the rising decan, the Greek system of planetary gods, sign ruler-ship and the four elements. The decans were a system of time measurement according to the constellations and led by the sacred star Sothis (or Sirius). The risings of the decans in the night were used to divide the night into 'hours'; the rising of a constellation just before sunrise (its heliacal rising) was considered the last hour of the night and over the course of the year, each constellation rose just before sunrise for ten days. When these calculations became part of the astrology of the Hellenistic Age, each decan was associated with ten degrees of the zodiac. Texts from the 2nd-century BC list predictions relating to the positions of planets in zodiac signs at the time of the rising of certain decans, particularly Sothis. The earliest version found in Egypt dates to the 1st-century BC.

Particularly important in the development of horoscopic astrology was the astrologer and astronomer Ptolemy, who lived in Alexandria, and his work, the *Tetrabiblos* set out the basis for the Western astrological tradition. It was one of the first astrological texts to be circulated in Medieval Europe after being translated from Arabic into Latin by Plato of Tivoli [Tiburtinus] in Spain in 1138. Greek influence played a crucial role in the transmission of astrology to Rome, although it was not always favourably received, being a popular pastime with the lower orders of society. For both the Greeks and Romans this resurrected term 'Chaldean star-gazers' gave some cause for concern and became so identified with astrology in a derogatory sense, that 'Chaldean wisdom' came to be a common by-word for divination using planets and stars in a derogatory sense.

The term 'magi' was also widespread throughout the Eastern Mediterranean until late antiquity and beyond: *mágos*, 'magian' or 'magician', eventually displacing the Greek *goēs* (the older word for a practitioner of magic), to include astrology, alchemy and other forms of esoteric knowledge. This association stemmed from the fascination for (Pseudo-) Zoroaster (a pen name), who was perceived by the Greeks to be the Chaldean founder of the 'Magi' and the inventor of both astrology and magic, a meaning that still survives in the modern-day words 'magic' and 'magician'.

The first definitive reference to astrology comes from the work of the orator Cato, who in 160BC composed a treatise warning farm overseers against consulting with Chaldeans. The 2nd-century Roman poet Juvenal, in his satirical attack on the habits of Roman women, also complains about the pervasive influence of Chaldeans, despite their lowly social status, saying: "Still more trusted are the Chaldeans; every word uttered by the astrologer they will believe has come from Hammon's fountain, ... nowadays no astrologer has credit unless he has been imprisoned in some distant camp, with chains clanking on either arm." One of the first astrologers to bring Hermetic astrology to Rome was Thrasyllus, who acted as royal astrologer for the Emperor Tiberius. Tiberius was the first emperor reported to have had a court astrologer, although his predecessor Augustus had used astrology to help legitimise his Imperial rights.

By the 13th-century, astrology had become a part of everyday *medical* practice in Europe. Doctors combined Galenic medicine (inherited from the Greek physiologist Galen - (129-216AD) with studies of the stars. By the end of the 1500s, physicians across Europe were required by law to calculate the position of the Moon before carrying out complicated medical procedures, such as surgery or bleeding. Nicholas Culpeper (1616-1654), the English botanist, herbalist, physician, and astrologer, whose books include *The English Physician* (1652); the *Complete Herbal* (1653), which contain a rich store of pharmaceutical and herbal knowledge; and *Astrological Judgement of Diseases from the Decumbiture of the Sick* (1655), which is one of the most detailed documents ever published on the practice of medical astrology in Early Modern Europe.

As far as the Inquisition was concerned, however, natural astrology was concerned with the general character of planetary influences in agriculture and medicine, and the calculation of natural phenomena, such as the measurement of time, prediction of tides and eclipses, and meteorological phenomena. Judicial astrology, on the other hand, was the art of judging the influences of the stars and planets upon human affairs and was officially prohibited by the Catholic Church during the Counter-

Reformation. The Council of Trent decreed that bishops should suppress astrological prediction in their dioceses and ensure the destruction of all books that cultivated the art.

Sixtus's Papal Bull against judicial astrology was one of the main instruments of the Catholic Church in its battle against any esoteric practice (including other forms of divination), ordering the confiscation of books on the subject – all of which probably landed up in the Vatican's vast esoteric library! The premise was that God had reserved unto Himself all knowledge of future events and therefore neither humans nor demons were able to forecast future events. Thus when trying to determine the future, often with the aid of demons, astrologers were actually defying God. As a result, judicial astrology acquired the status of heresy and the whole Inquisitorial apparatus was authorised to operate against it, condemning hundreds of people – including the likes of John Dee and Galileo – to hardship and suffering, if not death.

Nevertheless, medieval writers continued to use astrological symbolism in their literary themes. Dante's *Divine Comedy* builds in varied references to planetary associations when describing the architecture of Hell, Purgatory and Paradise, (such as the seven layers of Purgatory's mountain purging the seven cardinal sins that correspond to astrology's seven classical planets). Similar astrological allegories and planetary themes are pursued through the works of Geoffrey Chaucer. Chaucer's astrological passages are frequent and knowledge of astrological basics is often assumed through his work. He pinpoints the early spring season of the *Canterbury Tales* in the opening verses of the prologue by noting that the Sun *"hath in the Ram his halfe cours yronne"*. He makes the Wife of Bath refer to 'sturdy hardiness' as an attribute of Mars, and associates Mercury with 'clerkes'. Astrological references are also to be found liberally scattered through the works of William Shakespeare and John Milton.

Carl Jung managed to bring astrology into the forum of science via the back door, with his research into the symbolic meaning of his patients' dreams, conversations and paintings. Jung observed recurring mythical themes or archetypes, and maintained that 'these universal and timeless archetypes channel experiences and emotions, resulting in recognizable and typical patterns of behaviour with certain probable outcomes'. Jung claimed to observe a correlation between these archetypal images and the astrological themes or traditional 'gods' associated with the planets and signs of the zodiac, concluding that the symbolic heavenly figures attributed to the constellations were originally inspired by projections of images created by the collective unconscious.

Astrology is still considered a pseudo-science in the West, but not in other parts of the world, such as India for example, where in 2001, Indian scientists and politicians debated a proposal to use State money to fund research into astrology, resulting in permission for Indian universities to offer courses in Vedic astrology. In the West, 'star gazing' and 'star worship' followed a less favourable path with much confusion, denouncing, and demonising of astrology occurring during the early Christian period.

The Christian, or more specifically the Hebrew Bible contained repeated reference to astrolatry. *Deuteronomy* contained stern warnings against worshipping the sun, moon, stars or any of the heavenly host, and a relapse into worshipping the host of heaven, i.e. the stars, is said to have been the cause of the fall of the kingdom of Judah in *II Kings*. In 621BC King Josiah was recorded in *Zephaniah* as having abolished all kinds of idolatry in Judah, but astrolatry was continued in private. *Ezekiel* describes sun-worship practiced in the court of the temple of Jerusalem, and *Jeremiah* claims that even after the destruction of the temple, women in particular insisted on continuing their worship of the 'queen of heaven'.

It was common practice around the time the Israelites came into the 'promised land' that the native peoples would practice astrology and worship the heavenly bodies, but the Bible specifically warned the Israelites to keep away because 'those who are stargazers and make predictions based upon that are in error and will not be saved from judgment'. The kings (such as Josiah) were told to outlaw the worship of the heavenly bodies and did so; the seriousness of this offense was clear, since the penalty for this kind of idolatry was death by stoning. According to biblical writ, their God had destroyed the ten northern tribes of Israel because they indulged in astrology and other forms of demon worship and, as a result of this idolatry Judah was enslaved and dispersed as a nation, because of their involvement in astrology.

In other words, those who practice astrology fell under the judgment of their God and as in the Old Testament, the New Testament also roundly condemned astrology in *Acts of the Apostles*. Augustine of Hippo (354-430AD) criticized sun- and star-worship in *De Vera Religione* and *De civitate Dei* - despite the fact that his contemporaries often believed astrology to be an exact and genuine science, and its practitioners as true men of learning. Pope Leo the Great (400-461AD) also denounced astrolatry and the cult of *Sol Invictus* - the latter being later contrasted with the Christian nativity!

Sol Invictus ('Unconquered Sun') was the official sun-god of the later Roman Empire and often equated with Mithras as a patron and protector of soldiers. In 274AD the Emperor Aurelian gave it an official status alongside the traditional Roman cults. The god was favoured by the emperors after Aurelian and appeared on their coins until Constantine I: the last inscription referring to *Sol Invictus* dates to 387AD when there were still enough devotees that Augustine found it necessary to preach against them. The festival of *Dies Natalis Solis Invicti* was later syncretised with Christmas and this important pagan mid-winter festival (Winter Solstice) has retained its importance down through the ages until the present day with most of its symbolism still intact.

Fundamentally, the Old Testament contains the articles of faith for the three principal monotheist religions: Judaism, Christianity and Islam – all of whom decried stellar worship as idolatrous. The prohibition of astrolatry is mentioned in the Quran through the Prophet Ibrahim's observation of celestial bodies and whose worship was common in the Babylonian religion of that time. What all this demonstrates is that star worship retained its popularity right up until the 'Big Three' strengthened their strangle-hold on free thinking and stellar belief went underground. Nevertheless, the power that the stars retained over man's psyche was deeply ingrained – no one would preach against something that had no longer had any relevance or meaning; and neither can you legislate over something that doesn't exist. Mankind is still held in thrall to the stars ...

The Book of the Visions of Orm

Mystical writing can come from anywhere, at any time, and it doesn't necessarily have to relate to any particular religious Path or Tradition. We read a line, or an extract, and immediately we know we've plugged into something profound and important. We may have even read the book several times before but suddenly everything falls into place and makes sense in a way that never previously occurred to us. Just as Chet Raymo's mystical books are unexpectedly written by an American former Roman Catholic, professor of physics and astronomy, so a Scottish poet, novelist and dramatist, chiefly remembered for his attacks on the Pre-Raphaelites, Robert Buchanan's study in mysticism – *The Book of the Visions of Orm* – points us in the direction of the mysteries of stellar power.

In 'The First Song of the Veil' we are told how: '*Ere Man grew, the Veil was woven bright and blue,*' and how this veil '*the beautiful Master*' drew over his face – an account of how the creator-god distanced himself from mankind. In *Daily Life of the Egyptian Gods*, the authors offered a more ancient and tantalising glimpse of the ancients' concept of the heavens and the 'Unseen One' of Egyptian mythology. In *Starchild I,* we also discovered how "The sky, both the portion that man could see and the portion that remained hidden from them was incarnated by the body of a woman who took her place on high in the final stages of creation ... Beyond it were regions the sun never reached ... the Creator's ultimate refuge ..."

Then starry, luminous,
Rolled the Veil of azure
O'er the first dwellings
    Of mortal race;
—And since the beginning
No mortal vision,
Pure or sinning,
    Hath seen the Face

Yet mark me closely!
    Strongly I swear,
Seen or seen not,
    The Face is there!
When the Veil is clearest
    And sunniest,
Closest and nearest
    The Face is prest;

But when, grown weary
With long downlooking,
The Face withdrawing
    For a time is gone,
The great Veil darkens,
And ye see full clearly
Glittering numberless
    The gems thereon.
For the lamp of his features
Divinely burning,
Shines, and suffuses
    The Veil with light,
And the Face, drawn backward
With that deep sighing
Ye hear in the gloaming,
    Leaveth the Night.

And as mankind developed and expanded his boundaries, devouring friend and foe alike, with his constant warring and grasping need for riches, he moved further and further away from the Face. In the early days the priesthoods had the knowledge, wisdom and understanding that enabled them to tap into the magical/mystical power filtering down to them from these ancient deities. But with greed came ambition, and there were those who wanted the ability '*to gaze on the Face*' for their own ends; the stellar priesthoods were overthrown and the ancient stellar power went into the shadows. Mankind focussed on the images of the Sun-God and the Earth Mother.

Beautiful, beautiful, she lay below,
　　The mighty Mother of humanity,
Turning her sightless eyeballs to the glow
　　Of light she could not see,
Feeling the happy warmth, and breathing slow
　　As if her thoughts were shining tranquilly.
Beautiful, beautiful the Mother lay,
Crownèd with silver spray,

The greenness gathering hushfully around
　　The peace of her great heart, while on her breast
The wayward Waters, with a weeping sound,
　　Were sobbing into rest.
For all day long her face shone merrily,
And at its smile the waves leapt mad and free:
But at the darkening of the Veil, she drew
　　The wild things to herself, and husht their cries.
Then, stiller, dumber, search'd the deepening Blue
　　With passionate blind eyes;
And went the old life over in her thought,
Dreamily praying as her memory wrought
　　The dimly guess'd at, never utter'd tale,
　　　　While, over her dreaming,
　　　　Deepen'd the luminous,
　　　　Star-inwrought, beautiful,
　　Folds of the wondrous Veil.

And the poet tells us how mankind began systematically destroying the Earth Mother by pillaging the earth and enslaving his neighbours to such a degree that all the Old Gods turned their backs and disappeared from the sight of humans.

> *In the beginning, long ago,*
> *Without a Veil looked down the Face ye know,*
> *And Earth, an infant happy-eyed and bright,*
> *Look'd smiling up, and gladden'd in its sight.*
> *But later, when the Man Flower from her womb*
> *Burst into brightening bloom,*
> *In her glad eyes a golden dust was blown*
> *Out of the Void, and she was blind as stone.*

> *And since that day*
> *She hath not seen, nor spoken,— lest her say*
> *Should be a sorrow and fear to mortal race,*
> *And doth not know the Lord hath hid away,*
> *But turneth up blind orbs—to feel the Face.*

Realising their folly, the voices of the Children of Earth are heard crying for guidance, and for signs leading them back to the Path:

> *'O Mother! Mother*
> *Of mortal race!*
> *Is there a Father?*
> *Is there a Face?'*

> *She felt their sorrow*
> *Against her cheek,—*
> *She could not hearken,*
> *She could not speak;*

and although the Face answers from the thunder-cloud, '*I am God the Maker, I am God the Master, I am God the Father,*' the Earth Mother and her children neither saw nor heard him. The Wise Men were called in for a consultation, and *'looming there lonely'*, they searched the Veil wonderful '*with tubes fire-fashioned in caverns below,*' and we are told in a striking line that the Face withdrew backward again. After long searching, in which blindness met some, and death others, the remainder crept slowly back from the heights to which they had ascended, crying out:

'Bury us deep when dead—
We have travelled a weary road,
We have seen no more than ye.
'Twere better not to be—
There is no God!'

And the people, hearkening,
Saw the Veil above them,
And the darkness deepen'd,
    And the Lights gleamed pale.
Ah! the lamps numberless,
The mystical jewels of God,
The luminous, wonderful,
    Beautiful Lights of the Veil!

Different peoples at different times in their histories, and in different parts of the world, found their civilisation dominated by these stellar influences – the magical-mystical power that fuels the Universe. *The Book of the Visions of Orm* acts as an allegory for the vanishing of the belief of the original star-gazers, who had the knowledge, wisdom, wealth *and* human resources to create the wondrous monuments that still remain as a testament to their faith. The ancient astronomer-priesthoods were destroyed and dispersed by those who wanted the wealth and control of the people for their own ends, but no longer had the magico-mystical powers needed to maintain the equilibrium of universal chaos and harmony

Part Two: Burning Tapers of the Sky

"This morning I watched the sky burn, watched matter
flowing in the space between the stars ..."
The Soul of the Night, Chet Raymo

What we now need to ask is: where and how did this stellar-power manifest, so that early man could tap into it, harness that energy and use it to enhance his society? Surprisingly, the answer lies a long way from the familiar sites of Egypt, Mesopotamia and the British Isles. When European settlers first discovered ruins of great civilizations at Mapungubwe in South Africa and Great Zimbabwe in Zimbabwe, they erroneously concluded that these marvellous stone cities could *not* have been built by black Africans.

The Kingdom of Mapungubwe (1075–1220) was located at the confluence of the Shashe and Limpopo rivers and at its height the population was about 5000 people. In fact, until recently the official version of history maintained that southern Africa was an empty land, completely uninhabited until the first Dutch settlers arrived there in 1652! The government rationalised that the exquisite art and surviving architecture of the Shona and Bantu people of South Africa and Zimbabwe were actually the creations of Arabs, Phoenicians, or other non-African peoples, denying that the ancient city of Great Zimbabwe could possibly have been built by the indigenous people. In reality, however, Mapungubwe and Great Zimbabwe, as well as Thulamela, a more recent discovery, *were* black civilizations that developed sophisticated international trading economies and remarkable architecture in southern Africa as early as the 11th-century AD.

The ruined city of Great Zimbabwe is located in the south-eastern hills of near Lake Mutirikwe and the capital of the Kingdom of Zimbabwe during the country's Late Iron Age. Construction of the monument by ancestors of the Shona people began in the 11th-century and continued until the 15th-century, spanning an area of 1,780 acres which, at its peak, could have housed up to 18,000 people. One of its most prominent features are the walls, some of which were over thirty-six feet high and constructed without mortar, making it the largest ancient structure south of the Sahara Desert.

But that was before the discovery of the remains of a huge metropolis at Mpumalanga, approximately 90 miles west of port Maputo in Mozambique that covers around 1,500 square miles. It is part of an even larger community that is about 10,000 square miles and appears to show a site of extended settlement that appears to span c200,000-160,000BC! This remote region is well-known for the vast number of ancient goldmines discovered during the past five-hundred years, and suggests the 'existence of a vanished civilisation that lived and dug gold in this part of the world for thousands of years', comments Michael Tellinger, author of *Temples of the African Gods*. "And if this is in fact the cradle of humankind, we may be looking at the activities of the oldest civilization on Earth."

Researcher and author, Michael Tellinger, teamed up with local pilot Johan Heine, who had been looking at these ruins from years of flying over the region, in order to explore the area more thoroughly. An overview of the surrounding country revealed that the community had been developed by a highly evolved people, and suggested that these were the remains of ancient temples and astronomical observatories of a lost civilization that stretched back for many thousands of years. Therefore it was essential right from the beginning that the discoveries be put into some kind of historical perspective but dating was a problem – then came a startling break-thorough.

Johan Heine had discovered Adam's Calendar quite by accident. Having noticed a strange arrangement of large stones sticking out of the ground, he realised they were aligned to the four cardinal points of the compass. Three monoliths were aligned towards the sunrise, but on the west side there was a hole in the ground. After making extensive calculations, Heine deducted that the group was perfectly aligned with the solstices and equinoxes – but without the missing stone the puzzle was incomplete. A local man told him that a strange shaped stone had been removed from the spot many years previously but after an extensive search the pilot was able to track it down.

The monument is referred to as a 'calendar' because the stones are placed in such a way as to track the movement of the sun, which casts shadows on the rocks and still works perfectly today. The monoliths are aligned with each direction: north, south, east and west, as well as the equinoxes and solstices. The three rocks in the centre of the circle correspond with the star formation, Orion's Belt, and it appears that this unknown civilization was being guided by the same knowledge as the people who built the astronomically aligned monuments all over the world - many thousands of years later.

Not only are each of the stone circles uniquely designed and astrologically aligned, they demonstrate a great understanding of the movement of the earth and stars. Those who designed the structures understood about natural energy sources produced from within the earth that most people in our modern era have not even heard of. They knew that the core of the earth itself rings like a bell, which produces energy; and when building these stone circles, certain rocks were used that also ring like bells and produce a special energy force. Each stone was placed according to the sound it made in relation to another, as well as the precise astrological position.

The latest and most interesting discovery of the stone circles and Adam's Calendar is the sound frequencies of the rock formations from the earth beneath them. With modern technology, Michael Tellinger and his fellow scientists have been able to detect and measure incredible sound frequencies with acoustic properties coming from the earth inside the circles that conduct electricity. These sound frequencies are shaped as flowers of sacred geometry as they rise to the surface. They also measured electronic fields 200 metres underground with a heat of up to eighty degrees Celsius - as hot as volcanic earth - inside Adam's Calendar. There is no scientific explanation for this effect because there is no active volcano, and the temperature drops dramatically when measured from *outside* the circle - which is also unexplainable.

The first calculations of the age of the Calendar were made based on the rise of Orion, that constellation known for its three bright stars forming the 'Belt' of the celestial hunter. The Earth wobbles on its axis and so the stars and constellations change their angle of presentation in the night sky on a cyclical basis. This rotation, as we know is called 'precession' and completes a cycle about every 26,000 years. By determining when the three stars of Orion's belt were positioned flat (horizontal) against the horizon, it is possible to calculate the time when the three stones in the calendar were in alignment with these distinctive stars.

The first rough calculation was at least 25,000 years ago, but more precise measurements kept pushing the dating further back in time and based on the rise of Orion to 75,000 years. The most recent calculation suggests an age of at least 160,000 years - based on Orion being flat on the horizon - but also on the erosion of the dolerite stones found at the site. Some pieces of the marker stones had been broken off and remained on the ground, exposed to natural erosion. When the pieces were put back together about three centimetres of stone had already been worn away, which helped assess the age of the site by calculating the erosion rate of the dolerite.

Why dolerite?

The monoliths of Adam's Calendar are dolerite and the only dolerite vein is almost a mile away, meaning that rocks weighing as much as five tons were somehow carried all the way to that precise site for a particular alignment. Dolerite is typically found as an intrusive igneous rock (hypabyssal) formed from molten material that originated in the earth's upper mantle and solidified close to the earth's surface. It forms in 'dykes' or 'sills' commonly found in large groups known as 'swarms' and the most prolific swarms may contain more than a thousand dykes or sills radiating from a single volcanic centre. Karroo, one of the world's largest dolerite sites, is found at the tip of South Africa.

The term 'mafic' originally referred to minerals rich in magnesium and iron; these minerals are often dark, particularly if they contain a lot of iron. The vast areas of mafic rock associated with the Jurassic breakup of Gondwanaland in the Southern Hemisphere include many large dolerite sills and dike swarms. These include the Karoo dolerites of South Africa. In paleogeography, Gondwanaland, is the name given to the more southerly of two supercontinents (the other being Laurasia) that were part of the Pangaea supercontinent, which existed from approximately 510 to 180 million years ago. Gondwanaland began to break up in the early Jurassic period, accompanied by massive eruptions of basalt lava, as East Gondwana, comprising Antarctica, Madagascar, India, and Australia, began to separate from Africa.

Thousands of years and several continental shifts separate the construction of Adam's Calendar in South Africa and the creation of the celestial observatory at Stonehenge in England, but the common feature is the use of dolerite 'bluestones'. Constructed between 3000-2000BC, the bluestone was used for the outer ring of eleven large dolerites from the Preseli Mountains in Pembrokeshire, some 200 miles away. 'Bluestone' is the common name for spotted dolerite, an igneous rock that looks blue when broken and is spotted with small pellets of feldspar and other minerals that got into the molten matrix when the rocks were forming geological ages ago. While the particular reasoning and importance behind this choice of rock remains unknown, it was clearly justified by the considerable effort that was required to move it.

Despite there being some dispute over the actual site of the original quarry – either Carn Menyn or Carn Goedog a mile distant – it has been suggested that the dolerite stones may also have been selected because of their acoustic qualities. A recent study shows that rocks in the Preseli Hills have a sonic property where thousands of stones along the Carn Menyn ridge were tested and a high proportion of them were found to 'ring' when they were struck.

"The percentage of the rocks on the Carn Menyn ridge are ringing rocks, they ring just like a bell," said researcher Paul Devereux, the principal investigator on the Landscape and Perception Project. "And there are lots of different tones … you could play a tune. In fact, we have had percussionists who have played proper percussion pieces off the rocks." According to Devereux, the discovery of the 'resonant rocks' could explain the reason why they were selected for Stonehenge. "There had to be something special about these rocks," he said. "Why else would they take them from here all the way to Stonehenge?"

Dolerite was also extensively quarried in ancient Egypt since the Old Kingdom from the Fayum, and from Palaeolithic times at Rod el-Gamra. At the latter site, many unfinished *naoi* boxes were found: stone boxes that were placed in temple sanctuaries from the Middle Kingdom onward, typically to hold a statue of the god to which that particular temple was dedicated. The greenish dolerite porphyry at Rod el-Gamra is an extremely hard volcanic rock and there is ample evidence that the *naoi* were quarried by the use of iron tools. Iron tools may have partially replaced the good old stone and bronze tools of earlier times because the stone boxes were too hard for chiselling by bronze, and there can be little doubt that the extraction from bedrock was done by iron wedges.

Although there is no official evidence that the ancient Egyptians utilised the sonic qualities of dolerite, it was a stone that was used in a sacred setting – to contain the image of a god. Possibly the ringing sound was perceived to be the voice of the god when the stone *naoi* was struck by a priest – it would be unlike the Egyptians not to use this mysterious quality. At Adam's Calendar and Stonehenge, however, there is irrefutable evidence that the acoustic qualities of the dolerite stones played an important part in the celestial observances of the star-gazing people who gathered there. And even if a dating of 75,000 years pushes the boundaries of credibility too far, there is no doubt that the civilisation who constructed Adam's Calendar was the first to tap into the immense power of stellar-energy and harness it for the benefit of the people.

Fall From Grace

Africa has long been referred to as the 'cradle of civilisation' but like many other places around the world, it has always been a harsh environment, and its history is written in the rocks beneath our feet. Mpumalanga was, without doubt, an extremely wealthy gold-rich society, with its finger on the pulse of the Cosmos, and probably an abundance of knowledge in the occult sciences. So, what happened to those people? And why did they leave a territory that had been home to them for thousands of years?

History has a habit of repeating its mistakes and it's often only with the benefit of hindsight that we can hazard a guess as to what befell those ancient Mpumalangians. The answer is probably mirrored in the fall of the great civilisations of Greece, Prettani, Mesopotamia and Egypt; societies far in advance of their neighbours in terms of science and learning but which later became degenerate and complaisant. Life was good and the living was easy – the people didn't think they needed to worry about their gods and their boundaries any more – then the barbarians came and destroyed them.

Or there was a drastic climate change that altered the ancient Mpumalangians' ability to sustain themselves despite their vast wealth and knowledge, and which forced a mass exodus. The doomsday theorists of the time would have seen this as abandonment by the ancient gods as the surrounding plains became arid and inhospitable. According to Michael Tellinger, this remote region, some 150 miles inland in the heart of the vast *bushveld* that covers much of southern Africa, reveals undeniable geophysical evidence that the planet underwent a crustal shift, or crustal displacement at some turbulent time in its past: when the north-south axis of the planet actually moved to a different position. This is a natural geological occurrence and NASA scientists have explained that Earth's magnetic field has actually slipped its polarity many times over the millennia because the Earth's polarity is not a constant.

The matter governing the Earth's magnetic field moves around, and geophysicists are pretty sure the reason Earth has a magnetic field is because its solid iron core is surrounded by a fluid ocean of hot, liquid metal. The flow of liquid iron in the Earth's core creates electric currents, which in turn create the magnetic field. So while parts of the Earth's outer core are too deep for scientists to measure directly, they can infer movement in the core by observing changes in the magnetic field. The magnetic North Pole has been slowly creeping northward – by more than 600 miles since the early 19th century when it was first identified. It is moving faster now, as scientists estimate the pole is migrating northward about forty miles per year, as opposed to about ten miles per year in the early 20th century.

Even the smallest changes in the Earth's magnetic field are known to have an effect on climate, and shifts in polarity have been associated with major changes in temperature. Recent studies have provided evidence for five short-lived magnetic reversals during the past 470,000 years. The cause of a change in polarity would appear to be sudden convection plumes, or surges in the Earth's molten core, caused by subtle alterations in the Earth's orbit. When these interact with the weak electric currents generated by the circulation of the ocean currents, it alters the rate at which heat is distributed over the globe. A strengthening magnetic field is associated with a cooling of the Earth, while weakening is linked to warming.

So, even a slight planetary hiccup may have been enough to play havoc with those energy fields detected at Adam's Calendar and despite their advanced knowledge, the people would have been extremely superstitious when it came to interpreting what they would have seen as the 'wrath of the gods'. Was there a slow migration taking place over a number of decades before this ancient civilisation was covered by the dry dust of the savannah? The Mpumalangians didn't disappear overnight and as happens whenever there is a break-down in society, the wealthy and the intelligentsia are the first to leave; those at the bottom of the social ladder are the last to be affected.

Let us for a moment speculate that climate change did alter the African landscape and that there was a noticeable shift in the Calendar's energy fields. The astronomer-priesthood would probably be viewed with increasing scepticism as the land gradually became more inhospitable and the people more disillusioned. The buildings and circles would gradually have fallen into disrepair, eroded by the harsh climate of the encroaching savannah. Drastic measures would have been taken and it is possibly at this stage the priesthood (for they *were* the learned elite of their time) of Mpumalanga either decided, or may have even been forced, to leave this sacred landscape and move north. This breakdown of social order is echoed in the collapse of the stellar-priesthood in Egypt at the end of the Pyramid Age.

At Mpumalanga archaeological findings have discovered preserved artefacts that include coins, carvings, swords, symbols, head rests, bowls and statues to suggest that every ancient culture, including the Sumerians, Egyptians, Phoenicians, Romans, Greeks and Arabs, were trading here at some point in its long history. Unfortunately there are no human remains to help with the dating, but the artefacts reveal that Mpumalanga wasn't an insular community and that they were on familiar terms with the developing civilisations around them. In other words, they knew there was somewhere else to go ...

145

The Great Escarpment, which edges the central Southern African plateau, is a major geological formation that extends northwards to form the border between Mozambique and Zimbabwe, creating a natural barrier for a migrating people. While to the north there was another barrier: the Great Rift Valley that runs from Mozambique to the northern Jordan Rift Valley. All of the African Great Lakes were formed as the result of this rift, and most lie within the Valley, including some of the deepest in the world: up to 4,820 foot deep at Lake Tanganyika; and in this area the oldest human remains on the planet have been discovered.

The Mpumalangians didn't leave any noticeable traces along the way but we can find remnants of a strong stellar belief in the most unexpected of places. The African migration has also been scientifically proven via mitochondrial DNA to reveal evidence of a lighter-boned, more technologically advanced and artistic new arrivals in Europe from Africa. Professor Bryan Sykes tells us that all modern Europeans trace their ancestry back to these more progressive arrivals who crossed the only land-bridge into another continent. Were the Mpumalangians part of this drawn-out exodus?

The pre-dynastic beliefs of ancient Egypt were focussed on the stars and, as we have seen in *Starchild I*, the influence of an astronomer-priesthood was clearly evident right up until the end of the Pyramid Age when the Old Order was overthrown following massive civil unrest after years of famine, and a new religion established. Did the star-gazing Egyptians absorb the migrating people's penchant for massive stone-built monuments and then put their own spin on celestial temple building? Having discovered cosmic soul mates on the banks of the Nile, did the Mpumalangians linger in the land of Egypt until the fall of the Old Kingdom? The Egyptians were a hospitable society and from a very early period in its history, welcomed other cultural ideas from her neighbours - often incorporating them into the Egyptian way of life if the new knowledge was considered an improvement.

On the other side of the African continent, however, a different kind of stellar worship waited to be discovered. In Mali, West Africa, still lives a tribe of people called the Dogon whose ancestral belief is centred on the brightest star in the sky, S*igi tolo* or 'star of the Sigui', (with its two companion stars, *Pō tolo* and *Emmę ya tolo*, the female star), that anthropologists identified with the Dog Star, Sirius. According to Dogon traditions, S*igi tolo* has a companion star *Pō tolo,* which is invisible to the human eye, together with a third star, *Emmę ya tolo*, that was larger than *Pō tolo* but lighter and dimmer.

Unfortunately, these 20th century anthropological discoveries became embroiled in academic squabbling over the question of whether the Dogon had been primed by the original researchers to suggest they possessed this advanced astronomical knowledge. In late 1946, French ethnographers Marcel Griaule and Germaine Dieterlen spent a consecutive thirty-three days in conversations with the Dogon wiseman, Ogotemmêli, the source of much of Griaule and Dieterlen's future publications.

Having determined that Sirius A was, in fact, S*igi tolo* in Dogon belief, then it was only reasonable to assume that Sirius B, the companion star, could be identified as *Pō tolo*. Despite not being visible to the naked eye, when Sirius B is closest to Sirius, that star brightens: when it is farthest from Sirius, it gives off a twinkling effect that suggests to the observer several stars. This also alludes to suggestion that the Dogon knew of another star in the Sirius system, *Ęmmę Ya*. Nevertheless, Griaule and Dieterlen were puzzled by this 'mythical' star system, and prefaced their analysis with the following disclaimer: "The problem of knowing how, with no instruments at their disposal, men could know the movements and certain characteristics of virtually invisible stars has not been settled, nor even posed."

The experts were not, however, letting the researchers off that easily and the detractors were vociferous and venomous in accusing the French team of manipulating the facts. There was even the customary revelation that extra-terrestrial influences were behind the Dogon's astronomical beliefs; and that the tribe was of Egyptian descent with their astronomical lore going back thousands of years to 3200BC. In all fairness, neither Griaule nor Dieterlen had ever made such bold claims about any esoteric source for the Dogon's mythology. It has even been suggested that the Dogon may have had contact with astronomers based in the territory during a five-week expedition to study the solar eclipse of 16 April 1893.

A credible theory – but even supposing the notoriously superior Europeans bothered to discuss the intricacies of modern astronomy with a 'primitive' African tribe, would the Dogon have understood the jargon of this emerging science? Apparently Griaule sought informants best qualified to speak of traditional lore, and deeply mistrusted converts to Christianity and Islam, or people with too much contact with white influence. Griaule's daughter, Genevieve Calame-Griaule, also argued that later conflicting accounts may have come about because Dogon informants may have thought that subsequent researchers had been 'sent by the political and administrative authorities to test the Dogon's Muslim orthodoxy' – which is also a credible theory.

Sirius is part of a binary star system, whose second star, Sirius B, a white dwarf, is completely invisible to the human eye, and its existence had only been *inferred* to exist through mathematical calculations undertaken by Friedrich Bessel in 1844, and discovered by an American astronomer in 1862. In 1995, however, gravitational studies revealed the possible presence of a 'brown dwarf' star orbiting around Sirius (a Sirius-C), although more recent studies using advanced infrared imaging concluded that the probability of the existence of a triple star system for Sirius was 'low' but could not be ruled out because the region had not been fully explored.

Binary stars are double stars bound together in orbit; and more than half of stars are binary, or belong to multiple systems, with three or more components; brown dwarfs are stars that failed to get hot enough to generate nuclear burning. The name Sirius comes from the Greek word *seirios*, meaning 'scorching' because the Dog Star usually heralded unbearably hot weather. It is also the brightest star in the night sky, and, like Orion's Belt, would have been part of the predominant star system in the ancient sky, following as it does hot on the heels of the celestial hunter. It would have been impossible to ignore.

Just as anthropologists and archaeologists usually maintain anything they cannot explain as having 'religious' or 'ritual' connotations, so astronomers and pseudo-scientists either dismiss ancient theories as 'impossible', or the latter inject extra-terrestrial influences whenever ancient concepts reveal something incredible. Academics don't deny the existence of these double and multiple systems – they just don't want to admit that primitive [ancient] peoples were aware of them before Western scholars!

Nevertheless, further suggestion of a preserved African stellar cult comes from the same area. Starting out as a seasonal community, Timbuktu became a permanent settlement early in the 12th-century. After a shift in trading routes, Timbuktu flourished from the trade in salt, gold, ivory and slaves, becoming part of the Mali kingdom early in the 14th-century. By the 15th -century and after successive invaders, the Golden Age of the city was over and it entered a long period of decline, impoverishment and desertification.

During its Golden Age, however, the city's numerous Islamic scholars and an important book trade established Timbuktu as a scholarly centre in Africa. Several notable historic writers, including Leo Africanus, described Timbuktu to the outside world and the stories fuelled the city's reputation for being fabled and mysterious, since it was a centre with an established knowledge of astronomy and mathematics. Today there are close to a million of these ancient astronomical manuscripts found in Timbuktu as a testament to the people's fascination with the stars.

In *Astronomy Before the Telescope*, Brian Warner writes: "Throughout Africa, as on other continents, there was extensive traditional appropriation of celestial objects for mythological purposes. Commonly, their involvement was in religious rites, legends and folk-tales in which human personal and social relationships were reflected symbolically in celestial relationships ... or celestial bodies were endowed with male/female, positive/negative characteristics that are distillates of human character ... The brightest stars and a few of the most conspicuous constellations are recognised and named throughout Africa ..."

Of Stars and Serpents

The serpent is one of the oldest and most widespread of mythological symbols, having been associated with some of the most ancient rituals known to mankind, representing both good and evil. In some cultures, serpents symbolise the umbilical cord that joins humans to Mother Earth, and the Earth to the heavens. Among the classical archetypes, serpents and dragons were synonymous with each other, having similar symbolic functions and as such, were immortalized in the stars. The serpent, when forming a ring with its tail in its mouth, is a clear and widespread symbol of the totality of existence, infinity and the cyclic nature of the cosmos. The most well-known version of this being the Ægypto-Greek Ourobouros, believed to have been inspired by the Milky Way, as some ancient texts refer to a serpent of light residing in the heavens.

Hydra: The largest of the eighty-eight constellations, and also one of the longest with its southern end adjoining Libra and Centaurus, and its northern end bordering Cancer. It has a long history, having been included among the forty-eight constellations listed by the 2nd-century astronomer Ptolemy, and commonly represented as a water snake. Hydra is either the serpent thrown angrily into the sky by Apollo, or the Lernaean Hydra as defeated by Heracles for one of his Twelve Labours. The meteor shower, Sigma Hydrids peaks on December 11; it is a very active shower with an unknown parent body. The Alpha Hydrids is a minor shower that peaks between January 1 and 7.

Hydrus: A small constellation in the deep southern sky and was first depicted on a celestial atlas by Johann Bayer in his 1603 *Uranometria*. Its name means 'male water snake', as opposed to Hydra, the much larger constellation that represents a female water snake. It remains below the horizon for most Northern Hemisphere observers.

Serpens: 'The Serpent' is located in the northern hemisphere and one of the forty-eight constellations listed by Ptolemy. It is unique among the modern constellations in being split into two non-contiguous parts, Serpens Caput (Serpent's Head) to the west and Serpens Cauda (Serpent's Tail) to the east; between these two halves lies the constellation of Ophiuchus, the 'Serpent-Bearer'. Serpens represents a snake being tamed by Ophiuchus the 'snake-handler', identified with the healer Asclepius. There are two daytime meteor showers that radiate from Serpens, the Omega Serpentids and the Sigma Serpentids, with both peaking between December 18 and December 25.

Draco: A constellation in the far northern sky and its name is Latin for 'dragon'. Draco is circumpolar (that is, never setting) observed in the northern hemisphere, and another of the forty-eight constellations listed by Ptolemy. Thuban (α Draconis) was the northern pole star from 3942BC and the Egyptian Pyramids were designed to have one side facing north, with an entrance passage designed so that Thuban would be visible at night. Due to the effects of precession, it will once again be the pole star around the year AD21000. The traditional name of Alpha Draconis, Thuban, means 'head of the serpent'. The February Eta Draconids is a meteor shower that was discovered on February 4, 2011; its parent is a previously unknown long-period comet.

In ancient Egypt, where the earliest written cultural records exist, the serpent appears from the beginning to the end of their mythology. Nehebkau ('he who harnesses the souls') was the two headed serpent deity who guarded the entrance to the underworld. He is often seen as the son of the snake goddess Renenutet. She in turn, was often confused with (and later absorbed by) the primal snake goddess Wadjet, the Egyptian cobra, who from the earliest of records was the patron and protector of the country, all other deities, and the pharaohs. She was depicted as the crown of Egypt, entwined around the staff of papyrus and the pole that indicated the status of all other deities, as well as having the all-seeing eye of wisdom and vengeance. Hers is the first known oracle and she never lost her position in the Egyptian pantheon. There was Apophis the great snake who threatened the sun-god during his voyage through the netherworld; the primal, chthonic entities of the Ogdoad were sometimes depicted with snake heads and Kematef, the cosmogonic aspect of the god Amun, who took the form of a serpent.

But let us return to Africa proper, where the centre of serpent worship was Dahomey; at Whydah, the chief centre, there was a serpent temple tenanted by some fifty snakes. Every python of the *Danh-gbi* kind had to be treated with respect, because death was the penalty for killing one, even by accident. *Danh-gbi* was the god of wisdom to whom all things are known and a benefactor of the human race. In Dahomey-Benin mythology, the Great Snake of the Heavens, the serpent that supports everything on its many coils was named Dan. In the Vodou of Benin and Haiti, Ayida-Weddo (Aida-Wedo - 'Rainbow-Serpent') is a spirit of fertility, rainbows and snakes, and a companion or wife to Dan, the father of all spirits. As Vodou was exported to Haiti through the slave trade Dan became Danballah (or Damballah-Wedo). Because of his association with snakes, he is sometimes disguised as Moses, who carried a snake on his staff. He is also thought by many to be the same entity of Saint Patrick, known as a snake banisher.

The Fon people of Benin believe the rainbow serpent, Ayida-Weddo, held up the heavens. The creature had a twin personality as the red part of the rainbow was male, while the blue part was female. She is also portrayed as a narrow green snake and like Damballah, lives in the sky as well as in all the trees, springs, pools, and rivers. In some West African mythology, Mawu the creator, sent down from the sky the rainbow serpent Ayida-Weddo, and in Vodou she was syncretised with the Catholic figure of Our Lady of Immaculate Conception.

"In the beginning there was a vast serpent, whose body formed seven thousand coils beneath the earth, protecting it from descent into the abysmal sea. Then the titanic snake began to move and heave its massive form from the earth to envelop the sky. It scattered stars in the firmament and wound its taught flesh down the mountains to create riverbeds. It shot thunderbolts to the earth to create the sacred thunderstones. From its deepest core it released the sacred waters to fill the earth with life. As the first rains fell, a rainbow encompassed the sky and Danballah took her, Ayida Wedo, as his wife. The spiritual nectar that they created reproduces through all men and women as milk and semen. The serpent and the rainbow taught humankind the link between blood and life, between menstruation and birth, and the ultimate Vodou sacrament of blood sacrifice."
                                        The Book of Vodou, Leah Gordon

The rainbow-god of the Ashanti was also conceived as having the form of a snake. His messenger was said to be a small variety of boa, but only certain individuals, not the whole species, were sacred. The demigod Aidophedo of the West African Ashanti is also represented by a serpent biting its own tail. In many parts of Africa the serpent is looked upon as the incarnation of deceased relatives. Among the Amazulu, as among the Betsileo of Madagascar, certain species are assigned as the abode of certain classes, while the Maasai, regard each species as the habitat of a particular family of the tribe. In Yoruba mythology, Oshunmare was another regenerating serpent.

In esoteric circles, the 'Fire Serpent' is another name for the ancient Hindu concept of *kundalini*, a Sanskrit word meaning 'coiling like a snake'. The term *kundalini,* referring to the central magical power in the human organism; the nurturing intelligence behind yogic awakening and spiritual maturity leading to altered states of consciousness. The image of the serpent as the embodiment of wisdom was also a concept used by Gnosticism, especially those sects that the more orthodox characterised as 'Ophites' ('Serpent People'). The chthonic serpent was also one of the earth-animals associated with the cult of Mithras. There are a number of other interpretations of the term 'serpent power' – one suggestion being that the symbol of snakes coiled around a staff is an ancient representation of *kundalini* physiology. The staff represents the spinal column with the snake(s) being energy channels. In the case of the image of two coiled snakes crossing each other seven times, may possibly refer to the seven energy centres of the human body called *chakras*.

The picture begins to emerge that the only societies who considered the serpent to be evil were the knowledge-suppressing monotheistic faiths that also outlawed stellar-worship as a way of smothering free thinking. The serpent has long been viewed as the emblem of the Supreme Creator, who periodically reabsorbed His Universe back into Himself. This tradition is part of a current of magical force and occult lore dating back to Sumeria and pre-Dynastic Egypt where it was known as the Draconian Tradition: a magical current 'based on initiated knowledge or gnosis of the 'Fire Snake'. The Fire Snake is also known as the *kundalini*, or the Ophidian Current; the basis of *all* true initiation.

Kenneth Grant, writing in *Cults of the Shadow*, maintained that the 'mystical Qabalah' – the Tree of Life of the Western Esoteric Tradition, is "capable of illumining the arcane systems of classical antiquity by reference to the cults from which they originally emerged: the cults of Africa". He also maintains that the Ophidian cult of Inner Africa was continued and developed in pre-dynastic Egypt, where it was transformed into the god-cult of the Draconian tradition.

It also returns us to the claims made by Michael Tellinger in *Temples of the African Gods* that both Sumer and Egypt inherited their knowledge from the migrating, gold-mining civilization that lived at the southern tip of Africa more than 75,000 years ago. "These were also the people who carved the first Horus bird, the first Sphinx, built the first pyramids and created an accurate stone calendar right in the heart of it all. Adam's Calendar is the flagship among millions of circular stone ruins, ancient roads, agricultural terraces and thousands of ancient mines, left behind by a vanished civilisation which they now call the 'First People'. These were the ancestors of all humans today but with an advanced knowledge of the energy fields that run through planet Earth. They carved detailed images into the hardest rock, worshipped the sun, and are the first to carve an image of the Egyptian *ankh* – key of life and universal knowledge ..."

This archaic stellar knowledge also inspired some of the earliest myths and legends for the ancient peoples, including the Egyptian sky-goddess, Nut and her chaotic son ... Set. Gerald Massey, in *Ancient Egypt, the Light of the World*, correctly maintained that no successful study of Egyptian mythology, symbolism, thought or history is possible without first ascertaining to which of the four major strata of Khemetic evolution it pertains:

- The Stellar-Cult that carried over from Africa the totemic approach to the Egyptian Mystery Tradition. This was the cult of the Mother-Goddess of the Seven Stars plus her child, Sirius, the Dog Star. Sirius was represented by the god Set whose symbol was the Goddess – his own mother. At this period, the male role in procreation was unknown; time was measured by the risings and settings of certain stars.

- The Lunar Cult. The stars were replaced by the moon as a more precise mode of time-reckoning. The moon-god, Thoth, Lord of the Double Light, replaced Set as the keeper of time. The mechanism of paternity was still a mystery.

- The Lunar-Solar Cult heralded the enlightenment that the intervention of the male was necessary to procreation; lunar time gave way to solar time and the correct length of the year was calculated.

153

- The Solar Cult placed emphasis on the child as son of the father rather than of the mother, and caused a major upheaval in the history of humanity. In ancient Egypt, long before monumental times, conflict results from these important divisions: the Draconian elevation of the female principle, and the Osirian/Ammonite supporters of the male supremacy.

As Massey points out, it is important to realise that the Solar Cult was already flourishing in Egypt by the start of the Pyramid Age. Following the civic unrest of the 6th Dynasty, the victors remained and the vanquished left, and during this vast period of time, wave upon wave of migrants now left Egypt and swarmed across the known world, leaving in their wake remnants of all four magical traditions. The continual conflict between the 'Followers of Set' and the Solar cultists split the Kingdom of the Nile in two as first one then the other fought for supremacy – just as it was depicted in the mythology of the eternal battle between Horus and Set.

Finally the Solar-cult achieved victory but the Stellar-cult of the Draconian Tradition went underground [*The Setian*, Billie Walker-John] where it endured for centuries. Even the followers of the Solar-cult could not completely eradicate the ingrained beliefs of the people because this older faith could not be so easily ignored or banished; it was too powerful to discard especially when the King's immortal soul might be at risk if the Old Ways were discarded all together. The Osirian priesthood might have supplanted Set to the *outside* world but they were too afraid to deny the King proper funeral rites in which Set played an active part in the Mysteries as psychopomp. The seven stars of Ursa Major, together with the Dog Star, Sirius as the annual herald of the Goddess, continued to be reflected in the sixteen sanctuaries of Osiris – probably powered by the underground currents of the Setian priesthood.

The Draconian Tradition represents the first systemised form of primitive African Mysteries which the Egyptians elaborated into a highly sophisticated system of occultism that has always remained hidden to the present day. According to Kenneth Grant, the Tradition "evolved from a concentration of knowledge derived from careful observation of physical phenomena extending over enormous cycles of time".

In later Dynastic times, the Land of Khem was divided into thirty-six *nomes*, which represented an earthly transfer of the celestial symbolism of the heavens as the Circle of Nut, the Goddess of Infinite Space. Nut was a primordial deity represented by a constellation of seven stars (either Orion or Ursa Major)) symbolising Night and her stellar nursery, to which was later added the star of her first male child, Set or Sothis/Sirius. It was he who manifested in the south as the Light of the Mother who ruled in the North, and who was the first giver of light in the darkness and the first keeper of Time.

So powerful was this primeval African cult of the Mother of the Seven Stars that during the early days of Afro-Egyptian history the Draconian Tradition emerged as a magical entity; so true in its foundations that subsequent phases of Khemetic evolution could not totally eradicate the Ophidian origins of its esoteric wisdom. And there *was* a magical or esoteric element to the symbolism behind the beliefs, which was first celestial and astronomical - and afterwards terrestrial and synthetic.

The disintegration of the Draconian Tradition in Egypt never wholly destroyed the belief or its Mysteries. As Kenneth Grant observes: "It is true that it wiped them from the face of the land but numerous waves of Draconians throughout the centuries left Egypt and spawned the Cult far and wide so that it is traceable all over the globe in various stages, either of development or degeneration. In some cases it flowered into strange cults that persisted right down to modern times." This Draconian Tradition was never wholly about sex despite generating sexual energy as a means of awakening the serpent-power, or Fire Snake – the key to all cosmic consciousness. The ancient Egyptians were a sensuous people, in addition to being an intellectual and spiritual people; they recognised the importance of controlling and directing the mystical forces of the sub-conscious mind, the repository of infinite knowledge, wisdom and understanding.

Thus Nut, the Mother of the Seven Stars is the guiding, female principle – the archetypal mother with a highly sensual side to her nature as the early mythologies suggest – this is the Goddess of Infinite Space. When we see her supple body arched across the night sky and look upon her naked beauty, is there any amongst us – male or female – having once felt the touch of the mystic, who cannot but fail to be moved by all this celestial ecstasy? With her rampant, chaotic off-spring Set – God of Deep Space – the realm of black holes, cosmic radiation and distant quasars – and protector of the Bornless One, the Creator who resides *beyond* the Veil in Space and Time.

Nut and Set, however, should never be looked upon as beneficent and benevolent entities. There can be no supplication, no imprecation or appeasement – these are deities deaf and blind to human propitiates. Only after long and arduous service does anyone gain the benefit of wisdom and enlightenment but even then there is a price to pay in terms of personal suffering and, if we haven't got it right – death! Many claim to walk in the footsteps of Set but they do not carry the 'stigmata' that confirms a close encounter with this God of all Gods. We cannot, therefore, even begin to understand the beliefs of ancient Egypt without going back to the beginning and charting a course through the different layers of religion and history.

We also find subtle mirrored images of the Draconian beliefs in traditional British Old Craft's view that although it is not a religion, it *is* a belief – a belief in one's own abilities and in the 'Power' that fuels the Universe; and a faith – faith in one's self and in that 'Universal Power'. This Power not generally seen as gender specific but in truth, Old Craft does lean towards the male aspect since the female remains veiled and a mystery. In other words, in this case, the 'God' is the public face of traditional British Old Craft while the 'Goddess' remains in the shadows, revered and shielded by her protector. Not because she is some shy and defenceless creature, but because face to face – like the Egyptian Set – she would be too terrible to look upon. The secrets of these ancient mysteries come from the understanding of these things because it is not possible to convey the true meanings of these beliefs to an outsider, who has not experienced the Mysteries for themselves.

Strangely enough, we need look no further for the liturgy and 'prayer book' of the Draconian Tradition than in Aleister Crowley's *The Book of the Law* and the *Atus of Thoth*. Here we find the signposts that direct us to the Path of the Mysteries but it takes many years of searching before we can step through the cosmic portal, that allows us to look upon the face of Set – the God of Deep Space. But we can always find a way .

Part Three: Golden Fruit Upon a Tree

*"Whatever spot anyone may occupy, the universe stretches
away from him just the same in all directions without limit."*
Lucretius 1st century BC

In *The Mystical Qabalah*, Dion Fortune observed that the Tree of Life has
been described as the 'ground plan of the Western Esoteric Tradition',
and commented, quite rightly, that very few students of occultism know
anything at all about the fountain-head from where their traditions spring.
She also warns that no student will ever make any progress in spiritual
development if they persist in flitting from system to system, path to path,
tradition to tradition. If, as Fortune points out, we intend to take our
occult studies seriously then we *must* first find our Path and follow it
faithfully until we arrive, if not at its ultimate goal then at some
significant 'enhancement of consciousness'.

Any magical system has its value but only if pursued to its obvious
conclusion of developing the powers of the mind. And this value doesn't
lie in completing the prescribed exercises as results in themselves, but in
the powers that are developed as they are persevered with. Once we have
reached this level of understanding we may then experiment with other
methods that have been developed upon other Paths "but the student who
sets out to be an eclectic before he has made him or herself an expert will
never be anything more than a dabbler," warns Fortune. The seeker
looking at the Tree of Life is therefore better equipped to climb its lofty
heights if they have thoroughly explored their chosen Path at root level
before attempting to ascend its 'branches'.

The Qabalistic Tree of Life is a Path studded with Stars and Serpents
and in many myths the chthonic serpent (sometimes a pair) lives in, or is
coiled around the Tree whose branches reach up to the stars. In the
Genesis story of the Torah and Biblical Old Testament, the 'tree of the

knowledge of good and evil' is situated in the Garden of Eden, together with the Tree of Life *and* the Serpent. In Greek mythology, Ladon coiled around the tree in the garden of the Hesperides protecting the golden apples. Similarly Níðhöggr (Nidhogg Nagar) the dragon of Norse mythology eats from the roots of the Yggdrasil, the World Tree. Under yet another Tree (the Bodhi tree of Enlightenment), the Buddha sat in ecstatic meditation. When a storm arose, the mighty serpent king Mucalinda rose up from his place beneath the earth and enveloped the Buddha in seven coils for seven days, so as not to break his ecstatic state. The Vision Serpent was also a symbol of rebirth in Mayan mythology with origins going back to earlier Maya conceptions, lying at the centre of the world and the World Tree.

The Sumerian deity, Ningizzida, is the oldest known image of two snakes coiling around an axial rod; sometimes the Tree of Life is represented by a staff featuring coiled snakes such as the caduceus of Hermes, the Rod of Asclepius, the staff of Moses, and the papyrus reeds and deity poles entwined by a single serpent, Wadjet, dating to before 3000BC. In the Golden Dawn mystical (or magical) Qabalah the head of the Serpent of Wisdom is located at Kether at the top of the Pillar of Mildness, while its tail at the bottom of the descent of power, lies in Malkuth. The modern key to understanding, harnessing and utilising cosmic power is to learn how to climb the Tree of Life, by testing each of its levels.

The Hollow Tree

The problem in understanding the intricate workings of the Qabalah lies in the largely incomprehensible and exhaustive list of publications available to the beginner which automatically begs the question: *"Where do I start?"*

Firstly, by understanding the origins and antecedents of both the Tarot and the Qabalah as being *two completely different systems* that have undergone multiple translations, adaptations, additions and changes across the centuries. The Qabalistic Tree of Life has been around for well over 2000 years, representing an analogy for the Absolute, the Universe, Man and Everything - its very roots dig deep into the molten core of the Earth, while its uppermost branches reach out to Infinity. And vice versa because the energies of each individual *sephirah* are androgynous in that they can be and/either/or - male/female/androgyn, and that many of the attributes can be interchangeable between different locations on the Tree.

158

Like all things mystical, the origins of the Qabalah (from the Hebrew for 'that which is received'), are obscure. Traditionally, it is firmly rooted in Judaic inner teachings but it has been suggested (and with good reason) that there may have been a much earlier Chaldean influence. By the 2-3rd centuries AD, the Qabalah had evolved into an established 'tradition' that was being handed down by word of mouth, although it was still a long way removed from the esoteric/magical Western connotations that surround its modern usage. The origin of the system we know today, is accepted as one of Jewish (male only) mystical thought that was perfected in southern France and Spain during the 12-13th centuries. Christian interest in this form of Qabalistic learning grew during the 15th-century, but from the 17th-century onwards, the term became an umbrella for all manner of occult and esoteric doctrines which were not to be found in the original Hebrew texts.

The 'magical' version familiar to 20th-century occultists is the system expanded and revised by Eliphas Levi in the 19th-century, and by Dion Fortune and Aleister Crowley in the 20th. The 'Tree' finally metamorphosed into a mystical step-ladder by which means the seeker could unite himself with, or become the One, by rising up through the spheres, scaling the ladder of the ten *sephiroth* – crossing the Abyss in the process – to reach the Absolute. It could also represent an over-all blue-print of how the Universe came into being, in a cosmic game of 'snakes and ladders'.

Part of the romance surrounding the Tarot, is an 18th-century French theologian's claim that the cards were part of the Egyptian *Book of Thoth* and that they 'symbolised in a pictorial form the arcane knowledge of the initiates of Egypt'. This dubious claim re-appeared in the so-called 'writings of Iamblichus', a questionable translation by a student of Eliphas Levi that supported his master's theory that the twenty-two cards of the Major Arcana related to the twenty-two Paths linking the *sephiroth* together on the Tree. These mystical pathways required an intimate knowledge of related correspondences, all of which helped to guide the seeker on his or her way.

Which brings us to the systems used by Dion Fortune and Aleister Crowley, and since both were Initiates of the Hermetic Order of the Golden Dawn, there is a marked similarity in their respective interpretations of the subject. Having said that, there are now dozens of versions which never seem to agree on the assignment of the Major Arcana to the Paths of the Tree but at least Crowley explained why he placed several *Atus* in places which often differ considerably from other systems. Crowley maintained that every student should compile their own Tree as this is the most effective and individualistic method of understanding much of what passes for ritual magic in most of the modern Traditions.

> *"Never let your mind wander from the fact that your Qabalah is not my Qabalah; a good many of the things which I have noted may be useful to you, but you must construct your own system so that it is a living weapon in your hand."*
>
> [*Magick Without Tears*, Aleister Crowley]

In recent years, there has been a growing trend for 'dumbing down' occult teaching and there will be those who would claim that this simplistic approach can't go any further in taking the seeker down that slippery slope. There is, however, a vast difference in attempting to pass off dumbed-down material as in-depth esoteric knowledge - and that which gives a beginner a practical nuts-and-bolts approach to an often confusing and mind-numbing subject.

The Tree of Life is comprised of a series of ten spheres or *sephiroth* (eleven if we count Daath - the ' hidden' one) arranged on three columns or Pillars. Each *sephirah* can only be understood in relation to its neighbours, where it appears on the Tree and how it is affected by the 'descent of power', usually depicted as a coiled serpent, or a tongue of flame, reaching *down* from Kether to end in Malkuth - as all things must. The Tree is further divided into three triangles: the Supernal Triangle (Kether, Binah and Chokmah); the Ethical Triangle (Geburah, Chesed and Tiphareth) and the Astral Triangle (Hod, Netzach and Yesod) leaving Malkuth standing alone at the foot of the Tree. The whole Tree is criss-crossed by a mystical system constructed from the twenty-two Paths, each one symbolised by a card of the Major Arcana.

Each of the *sephirah* also has its own set of individual correspondences relating to colour, perfume, flora, fauna, gemstones, etc., and a thorough grounding in these enables us to evoke the right 'essence' for a particular working. It is often obvious why particular correspondences are assigned their place on the Tree but many are equally obscure. The various different sources will all have their own particular attributions and, although Aleister Crowley's *Liber 777* has the most comprehensive listing, a degree of experimentation is permissible once you've learned the ground rules.

This is the framework on which the seeker must build if they wish to explore the secrets of stellar-wisdom within their own system of magical workings. And if the seeker asks: what use is all this? What is the point of all this study? Dion Fortune gives us her answer in *The Mystical Qabalah*, "... I have used its methods both subjectively and objectively till they have become a part of myself, and I know from experience what they yield in psychic and spiritual results, and their incalculable value as a method of using the mind." Or conversely in the words of Louis Armstrong when asked to define jazz: *"If you gotta ask, you ain't never gonna know."*

The 'practical' Qabalah, then, is the root system for all talismanic, ritual and ceremonial magic; without it there will be no understanding of either the Universe, or one's own Self. Add the magical correspondences and, together with the Tarot, we have a system of visual stimuli which trigger off instant images in the sub-conscious. This is why Aleister Crowley considered it important that everyone should construct their own version in order that it becomes a constantly growing and expanding personal cosmic i-Pad. And, once conditioned, an image or perfume will be all it takes to kick our Qabalistic sub-conscious into over-drive as we set out to rediscover the wisdom of the ancient star-cult.

But first we need to find our way around the *sephiroth* and in this extract from *The Hollow Tree* we will be starting with Malkuth, although nearly all books on the Qabalah will begin at Kether. Most students are aware of the adage "As above, so below" and this is aptly applied to the Tree from either the point of view of Kether or Malkuth - both are equally holy. We are starting with Malkuth because every magical operation has its end results at this level - not the other way around. Magical workings bring power *down* through the different levels to enable the seeker to utilise the energy for whatever purpose and no working can be considered complete unless it manifests in Malkuth, i.e. the physical plane. If this 'earthing' process has not been carried out correctly, then a 'loose force is left lying around' which can have devastating long-term effects of future magical workings and result in something nasty left lurking in the mystical woodshed.

These effects are often felt in terms of psychic disturbance, unexplained runs of bad luck, ill-health or depression, the unpleasant feeling of something in the house, irritability or tiredness. As Dion Fortune points out, these difficulties are caused by 'faulty techniques' on the part of the practitioner, and not because magical practice is dangerous or anti-social. The same effects can be caused if a beginner forgets to close the 'doors', or gateways properly after meditation.

It is therefore imperative that the seeker is familiar with *all* the relationships between the different *sephiroth* before engaging in any form of magical ritual. Once this learning process has been completed and the seeker's personal Tree is in the sapling stages of growth, then and *only then*, can they begin to explore the *sephiroth* under the protection of their own traditional deities. Do not operate under the popular pagan myth that

161

we can proceed with impunity because 'deity' will protect a beginner from harm. It doesn't work like that - ignorance can reap some extremely dire results.

Knowledge of the Tarot will also provide suitable images for the purpose of meditation, visualisation and conceptualisation, and it is important to provide ourselves with a carefully chosen Tarot deck with designs that complement our own Tradition, whether it is drawn from Craft, ritual magic or any other Path. Understanding the basic mechanics of the Qabalah, enables a seeker to realise why every authentic magician of note since the Renaissance has made its study a life-time's commitment. The more we work with the Tree, the more we come to realise that this is a living, breathing thing that enables us to explore and comprehend the Cosmos, from our inner-Self to the 'furthest reaches of the most abstract infinity' ...

Malkuth
The Tenth and final *sephirah* of the Tree, located at the base of the Pillar of Equilibrium. It represents the densest manifestation of the cosmic current and the 'Kingdom' in its widest sense, i.e. everything that is physical or matter.

Planetary Attribution: Earth - represented by nature, earth and grain deities.

Magical Image:
A young woman, crowned and throned - for purposes of meditation, the magical image can be represented by the **Princess of Disks** (the Earthy part of Earth) as the element on the brink of Transfiguration. Crowley's own *Thoth Tarot* depicts her with a ram's horn helmet, with her sceptre descending into the Earth where the point becomes a diamond; her shield denotes the twin spiral forces of Creation in perfect equilibrium: "She is strong and beautiful, with an expression of intense brooding, as if about to become aware of secret wonder." Or focus on the **Prince of Disks** (the Airy part of Earth) who is the element of Earth become intelligible with his chariot drawn by an ox, the sacred symbol of Elemental Earth.

Spiritual Experience:
Since Malkuth is magically and mystically the last *sephirah* - this is where we encounter the Vision of the Holy Guardian Angel - our inner, divine Self that protects during those dark nights of the soul. The attainment of the Knowledge of the Holy Guardian Angel is the

foundation of a seeker's power and constitutes the most critical stage of his/her development.

Summary
Although Malkuth is considered to be the Sphere of the Earth, it would be a mistake to limit this concept to the thin 'skin' we refer to as Nature. From its molten core to the outermost reaches of its atmosphere, Malkuth represents the Earth-soul - the 'subtle, psychic aspect of matter' and the elemental energies of Earth, Air, Fire and Water - in which many other faiths reject the idea of divinity in physical matter. This, then, is what is meant by 'the Kingdom': the end-result of all operations since everything ends in Malkuth as everything has its beginning in Kether.

The titles given to Malkuth indicate that having been seen as the 'Gate and the Mate' it represents the Gate of Life and the Gate of Death since birth into the plane of form is considered death to higher things. We enter Malkuth when we are born into the physical world and exit when our physical body dies. It is the Gateway to both Inner and Outer Planes. Full comprehension of Malkuth cannot be achieved except by an understanding of its nearest neighbour Yesod, although Malkuth receives all emanation of ideas and potentials from all the other *sephiroth*.

Making no bones about it, Malkuth is the level at which we take the decision to make the first irreversible step on the Stellar-Path. With this decision should also come the realisation that by giving 'every drop of blood for the cup' we will be shortening this present life-span on the Wheel of Life by direct and deliberate action. With this in mind, the seeker still needs to put in place those elementary safety precautions that will become second nature at whatever level they are working. The first basic exercise will, therefore, be to construct an astral **Temple of Malkuth** - from which all journeys begin and where all journeys end.

For the purpose of the exercise, sit quietly in a candle-lit room. Visualise a room with a floor made up of black and white squares; in the centre is the altar constructed from a double cube (one on top of the other) and covered by a white cloth. On the altar is a deep blue crystal bowl in which burns the sacred flame; this is the symbol of all Mystery Paths regardless of the Tradition since without this light no Temple can make its contacts. This light guides us out onto the astral and acts as a beacon for our return. Overhead is the bronze lamp for the burning of incense and the Temple is filled with the perfume of Dittany of Crete. At the four quarters a light burns for each of the four elements. On the eastern wall there are two pillars flanking three doors - a black one to the left and a silver one to the right.

The seeker should practice constructing this Temple through visualisation until it becomes as familiar as a room in his or her own home. Using the same techniques, we will build a Temple for each of the *sephirah* and for this exercise you might find that it aids concentration if you burn the appropriate incense (see above). Malkuth is, of course, the *sephirah* with which we are the most familiar, and the one we see through a microscope or a powerful telescope.

Having said all this in such a grandiose manner, we should never lose sight of the Path of the Hearth Fire which often gets abandoned in the search for Cosmic wisdom. The Hearth Fire is Love in *all* its various aspects; the source of womanly power and manly energy in its most sacred but most simplistic forms, and without it no other fire can come into existence. This is a warning that all would-be seekers, *both male and female,* ignore at their peril because the correct sexual balance is an essential ingredient for Qabalistic working. The majority of Qabalistic literature with which we are familiar today was compiled and published during the Victorian era when it didn't take much to frighten the horses. Consequently, any 'sexual' references would have been deleted by the publishers for fear of imprisonment.

The Qabalah *isn't* about sex but it *is* about harmony and balance of the senses, and without an understanding and acceptance of this, successful working with the Tree of Life could result in stunted spiritual growth. Unfortunately, much of this dated philosophy came from early Theosophical writings which coined those rather nebulous references to 'left-hand path' that have confused esoteric writing for the last 150 years. As a result, over the decades the term 'left-hand path' has erroneously been taken to mean:

- anything of a sexual or orgiastic nature
- any reference to female-only magical working
- satanism or black magic

The three columns or Pillars of Severity - Mildness and Mercy (attributed to Feminine) and Equilibrium (attributed to Masculine) - are the balancing and tempering of male and female energies. The practice of magic is the harnessing of *natural* energies, whether it is derived from the forming of new galaxies at the furthest reaches of the Universe; or through the arousal of passion. In true Qabalistic learning there is no place for contaminating or restricting attitudes about what is, and what isn't considered 'nice'.

At this point we should reflect for a moment on Dion Fortune's comment in *The Mystical Qabalah*: "It is truly said in the Mysteries that no degree becomes functional until one has taken the next." This means that the true nature of Malkuth cannot be fully understood until the seeker has ascended to Yesod; the secrets of Yesod will not be revealed until the door to Hod, the Sephirah of Magic, has been unlocked, and so on. Imagine looking backwards at the Earth from Space and seeing it clearly for the first time ... before we move on.

NB: An ideal introduction would be Alan Richardson's *Introduction to the Mystical Qabalah*, which is possibly the best beginner's guide ever written.

Yesod

The Foundation and the Ninth Path of Pure Intelligence - and the *sephirah* most easily reached from physical manifestation, just as the Moon, its planetary attribution is the nearest to Earth.

Planetary attribution: Moon – represented by lunar deities.

Magical Image:
A beautiful naked man, very strong, **The Prince of Disks** (the Airy part of Earth) can be interchangeable with Malkuth because he holds in his hand the sceptre to symbolise the bringing forth of that which is sustenance of the Spirit into the physical plane from above. Or try using **the Princess of Cups** (the Earthy part of Water) who represents the power of the Water to give sustenance to the idea, to support life, and to form the basis of chemical combination ... "On a superficial examination she might be thought selfish and indolent, but this is a quite false impression; silently and effortlessly she goes about her work."

Spiritual Experience: Vision of the Machinery of the Universe

Summary:
Yesod is a confusing *sephirah* because of the conflicting messages we find in its symbolism; on one hand it is the Foundation of the Universe, on the other the apparent fluid state of illusion. Many authors also ignore the potent sexual energy that is focused at this level. Again, we are not

looking at base sexual activity but the more subtler aspects of sex which is only just being rediscovered in the West, having been an important and intrinsic part of Eastern mysticism for thousands of years.

From the seeker's point of view, Yesod is of supreme importance in the seeker's magical development because this is the level at which they begin to elevate the consciousness and rise through the planes. A word of warning, however, relates to the fact that although this 'Treasure House of Images' offers up a wide panorama of magical concepts, the seeker is unable to command or control them, because she/he has not yet learned the words of power. Together with Hod and Netzach, Yesod forms the Astral Triangle and these three *sephiroth* form an area of power within the World of Assiah (Elements and Action). The power of Yesod is greatly influenced by the duality of Hod *and* Netzach, having as it does, a dualistic side to its nature.

In Qabalistic terms, these magical images symbolise both the rhythmic nature of the Moon and the rhythmic sexual urges in the female, although these are etheric, not physical conditions. Magically these energies will always balance each other *when applied correctly.* There are times during magical workings when the polarity of power requires a reversal of focus; on the inner planes the negative energy does the work while the positive energy provides the stimulus. This refers to the male/positive and female/negative energies, and the magical partners who have perfected this 'harmony' generate an obvious aura of power to the trained 'eye'.

To reach the **Temple of Yesod** we will have begun in the Temple of Malkuth and travelled the 32nd Path. Sit quietly and visualise the room as shimmering quartz, reflecting the misty violet colours of the veils that line the walls. The floor is veined violet, mauve and purple marble. In the centre is a square altar of quartz and on top, a huge pearlised sea-shell holding the sacred flame. This time there are four doors flanked by pillars of violet and silver; the scent of jasmine fills the air.

In human terms, Yesod - the Foundation or Image of the World is the *sephirah* nearest to us and still represents the world of illusion because we submerge our potential (Kether) beneath a cloak of social, family or professional habits and attitudes. The word for *persona* is Latin for 'mask', and a rather good description of what we offer to our friends and acquaintances under the guise of our 'personality'. Yesod is the store-house of library images from the physical and psychological planes and when we sleep we might find we have an action-replay of the day's events; or a completely different scenario with unknown people or places which are transmitted from the other *sephiroth*.

Another important aspect of human action that we have already mentioned, is Yesod's correspondence to the sexual act; this *sephirah*

166

also receives energy, via Tiphareth, from Daath and Kether - and extremely potent energy it is - because only the central *sephiroth* can produce the necessary transformation or conception for physical or spiritual birth.

Hod

The Splendour and the Glory. This Eighth Path is called the Absolute or Perfect Intelligence because it represents all the intellectual activities of the mind.

Planetary Attribution: Mercury – represented by messenger and teaching deities.

Magical Image:
A Hermaphrodite. Try Crowley's *Thoth Tarot* for meditation using the **Queen of Cups** (the Watery part of Water) with its power of reception and reflection. This image is of 'extreme purity and beauty with infinite subtlety; to see the Truth of her is hardly possible, for she reflects the nature of the observer in great perfection'. By contrast, the **Knight of Swords** (the Fiery part of Air) represents the 'violent power of motion to an apparently manageable element ... he is fierce, delicate and courageous, but altogether the prey of his idea, which comes to him as an inspiration without reflection'.

Spiritual Experience:
Vision of splendour - the glory of God manifesting in the created world.

Summary:
Hod is the *sephirah* of the rational intellect. Working with Hod stimulates the intellectual processes and encourages a tremendous talent for logic and honesty and because the *sephirah* is governed by Mercury, the aspects of negative virtue, deceit and cunning are all part of the package. The budding seeker must quickly come to grips with the difference between self-deception and the magician's natural talent for dissembling and shape-shifting. The search for knowledge is a dangerous Path and we've all discovered the publishing garbage that passes itself off as rare esoteric wisdom but which, in reality, stunts our psychic growth.

Hod and Netzach (together with Yesod) are the components of the Astral Triangle, and form a powerful energy balancing act by merging to form the Hermaphrodite - the magical image of Hod. These are the

167

sephiroth closest to physical manifestation and are located at the bases of the Masculine and Feminine Pillars. On a magical level, Hod governs esoteric studies, books and forms of ritual, while Netzach controls natural and instinctive magic, and the performance which energises the ritual.

As Dion Fortune points out: "For the full understanding of the philosophy of magic we must remember that single *sephirah* are never functional; for function one must have the Pair of Opposites in balanced equilibrium, resulting in an equilibrated Third which is functional. The Pair of Opposites by themselves, are not functional because they are mutually neutralising ..." It is at this level that any serious magical practitioner must get his or her head around the fact that balance is *the* most essential ingredient in magical practice and that without this acceptance, the process of learning will be an uphill struggle at best, or a magically sterile vacuum at worse.

Sit quietly and visualise the walls of the **Temple of Hod** as being lined with books of learning from across the ages, while the floor comprises pearl and azure tiles. In the centre burns the sacred flame of knowledge on the shimmering crystal altar. There are five doors flanked by pillars of dark blue and silver, and the air is perfumed with cinnamon. You will be spending a lot of time in this Temple, so mark the details well before moving on, for this is the seat of learning and none of us ever know anything in terms of Cosmic wisdom - no matter how long we've been seeking.

In human terms, Hod (Voluntary Processes) checks the excesses of the Involuntary Processes of Netzach and prevents the hearts (and very often the genitals) from ruling the head. This is the *sephirah* of mental input and learning which are 'stored in the brain to become conditioned memories and reflexes'. A good analogy is the soldier's training which becomes second nature and belongs to Hod; his desire to survive is found in Netzach (the primordial urge); in a theatre of war his actions (hopefully) are governed by Tiphareth (consciousness) and Chesed (mercy) but, if allowed to run unchecked they can become lost in Geburah (cruelty).

In the long-term, although the *basic* principles of magic can be defined and classified, the only real learning comes from individual experience, and involves disciplined self-development. Experience itself is the *real* initiator and the ground-rules we are looking for to provide the astral safety measures for our continuing journey can be found in Hod - for those who have the eyes to see.

Netzach
The sphere of Victory and the Seventh Path of Occult Intelligence because it represents intellectual virtues and love in all forms.

Planetary Attributions: Venus – represented by all love deities.

Magical Image:
A beautiful, naked woman. From the *Thoth Tarot* try meditating on either the **Princess of Swords** (the Earthy part of Air) who represents the influence of Heaven upon Earth; she is firm and aggressive, with great practical wisdom and subtlety in material things. Or the **Queen of Wands** (the Watery part of Fire) whose face 'expresses the ecstasy of one whose mind is well in-drawn to the mystery borne beneath her bosom'.

Spiritual Experience: Vision of Beauty Triumphant

Summary:
It is easy to dismiss Netzach as the *sephirah* of physical or romantic love, but this would be a grave error of judgement. The Queen of Wands and the Princess of Swords are much more realistic interpretations of the power of Netzach than the sweetness and light normally used to represent this *sephirah*. As Ellen Cannon Reed observed in *The Witches' Qabala*, "This spark of genius that touches us when we are being creative ... Netzach is energy, creative energy, the energy you put into rituals to make them effective," and the instincts and emotion which need to be checked by the rational intellect of Hod.

According to Dion Fortune, it is the Netzach factor in ourselves that provides the basis for instinctive behaviour which, when uncontrolled by rationality, give rise to the spontaneous reflexes. These lower *sephiroth* of the Planes of Illusion are densely populated by every thought-form the human imagination is capable of creating. The more the mind conjures up these 'creations of the created', the more concrete the image becomes, thereby confusing the 'reality' of the image. "All god-forms in Netzach are worshipped by means of the arts, not conceived by means of philosophies ... perceived far more by the 'contemplations of faith' than by the 'eyes' of the intellect," she warns in *The Mystical Qabalah*.

Sit quietly in the candle-light and visualise the walls of the **Temple of Netzach** shimmering like sun through the leaves of a green wood, while the floor is inlaid with jade and copper. The altar is a darker jade and the sacred flame burns inside an oyster shell. There are five doors flanked by pillars of emerald and silver while the air is perfumed with sandalwood.

In human terms Netzach (Eternity) - Involuntary Processes - is the first *sephirah* to actually be seen to work on the physical plane, and the control centre for all the vital bodily and instinctive functions without which we could not survive. Netzach governs the primordial urge, bodily organs and those 'gut reactions' that influence our decisions over people and situations. It is the biological (and often illogical) urge that has been described as 'eternally repeating the Spring festival in the body of mankind', so it is not surprising that this feminine *sephirah* is governed by the goddesses of love.

Tipareth
represents Beauty and Harmony, being the Sixth Path, called the Mediating Intelligence because it is the sphere of the Dying God and the Sacrificial King.

Planetary Attributions: Sun – represented by all solar deities.

Magical Image:
A king and a sacrificial god. Crowley's **Prince of Swords** (the Airy part of Air) epitomises the glorious sun-king whose sacrificial death and re-birth represents the Intellect. The sword in the right hand symbolises creative force; the sickle in the left hand destroys what has been created.

Spiritual Experience:
Vision of the harmony of things; an understanding of the mysteries of sacrifice.

Summary:
This is the third *sephiroth* of the Ethical Triangle with Chesed and Geburah; the pivotal point of the Tree and the sphere from which emanates the popular images of deity in the form of the Sun - and the sacrificial-gods who reach out from ancient times to the present day. There is a strong multi-faceted aspect to this *sephirah* and the focus selected for magical working would be governed by the deity most closely related to the desired outcome. It is also important to realise that this *sephirah* is at the very nerve centre of the whole Tree, at the point of 'transmutation between the planes of force and the planes of form' linking as it does, eight Pathways from the highest to the lowest levels.

The central Pillar of the Tree is the Pillar of Consciousness, harmonising the active and passive powers of the left and right-hand columns. The Sun-*sephirah* therefore represents the Giver of Life and the source of all-being which, in Qabalistic terms, symbolises all sun-gods and healers, and all healers are solar deities. Another universal symbol is, of course, gold - the mineral that can be dulled by grime and filth but cannot be naturally corroded. At both spiritual and temporal levels, sun/gold can be seen as manifesting energy, the driving force behind all manner of actions and reactions. The sun is vital to our health and well-being; it fosters growth and vitality; gold (money) is the universal language which is 'representative of externalised life-force' on the planet in terms of economics and commerce.

The Hebrew word for Tiphareth is 'beauty' which should be of beauty in things that are balanced or harmonised. Not surprisingly, the vision for this level is the Vision of the Harmony of Things, corresponding with the Japanese state of *wa* and ancient Egyptian *ma'at*. It also means that we must re-double our efforts to look at things from different angles - and approach matters from a lateral viewpoint, rather than taking a linear stance. Tiphareth enables us to be objective without holding a jaundiced opinion of the micro/macrocosm: this is the true level of "As above, so below".

Here we also need to understand and appreciate the true meaning of sacrifice, which bears no resemblance to the popular theory of newspaper journalism and commercial paperback books. Sacrifice in true esoteric language is the translation of force from one form to another - a very basic example is the offering of incense which begins in the solid form of wood, resin and herbs to be translated into smoke when it is burned. A sacrifice in any form breaks up the form that imprisons static energy and releases it into the cosmos, thereby converting one form of energy into another.

Visualise the **Temple of Tiphareth** as a vaulted eight-sided room with a door set into each panel. Here the walls shimmer with a bright intensity that appears to reflect every colour in the spectrum just as sunlight through raindrops creates a rainbow. The floor appears to be liquid gold; the altar is gleaming white marble with a gilt filigree chalice to hold the sacred flame. The air is perfumed with frankincense.

On a human level, Tiphareth represents the Essential Nature of man with which he is born. Located at the junction of eight Paths, Tiphareth absorbs the influences of the realms above and from the kingdoms below with direct access to all *sephiroth* except Malkuth. This shows why, although human essential nature cannot be seen in the physical world, its character can be traced by human action. This is the essence which exhorts you to "Know thyself" and recognise this essential nature in others. This is the place into which things flow from all directions and flow out again: a holding centre for every action, emotion, or experience on both the physical and spiritual planes.

Look upon Tiphareth's physical correspondence to the chakra located in the solar plexus and see how poorly we function if there is a blockage in this area. This is not a New Age theory, it is an extremely ancient one and recognises (in modern terms) that if there is a central blockage within the system, then eventually everything will break down. We, therefore, need to keep our channels open and pure, so that the flow of energy remains unhampered both on the physical and spiritual planes.

Geburah
Symbolises Might and the Fifth Path known as Radical Intelligence because it unites with Binah (Understanding) and Chokmah (Wisdom).

Planetary Attributions: Mars – represented by all war, protector and avenger deities.

Magical Image:
A mighty warrior in his/her chariot would be ideally represented in the *Thoth Tarot* by the **Princess** (the Earthy part of Fire) and the **Prince** (the Airy part of Fire) **of Wands**. Meditate on the swiftness and strength of the Prince in all his vigour and activity but bear in mind that he is inclined to act on impulse. The Princess is the fuel of the Fire, which implies the 'irresistible chemical attraction of the combustible substance'.

Spiritual Experience: Vision of Power

Summary:
When working with Geburah it is essential that the seeker maintains a tight hold on the reins. Although we stand in awe of the sheer martial power of this *sephirah*, we must conquer our fear because this is the might of defence and punishment rather than wanton destruction. It is easy to misunderstand the driving force of Geburah and Dion Fortune uses the following analogy: "Chesed, the king on his throne, the father of his people; but it is Geburah, the king in his chariot going forth to war, who commands our respect ... whose strong right arm protects his people with the sword of righteousness and ensures that justice shall be done."

Qabalistic teaching is adamant that this *sephirah* should not be looked upon as evil, since evil is simply misplaced force. It can be misplaced in time: like the violence that is acceptable in war, is unacceptable in peace.

172

It can be misplaced in space: like a burning coal on the rug rather than the fireplace. Or it can be misplaced in proportion: like an excess of love can make us overly sentimental and possessive, or a lack of love can make us cruel and destructive. Those working in the Mystery Traditions have learned that 'good' and 'evil' in themselves do not exist and that dynamic energy is equally as important as compassion.

In the candle-light visualise the **Temple of Geburah** with its walls flickering with the reflection of an unseen fire. The floor is black marble, shot through with gold; the altar is citrine, on top of which is a sphinx with the sacred flame burning between its paws. There are four doors flanked by massive pillars of black and gold. The perfume of patchouli scents the air.

In human terms, there is a balance of opposites in Geburah (Might) and Chesed (Mercy). Geburah is the realm of Outer Emotion; impartiality created by the balance and interaction between the positive and negative sides of the Tree. This is the equilibrium that all magical practitioners should strive to achieve since this governs the Law of Equilibrium so necessary in magic. If Geburah is allowed to reign unchecked it will become aggressive, bigoted or cruel; harnessed as a creative energy it can give an impetus to our actions which carries all before it. Here we find the ability to draw on the strength of the *sephirah* when it is necessary; to cut away that which has outlived its usefulness - the conviction that allows us to be cruel in order to be kind. Fortune maintains that Geburah is the best friend we can have, if we are honest, because sincerity has no need to fear its activities

Remember that we are climbing the Tree *against* the natural flow of energy because it emanates from Kether travelling *down* to Malkuth. In Chesed we discover the point where we pass from the realm of pure spirit into the physical world of form and matter.

Chesed
is Mercy and the Fourth Path known as Cohesive or Receptive Intelligence because it contains all the holy Powers, and from it emanate all the spiritual virtues.

Planetary Attributions: Jupiter – benevolent ruler deities.

Magical Image:
A mighty crowned and enthroned king. **The Prince of Cups** (the Airy

part of Water) from the *Thoth Tarot* is a possible focus for meditation as this is a card of immense power, representing on one hand 'elasticity, volatility, hydro-static equilibrium' and on the other, 'the catalytic faculty and energy of steam'. Or the **Knight of Cups** (the Fiery part of Water) who is sensitive to external influence but not very enduring.

Spiritual Experience: Vision of Love

Summary:
Chesed is the *sephirah* of order and the level at which abstract and form begin to merge -where we pass from the realm of pure spirit into the physical world of form and matter. All the creative work of the world has its origins in Chesed, and it is to this level that the seeker must aspire. Many occultists are fooled by the Veil of Illusion which conceals this *sephirah,* and believe themselves to be climbing the Tree when, in fact, when they are still functioning at the level of Yesod or even Malkuth. To work successfully in Chesed we must be able to see beyond the Veil, or the attempts to translate the images into 'terms of the higher plane and learn what they really represent' will prove to be a futile exercise.

Here we stand on the brink of the World of Briah (Creation) where we need to contemplate the crossing of the Abyss - Daath. This is the level, according to Dion Fortune: "To which the Adept rises during meditation, because "it is here that he receives the inspirations which he works out on the planes of form."

Visualise the **Temple of Chesed** as being filled with a brilliant blue light; the floor is a deep blue, inlaid with crystal stars in the shape of the constellations. The altar is a block of pure crystal on which stands a bowl of amethyst holding the sacred flame. There are four doors set into the walls flanked by pillars of lapis lazuli and silver. The air is scented with the perfume of opium.

On a human level, Chesed represents Inner Emotion which stems from deep emotional experiences that are stimulated by such happenings as an intense love affair, or a profound religious awakening. From this *sephirah* comes the powerful creative urges – "The deep-water current that a man draws on for resource when ordinary emotions are inadequate," writes Dolores Ashcroft-Nowicki. Although Chesed has the benevolent qualities of mercy and generosity, it needs the heavy hand of Geburah to temper the balance and prevent too much license. This is why we must learn obedience and be willing to sacrifice independence and individualism for the sake of others and not be ruled by the ego. Obedience to 'the system' means the preservation of order in that we do not allow 'unrestricted self-will' to result in chaotic mis-management on a domestic or social level. It is interesting that all the negative virtues assigned to Chesed are social no-no's - i.e. bigotry, hypocrisy, gluttony and tyranny. At no other level is it quite so important to observe the seeker's credo to "Know thyself!"

Binah
is Understanding and the Third Path known as Sanctifying Intelligence and the Foundation of Primordial Wisdom. It is also called the Creator of Faith from which faith emanates.

Planetary Attributions: Saturn – represented by ancient mother goddesses and Saturian gods.

Magical Images:
A mature woman. For meditation purposes concentrate on the **Queen of Disks** (the Watery part of Earth) from the *Thoth Tarot* since she is the embodiment of the dogma that the Great Work is fertility, and represents the ambition of matter to take part in the great work of Creation.

Spiritual Experience: Vision of Sorrow

Summary:
Binah represents negativity, receptivity and passivity and is located at the top of the Feminine Pillar. Although it may seem like a contradiction, all the principal Mother Goddesses are assigned to this *sephirah*, especially those who were known in ancient time as creator/destroyer goddesses, deities. In this context the 'dead' can also be looked upon as the 'yet to be born'. This is the Circle of Life and at the end of each incarnation we return to Binah as part of the continuing process of birth/death/rebirth. This is the true explanation of the 'Vision of Sorrow' as part of the Mysteries enacted in the Isis/Osiris, Demeter/ Persephone, Ishtar/Tammuz mythologies.

Binah is the third *sephirah* in the Supernal Triangle and paired with Chokmah - the Great Father and Great Mother representing the universal ebb and flow of opposites which is the base for all magical working. It is the female potency of the Universe and some express unease that this *sephirah* is located at the top of the Pillar of *Severity*, since they feel that female attributes are more akin to mercy. As Dion Fortune points out, however, here we are dealing with *cosmic* principles, not personalities and this is where many would-be magicians go astray, in that they want to look upon the Great Mother as a flesh and blood entity - not an abstract source of power. And, as we discovered with Malkuth and Yesod, Binah,

(Understanding) cannot be understood without its relationship with Chokmah (Wisdom). It may also appear strange that it is at this level, that the *roots* of faith are located. At the mundane level, faith is often a product of conditioning, something that is learned by rote and accepted through habit, but the Faith that stems from our contacts with Binah is 'the conscious result of super-conscious experience which has not been translated into terms of brain-consciousness'.

Visualise the **Temple of Binah** as having been hewn from bare, living rock and giving the impression of Timelessness since it reaches back to when the Waters of Nun receded, exposing the Mound on which the Temple was built. The floor is hard-packed earth and the altar is a large boulder with a natural hollow at the top which holds the sacred flame. There are four doors flanked by pillars of stone and the air is perfumed with myrrh.

On a human level, Binah represents our quest for Understanding - the feminine Outer Intelligence which resolves receptive intelligence by transmuting it into understandable principles. Experience in the outer world accumulates in Binah with the energy coming from above *and* below to fuse in Understanding (Binah), out of Knowledge (Daath) and Wisdom (Chokmah). Accepting that Chokmah and Binah represent the 'essential male-and femaleness' in their creative aspects is the first step to understanding the Mysteries. We are not talking about orgiastic sex of the tabloid press but the dynamic principle which derives its energy direct from the source of all energy - and sex represents only one aspect of this factor. The seeker keeps the different energies at their correct levels/places - ensuring that one does not invade the other - and understanding the true significance of 'life-force' is a step on the right Path.

Chokmah
is Wisdom and the Second Path known as the Illuminating Intelligence and the Splendour of Unity.

Planetary Attributions: the Zodiac – represented by all Father gods, and goddesses of Wisdom.

Magical Image:
A bearded male figure. Try meditating on the **Knight of Disks** (the Fiery part of Earth) from the *Thoth Tarot*, who represents gravitation and the activity of Earth as a producer of Life. He is clothed as a warrior and his helmet is crested with a stag.

Spiritual Experience: Vision of the Source we seek

Summary:
Chokmah is at the top of the Masculine Pillar as the concept of pure spiritual force and fertility in its abstract form - this is the Great God Pan in all his glory, rather than the Earthy Pan of Malkuth. Chokmah is part of the first pair of *sephiroth* on the Tree (which must always be considered in relation to each other otherwise there can be no understanding) and part of the Supernal Triangle with Kether and Binah.

Chokmah is traditionally assigned the planetary attribution of the Zodiac represented by the zodiacal band around the sky, centred on the path of the Sun and enclosing the orbits of all the other planets - defining the twelve phases of a continuous cosmic process. Chokmah is pure energy, limitless and tireless and, as explained in *The Mystical Qabalah*, incapable of doing anything on its own except radiate off into space unless Binah draws off the impulses of energy and directs it. As in all balanced magical working, Chokmah (male) supplies the energy, and Binah (female) supplies the machine. Holding these two *sephiroth* in the balance, we must look at the human sperm as a simple unit of energy, incapable of no more than the briefest life — until it encounters the reproductive system of the womb. 'As above, so below'.

Visualise the **Temple of Chokmah** appearing like a huge stone-henge monument constructed in granite; the floor is polished granite and so is the altar, on top of which burns a simple wood fire - the first flame. There are four doors flanked by granite columns and the air is perfumed with musk.

On the human level, Chokmah represents Wisdom or the masculine Inner Intellect; the deepest part of the mind, the highest intellectual centre. This *sephirah* stimulates the most 'profound ideas and observations' seeing, as it does, with the 'inner eye of illumination, and speaks without words as Wisdom' - illustrating the Zen question: What is the sound of one hand clapping? The essence of Chokmah has an almost divine quality since it *is* the direct link with the Divine World.

The Wisdom we have gained as we slowly climb the Tree (and begin to understand the subconscious impulses that filter *down* through all the levels), should start to manifest in the physical plane. Even with this basic, elementary study we can begin to see how necessary balance and harmony is to us in our everyday life - not to mention our magical one. If we learn to harmonise these energies during our daily interaction with family, colleagues and friends, the chalice will spill over into our magical workings - and vice versa.

Kether

the Crown, is the First Path known as the Admirable or Hidden Intelligence because it is the Light, giving the power of comprehension of the First Principle, which hath no beginning.

Planetary Attributions: First Swirlings – represented by all creator/creatrix deities.

Magical Images:
An ancient bearded king, usually depicted in profile although the *sephirah* is androgynous, i.e. *both* male and female energy. Try meditating on the **Queen of Swords** (the Watery part of Air) from the *Thoth Tarot* which represents the elasticity of that element and its power of transmission in the form of a Queen seated on a throne of cloud. Or, on the **Knight of Wands** (the Fiery part of Fire) clad in black armour astride a black horse, for which Crowley could provide no description, except that it is purely the male creative force in fire or spirit.

Spiritual Experience: Reunion with the Source. The completion of the Great Work.

Summary:
Kether is the cause or source of all manifestation and before Kether there is nothing. The planetary symbolism for this *sephirah* is 'the first swirlings' and if you have difficulty grasping this concept, imagine outer space at the time of the Big Bang, before this galaxy (or any other) came into being. This is where the descent of power begins. In purely human terms, Kether is seen as the 'unknown full potential of man' following the descent of power as it zig-zags down through the *sephiroth*. This 'potential' either diminishes or develops depending on the spiritual growth of the individual.

There is no Temple image for Kether - just pure Light.

Daath

is Knowledge symbolised by an invisible sphere between the Supernal and Ethical Triangles in what is commonly referred to as The Abyss.

Planetary Attributions: Uranus – represented by all primordial or Otherworld deities.

Magical Image: A dark brooding king – often in the image of Set, or Anubis in his role as psychopomp.

Spiritual Experience: Vision of Profound Transformation.

Summary
Daath is the invisible *sephirah* on the central Pillar which 'always belongs to another plane to that on which the Tree is being considered'. It is the gateway to other dimensions and much of the occult literature concerning this *sephirah* is only accessible by those who have experienced a high level of esoteric instruction; although several books by Kenneth Grant offer a broad overview for those wishing to understand more about this 'eleventh' *sephiroth*.

Although Daath is accorded Uranus as its planetary attribution, there is something definitely 'Saturnian' about this plane. As Knowledge, Daath is the child of Chokmah (Wisdom) and Binah (Understanding) and the seat of conceptual knowledge as opposed to Absolute Knowledge. Many teachers try to dissuade their pupils from working with Daath by referring to it as part of the Dark Tree or the Tree of Evil; a large number of authors refrain from mentioning it at all - as if it doesn't exist. To quote Crowley's philosophy, however, this caution exposes the seeker to the danger of formulating an incomplete and unbalance Universe.

In *The Mystical Qabalah*, Dion Fortune describes it as being the 'secret of generation and regeneration, the key to the manifestation of all things … and conscious awareness of another dimension', which is neither dark nor evil - unless you have a problem with the mind being receptive to all things. If it is possible to relate to Daath in human terms, it can only be described as the instant when individuality vanishes and merges with the Divine - often described as the annihilation of Self, the Abyss into which the ego vanishes. The state can be achieved by meditation and last for seconds, or eternity. Daath is usually described as 'the Veil', beyond which lies Knowledge but it is only 'dark' to those who have not experienced enlightenment.

Since this is an elementary text, it would be fool-hardy for the untrained mind to use it as a guide to wander in this region before developing an understanding of what the rest of the Tree holds in store.

Hopefully, we have seen that the ten (or eleven) *sephiroth* are arranged in a system of pillars, worlds and triangles, and it is important to understand that a study of the *sephiroth* as isolated units is a futile and meaningless pursuit. Whilst it is necessary to fully understand the meaning of each sphere and its correspondences, it must also be studied in relation to everything else on the Tree.

It is just as important to realise that the Names of Power, i.e. the god/goddesses, can often be assigned to more than one *sephirah*. This is because the deities themselves often have more than one aspect. Pan, for instance, fits quite comfortably in Malkuth as an Earth god but he is equally at home in Chokmah as the Great God - his influence can also be found in Daath. This is why it is essential to have a good grounding in the classical mythology of other Traditions besides your own before beginning to identify particular deities with your own personal Tree.

And while the different attributes and correspondences permit a certain degree of flexibility, there are certain elements of the Tree that remain fixed. There are the *sephiroth* themselves, the Veils of Negative Existence, the Pillars, the Triangles, the Four Worlds and the twenty-two Paths - all linked by the coiling Descent of Power from Kether down to Malkuth

As Allan Chapman observes in *Gods in the Sky*, an understanding of ancient astronomy and cosmology reveals how ancient people believed the Universe to be constructed and arranged in physical terms. What most have in common is the belief that everything was arranged in a system of layers or spheres – a perfect example of which was incorporated in the original mystical Qabalah. And we don't need to be an astrophysicist or an Adept in the Western Mystery Tradition to understand the basic lessons of the Tree of Life. The structure of the Tree gives an overview of the Universe and its inhabitants both corporeal and otherworldly on many different levels

The Tree offers us a glimpse behind the scenes, as it were, so that we have a greater understanding of the Law of Equilibrium, or Opposites and its necessary catalyst. That for every positive there is a negative – active/passive – male/female – night/day – good/evil – love/hate – chaos/harmony. Dion Fortune frequently explains – and we repeat – that evil for example, is simply misplaced force that can be misplaced in time; like the violence that is acceptance in war is abhorrence in peace time. Or like a burning coal in the hearth brings us warmth but a burning coal on the rug becomes life threatening. An imbalance of emotion such as the lack of love that can turn a person cruel and destructive, while in excess can make an individual overly sentiment and weak.

The Tree of Life can offer a view of the multi-dimensional Universe and as Richard Cavendish wrote in *The Magical Arts*: "Modern occultists are attracted to the Qabalah because of its age and its mystery, and because they can draw from it the great magical principles that the Universe is a unity, that man is God and the Universe in miniature, and that man can develop the divine spark within him until he masters the entire Universe and himself becomes God." And in doing so we learn how to draw on those powerful energies from Deep Space ... the ultimate goal of the archaic stellar-wisdom of the ancients.

Part Four: Mistress of Melancholy

"You darkness, that I come from, I love you more than all the fires that fence in the world."
Rainer Maria Rilke

Chet Raymo points out that scholars of mystical thinking and early religion have repeatedly shown that the concept of time in traditional cultures is based upon recurring cycles rather than linear succession. The recurring cycles are closely associated with celestial phenomena – the stellar, lunar and solar cycles that impart forcefully upon every aspect of traditional human life. Traditional time is the eternal repetition of a reverberating cosmic rhythm.

The Moon, however, is the true mistress of melancholy and illusion. It is the nearest heavenly body to the Earth and often blinds us with her beauty so that we are deflected from thinking about the mysteries of Deep Space. For aeons the Moon has been a focal point of homage, with even poets and pagans of the modern era being fooled by her loveliness, and yet in reality and despite the gravitational pull, it is a desolate, sterile lump of rock that only glows with reflected light from the Sun.

The Moon is a magical analogy for all not being as it seems, and often the permanent mystical resting place for those with an inability to penetrate its veil of illusion. Nevertheless, if we meditate upon the Moon card from Crowley's *Book of Thoth*, we see the Moon from a different perspective ...

"The Moon, partaking as she does of the highest and the lowest, and filling all the space in between, is the most universal of the Planets. In her higher aspect, she occupies the place of the Link between the human and the divine ... In this Trump, her lowest avatar, she joins the

earthly spare of Netzach with Malkuth, the culmination on matter of all superior forms. This is the waning moon, the moon of witchcraft and abominable deeds. She is the poisoned darkness which is the condition of the rebirth of light ..."

This card when drawn as part of a Tarot spread represents illusion and deception; bewilderment and hysteria; while standing on the brink of important change. At the bottom of the card moves the Sacred Beetle, bearing the Sun through the darkness of the night. Above is the 'evil' landscape of the Moon. A stream or path of Serum, tinged with blood, flows between the two barren mountains. On the hills are dark sinister towers. On the threshold stands the jackal-headed god, Anubis, in double form: at his feet are the jackals waiting to devour those who have fallen by the way.

"Upon the hills are black towers of nameless mystery, or horror, and of fear. All prejudice, all superstition, dead tradition and ancestral loathing, all combine to darken her face before the eyes of men. It needs unconquerable courage to begin to tread this path ... The knight upon this quest has to rely on the three lower senses: touch, taste and smell. Such light as there may be is deadlier than darkness, and the silence is wounded by the howling of wild beasts."

This is the realm of Anubis, the Watcher in the Twilight, the god that stands on the threshold of life - and the threshold of death. Here all is doubt, all is mysterious, all is intoxicating such as we experience during the Dark Night of the Soul. But as Crowley observes: "Whatever horrors may afflict the soul, whatever abominations may excite the loathing of the heart, whatever terrors may assail the mind, the answer is the same at every stage: *"How splendid is the Adventure!"*

The Moon then either lures us into a soporific, dreamy state of being, during which we remain blind to the existence of the Veil of Light; or we walk on under the protection of the Watcher in the Twilight and brave the terrors of the darkness to pass beyond the Veil. It is only when we arrived at the sphere of the Moon (Yesod), that we can look back at Malkuth and our encounter with the Holy Guardian Angel – that inner element of the divine Self that protects us during those long dark nights of uncertainty – and begin to understand that it was merely the preparation for the next stage of our mystical journey where we experience the vision of the 'machinery of the Universe' and pass through the portal to the gateway of Initiation.

And yet the Moon is more than just a powerless lump of cosmic rock. As Dion Fortune explains, from the point of view of magic, the Moon/Yesod is the all-important *sephirah*, just as the Sun/Tiphareth is the functional sphere of mysticism. Yesod is also of importance to the seeker because it is the first sphere with which we make contact and consciously lift above Malkuth.

"Yesod is also the Sphere of the Moon; therefore to understand its significance we must know something about the way in which the Moon is regarded in occultism. It is held by initiates that the Moon separated from the Earth at a period when evolution was on the cusp between the etheric phase of its development and the phase of dense matter ... The Moon and the Earth, according to the occult theory, share one etheric double, though their two physical bodies are separate, and the Moon is the senior partner; that is to say, in etheric matters the Moon is the positive pole of the battery, and the Earth is the negative one ... It is the light of the Moon which is the stimulative factor in these etheric activities, and as Earth and Moon share one etheric double, all etheric activities are at their most active when the Moon is at its full. Likewise, during the dark of the Moon, etheric energies at its lowest, and unorganised forces have a tendency to rise up and give trouble ... The Dragon of the Qlipoth raises his multiple heads ... In consequence, practical occult work is best let alone during the dark by all but experienced workers ..."

As with all journeys into Deep Space, the Moon is the launch pad for our mystic wanderings. Unless we make all the right magical preparations at the beginning stages of our voyage, we will have insufficient power to maintain us during the mystical hardships that lie ahead. If we do not have total belief in ourselves, then the 'heat-shield' of our magical preparations cannot be deployed and our efforts – like those of Icarus – will see us plunge back to the earthly sphere of Malkuth.

The Veils of Negative Existence

In Qabalistic terms there is both an Absolute and a Relative Universe – and in between them lie the Veils of Negative Existence. These are the *Ain* (Void – the Absolute); the *Ain Soph* (Infinity or Endlessness - Set) and *Ain Soph Aur* (Infinite or Limitless Light - Nut) through which energy filters down into Kether from the Absolute. This Absolute is timeless and without form or substance and is even beyond Eternity – the

Bornless One of the Egyptian Mystery Tradition. It is nothing and everything.

In his book on the Tree of Life, Hebrew scholar Z'ev ben Shimon Halavi describes this in the following terms: "The Absolute has no direct contact with Creation yet Being permeates through the matrix of the Universe, supporting it like the silence behind every sound. Without this negative reality nothing could come into existence; as shadow cannot manifest without light." Something of the nature of negative reality can be discovered in the words of an old Zen poem:

"When one looks at it, one cannot see it;
When one listens for it, one cannot hear it;
However, when one uses it, it is inexhaustible."

The Relative Universe is defined within the Tree of Life at all levels with Negative Existence acting as a cosmic bridge between the Creator and his Creation. The spheres of Negative Existence lie behind time and space - without it there could be no galaxies and no humans. The first or that nearest to the Relative Universe is *Ain Soph Aur*, the Limitless Light which penetrates even the densest matter, represented by the goddess Nut. The second is *Ain Soph,* which is the first step towards manifestation of the Creator, represented by the most primordial of gods, Set. Beyond that there is Nothing - and beyond that the Absolute.

In Aleister Crowley's mystical prose-poem *The Book of the Law*, he guides us towards the Veil of Light with his evocative imagery of the 'unveiling of the company of heaven'. The company of heaven is mankind, and its 'unveiling' is the assertion of the independent godhead of every man and woman: *Every man and every woman is a star*. That each of us is not only part of God (the Absolute), but *the* Ultimate God - a concept that can only be understood by the Initiate, since it is necessary to acquire certain higher levels of consciousness to appreciate it.

In *The Law is for All*, Louis Wilkinson breaks down Crowley's *Liber AL vel Legis sub figura CCXX* line by line so that we can get to grips with this enigmatic piece of writing. Each line is a magical revelation that only becomes apparent at each stage of our magical journey to the stars but reminds us that our minds and bodies are veils of light in themselves, and that the nature of this magical power is quite incomprehensible to those standing on the outside of its gleam.

"Now, therefore, I am known to ye by my name Nuit, and to him by a secret name which I will give him when at last he knoweth me. Since I am Infinite Space, and the Infinite Stars thereof, do ye also this ..."

And in the second chapter:

"I am the flame that burns in every heart of man, and in the core of every star. I am Life, and the giver of Life, yet therefore is the knowledge of me the knowledge of death ..."

The Book of the Law gives us a liturgy for stellar worship that cannot be found elsewhere in esoteric literature, and gives us an opportunity to see beyond the Veils of Negative Existence to glimpse the *Ain Soph Aur* (Infinite or Limitless Light - Nut) and *Ain Soph* (Infinity or Endlessness - Set) ... and to stand where energy and light filters down from the Absolute.

The Three Triangles & the Four Worlds

Just as there are four elements in the physical world - earth, air, fire and water - so there are four corresponding levels within the Relative Universe, with each level being a fainter mirror image of the one below:

Atziluth - the World of Emanations - Kether, Chokmah and Binah. Situated close to the Endless Light, this is the level at which the Tree is found in its purest state.

Briah - the World of Creations - Chokmah, Binah, Geburah and Chesed. This is the level of creation or 'intelligences' that are concerned with implementing the Divine instruction and often referred to as 'archangels' by Qabalists.

Yetzirah - the World of Formations - Chesed, Geburah, Netzach and Hod. This is the level of form where the creative process is manifested albeit with endless variations and permutations.

Assiah - the World of Substance and Action - Netzach, Hod, Yesod and Malkuth. This is the level of the elements and the world in which we live, on both the physical and metaphysical levels. Here the elements evolve through an ever-changing cycle which manifests as flora or fauna - and even the smallest atom belongs to the world of Assiah.

Man, in his physical body, is confined to the Assiatic World but, by a series of spiritual evolutions, he can ascend to the upper Universe. This can be achieved by harnessing the energy generated by a rare single-mindedness in the serious seeker and effectively by-pass the arduous zig-zag path and climb straight up the centre column of Mildness. In doing so, however, we will miss the challenge of travelling the more arduous Path and not experiencing the trials and tribulations of some of the more spiritually interesting *sephirah* on the Pillars of Severity and Mercy.

As well as spheres and columns, the Tree is also divided into three separate Triangles: **The Supernal Triangle**, incorporating Kether, Chokmah and Binah, that sets Creation in motion by energy entering the equation where it becomes a rarefied 'form'. After this first creation there is a momentary pause as the newly formed energy slows down to cross the Abyss (Daath). If this void is not crossed, the creation process stops there and is re-absorbed into itself.

Once the Abyss has been crossed, we come to **The Ethical Triangle** of Geburah, Chesed and Tiphareth, representing the stage at which nothing can be changed in the creative process. Only by destroying the creation and starting again from scratch can the alterations or change be implemented.

The Astral Triangle of Netzach, Hod and Yesod is the level at which consciousness enters the equation and presents a clear image of past, present and future concepts because the course is already set and the results fixed.

As we can see, there are various groupings of the *sephiroth* upon the framework of the Tree, each serving a different purpose in revealing the meaning of the associations and equilibrium of the individual *sephirah*. We must also be clear about the significance of the left and right sides of the Tree: the Pillar of Severity (left) is considered to be negative, or feminine; and the Pillar if Mercy (right) to be positive and masculine. On a superficial level these attributes might be thought of as 'incompatible symbolism' but a combined study of the Pillars, Triangles and Four Worlds reveals that the incompatibility is purely cosmetic.

Qliphoth

When working with the positive aspect of a *sephirah*, we must also remember that it also has a negative aspect. As Dion Fortune points out, if we cannot maintain the necessary equilibrium of natural energies during a magical application, then the negative aspect is liable to come uppermost and swamp the operation. "There is a point in every magical operation when the negative aspect of the force comes up to be dealt with, and unless dealt with will lure the experimenter into the pit which he had digged [*sic*]. It is a sound magical maxim not to invoke any force unless you are equipped to deal with its averse aspect."

The identity of these negative aspects is the 'Qliphoth' - the name given to a twilight world of soul-less entities which are not truly living, but animated astral shells prolonging their existence by absorbing the vitality of the living in the true vampiric sense. This is the realm of distortion, imbalance and atrophy in corresponding forces **at every level of the Universe** which are out of line with general evolution. Often described as the flotsam and jetsam of the astral world, Qliphotic phenomena usually manifest when there has been some sort of disturbance within the natural inter-play of magical-astral working.

Fortune maintains they *are* evil because they are not independent principles in the cosmic scheme but the unbalanced and destructive aspect of the *sephiroth* themselves; the Qliphah merely being the reverse of a coin of which the obverse is a *sephirah*. Other sources infer that Qliphoth are demons but, in reality, these entities are neither good nor evil. The origin of the word '*qliphah*' means 'husk' and is the representation of evil or impure spiritual forces in Jewish mysticism; in the Western system it refers to an emanation of imbalanced force from its corresponding *sephirah* on the Tree. Other sources consider the Qliphoth to be, quite simply, the spirits of the dead, but this is not the case. They may consist of the spiritual energy *obtained* from either the living, or the dead, and encase themselves in the lighter, etheric shell-bodies of the dead, but they are not actual souls of the dead. They are synonymous with idolatry, the root of impurity through ascribing false dualism in the Divine, the perceived realm opposite to holiness.

"The unbalanced force of each sephirah then, which arose unchecked during the temporary phases of disequilibrium that occur periodically in the course of evolution, forms the nucleus around which were organised all the thought-forms of evil arising in the consciousness of sentient beings or through the operation of blind forces that happen to be out of equilibrium, each kind of harmony seeking its own place. It will follow, then, that what was at first a mere overplus of a force, both pure and good in its intrinsic nature, nay, if not compensated, become in the course of ages a highly organised and developed centre of positive and dynamic evil."

[*The Mystical Qabalah*, Dion Fortune]

In more modern parlance, Qliphoth can be viewed as a kind of astral parasite that latches on to any astral voyager just as easily as a tick or flea can latch onto a dog out on a country walk. Bob Clay-Egerton likened them to 'extra-terrestrial intelligences – neither good nor evil – but influenced by the energy they encounter once brought through to the earthly realm where they can grow and develop into a more tangible form. Looking at a worse-case scenario: how many cases of a sudden homicidal outcome may have actually been the result of possession by an entity of low grade and/or malignant ability or intelligence? For example: If we invoke the fiery energy of Mars (Geburah) into a magical working, we must be sure that we can prevent the negative Martian force of cruelty and destructiveness from manifesting.

> *"By opening a psychic doorway through which these extra-terrestrial intelligences may enter, a seeker may have no control over what level of astral entity takes the advantage. Such entities will also induce illogical annoyance against anything which threatens to interfere with the continuance or increase of opportunities for such stimulus; and will induce illogical and emotional reactions against anything and/or anyone who criticises the need for such stimulants. In more simplistic terms, these can be identified as the Negative Virtues, or vices, since when attempting to work with the positive aspects of a sephirah, it is equally as important to consider the negative aspects in order to maintain the necessary equilibrium."*
>
> [*The Collected Writings of A R Clay-Egerton*]

These astral entities are, of course, the entropic (or lost energy), unnatural force in the Universe which drives people towards death, self-destruction, and suffering, because this level of control is what the Qliphoth craves as food. This 'lost energy' is the residue of existing power left over from a now extinct source that adheres to another surviving energy generating source, i.e. a human. Like the 'lost light' in the underground tunnels in Vietnam, reported by US military veterans, it is a pocket of existing weak energy trying to get back to the light side of the Tree of Life. Because of the adhesive nature of these pockets of discarnate energy, only a magician of Adept level should attempt to investigate their identities. Kenneth Grant contends that "we are only now beginning to understand that these [names] contain formulae of immense magical and scientific potency." He points out that this is also the 'habitation of the phantom forms generated by sexual desires and morbid cravings constantly produced by dwellers on earth'.

Nevertheless, we may now have a greater understanding of the astronomical origins of how the various different deities were assigned to the *sephirah*; how gods, goddesses, and demons were often

190

personifications of astronomical phenomena such as lunar eclipses, planetary alignments, and apparent interactions of planetary bodies with stars. And how early astro-theologians thought that the stars were openings in the firmament through which they thought they saw the Empyrean Heaven – the place in the highest heaven, which in ancient cosmologies was believed to be occupied by the Element of Fire, or the realm of Pure Light – i.e. **Kether**.

Part Five: Viral Mythology

According to Maspero, Set formed one of the divine dynasties at Annu, and the northern stars seem to have been worshipped there ... In short, in Lower Egypt the temples are pointed to rising stars near the north point of the horizon or setting north of west. In Upper Egypt, we deal chiefly with temples directed to stars rising in the south-east or setting low in the south-west ... Now with regard to the northern stars observed rising in high amplitudes, we found traces of their worship in times so remote that in all probability at Annu and Denderah Ursae Majoris *was used before it became circumpolar.*

We've come a long way since Adam's Calendar was constructed on those vast African Plains. And previous generations of spiritual seekers would have committed murder for the depth of knowledge we now possess about the Universe. As cosmology consultant Marcus Chown points out, once upon a time we thought the world rested on the back of a turtle and the Sun was a ball of molten iron not much bigger than Greece. "For the first time in history, we have a good idea of the extent of the Universe – we can see all the way to the 'light horizon' that forms the boundary of observable space, where we find super-bright quasars, whose light has taken so long to travel across space that we see them as they were when the Universe was in its youth, many millions of years ago."

And yet for all our Deep Space probing, our inner spirituality and mystical leanings are governed by primitive archetypes that are rooted in the images of the past and concealed by the veil of our own collective unconscious. These pictures and images still have the power to create all manner of responses in human beings. We are stirred by them, soothed by them, we pay homage to them and expect to be uplifted by them; and are moved to the highest levels of empathy and fear. Humans have always responded in this way and we still do. These responses are evident in societies we would possibly consider superstitious - and in modern hi-tech societies, too. They make us aware of our kinship with the instinctive, the primitive, the coarse, the esoteric, the erotic – and have psychological roots that we often prefer not to acknowledge.

All these ancient images are rooted deep within the mind-set of national cultures and folklore, and from a magical perspective there is a valid reason why we continue to use what might be viewed as the out-dated symbols of sorcery and superstition. As Kenneth Grant explained in *Hecate's Fountain*: "The answer is that the occultist understands that contacts with these energies may be established more completely through symbols so ancient that they have had time to bury themselves in the vast storehouse of racial subconsciousness. To such symbols the Forces respond swiftly and with incalculable fullness, whereas the pseudo-symbols manufactured in the laboratory ... the intellectual formulae and symbols of mathematics have been evolved too recently to serve as direct conduits. For the Old Ones, such lines of communication are dead. The magician, therefore, uses the more direct paths which long ages have mapped out in the shadowlands of the subconsciousness."

Archetypal imagery

These ancient archetypal images remain relatively constant in the twenty-two Tarot cards of the Major Arcana, although the choice of Tarot deck is a very personal one and must be acquired by intuition rather than recommendation. This is because the designs vary widely from the old Marseilles (French), Thoth Tarot or Rider Waite decks, to a whole range of more contemporary pictorial offerings – the latter not always reflecting the deeper esoteric meanings of the more traditional cards. The seeker should choose the version that 'speaks' to them personally since there are no standard pictures or presentation, and even the attributes, may vary from deck to deck.

A full Tarot pack consists of fifty-six cards of the Minor Arcana divided into four suits of wands, clubs, pentacles and cups and twenty-two trumps of the Major Arcana. The Major Arcana consists of universal archetypal symbols, and each card equates with a particular 'path' on the Qabalistic Tree of Life ... which can be used as meditational doorways to specific areas of the Tree at a later stage. By familiarising ourselves with these archetypes and their place in the heavens, we won't go far wrong in beginning to learn the esoteric meaning of the cards together with their celestial correspondences, For example:

194

0 - The Fool: The universal concept of the Trickster, who is a subtle blend of innocence and cunning, like the eternal child. [Constellation: Aquila]

I - The Magus or the Magician of myth and legend, who is also our mentor and guide. [Constellation: Draco]

II - The Priestess or the Wise Woman and the female counterpart of the Hierophant, who instructs in the art of occult knowledge. [Constellation: Ursa Major]

III - The Empress or the beneficent Queen and the epitome of charity and kindness. [Constellation: Cassiopeia]

IV - The Emperor or a great King, a wise and powerful ruler: all that is positive in the masculine persona. [Constellation: Aries]

V - The Hierophant or the Teacher who imparts esoteric knowledge to the people, in a practical and oral way they can understand. [Constellation: Taurus]

VI - The Lovers who represent the alchemical Union of man and woman on all levels. Yin and Yang and the Law of Opposites. [Constellation: Gemini]

VII - The Chariot - a martial symbol of Victory in the face of overwhelming odds. [Constellation: Cancer]

VIII - Strength - the inner Strength that can unexpectedly come to the surface in the most unlikely of persons or situations. [Constellation: Leo]

IX - The Hermit who signifies the silence surrounding Inner Knowledge and that which must be sought after. [Constellation: Virgo]

X - The Wheel of Fortune that represents a change of Fortune or circumstances - and usually for the better. [Constellation: Ursa Minor]

XI - Justice or Equilibrium. The concept of Justice being tempered with Mercy; and Mercy tempered with Justice. [Constellation: Libra]

XII - The Hanged Man who represents Redemption through sacrifice and submission to the Divine Will; as in the universal myth of the sacrificial god. [Constellation: Hydra]

XIII - Death - in esoteric terms, the Passing from one stage to another; the universal link between material and spiritual. [Constellation: Scorpio]

XIV - Temperance or Personal Control over an indulgence of the natural appetites and passions. [Constellation: Sagittarius]

XV – The Devil - the card often referred to as Pan, and the force of unbridled Nature. [Constellation: Capricornus]

XVI – The Tower - the symbolic Destruction of all that is important/prominent … but not always in a negative form. [Constellation: Lupus]

XVII – The Star - the symbol of timeless Mystery and the ever-turning cosmos. [Constellation: Aquarius]

XVIII - The Moon - the archetypal suggestion of Illusion, often representing the standing on the brink of important change.

XIX - The Sun - the ultimate symbol of Light, warmth and strength.

XX - Judgement or Final Decision concerning the past and a new current for the future. Life progressing a little further along the Path. [Constellation: Pisces]

XXI – The Universe - representing the macrocosm and the microcosm – All.

Tarot decks usually come with their own booklet giving details of suggested layouts (or spreads) for reading, and the traditional interpretation of the cards, both in the upright and reversed positions. Ultimately the cards *will* speak to you – but the messages may not be those given in the popular books. The more familiar you become with the Tarot, the easier it will for you to interpret the signs and become a competent reader – if only for yourself.

The basic archetypal associations given above are but one of the many meanings behind each design, and we have to learn how to read that intricate multi-layering. Not to mention the various correspondences governing that card as it directs you along the Path. Begin by working solely with the Major Arcana and become completely familiar with the design of each of the twenty-two cards. Eventually one or two will have a stronger 'voice' than the others and this/these will become *your* card(s), regardless of the representation or traditional interpretation. Drawing this card will always have a special significance for you alone, and can be used as a personal gateway for visualisation and meditation – or act as a warning.

Each of those cards of the Major Arcana/Paths are aligned with the elements, planets, stars, constellations and signs of the Zodiac; and another of the most novel means of finding our way around the heavens is the ingenious use of Urania's Mirror. *Urania's Mirror*; or, *a view of the Heavens,* is a set of thirty-two astronomical star-chart cards, first published in November 1824 and packaged in a box depicting Urania, the Muse of astronomy together with a book entitled *A Familiar Treatise on Astronomy* ... written to accompany the set. The illustrations were re-drawn from Alexander Jamieson's *A Celestial Atlas* but with the addition of holes punched in them to allow each card to be held up to a light to see a depiction of the constellation.

Although Jungian psychology is currently unfashionable, nevertheless, it is Carl Jung's identification of archetypes and the highly developed elements of the collective unconscious that resonates long and loud to the seeker of arcane stellar-wisdom. By examining behaviour, images, art, myths, religions, and dreams, Jung saw these archetypes as universal, archaic patterns and images that derive from the unconscious mind, which he described as the psychic counterpart of instinct. These images have entered the subconscious as autonomous and hidden forms that are transformed to produce specific expressions in individuals and their cultures.

In psycho-babble, Jungian archetypes refer to those 'indefinable, underlying forms from which emerge the classic images or motifs' such as the mother, the child, the trickster, the wise/holy man and the flood. Nevertheless, it the *ancient* historical and cultural context that gives these images their universal meaning when viewed as mystical representations. Unfortunately popular and new-age appropriations have condensed these distinctive cultural images into stereotypical *modern* pagan imagery instead of retaining the deeper, instinctual sources – 'the 'archaic remnants' of these primordial images. Mistakenly, local myths are seen as being universal and separated from the history of their actual creation and cultural context by turning a complex reality into something simple and easy to grasp.

197

An exploration of the celestial Paths of the Tarot requires that these archetypal images be restored to their original indefinable, underlying forms before we can begin to understand what the images mean when they appear before us in moments of highly charged mystical or magical manifestation.

The Paths of the Tarot

The original allocation of the individual Paths of the Tarot has been subjected to a great deal of fabrication and fairy tale but from the star-seeker's point of view, the attribution of the twenty-two cards of the Major Arcana was perfected (but not invented) by Eliphas Levi. All concepts and explanations must be taken into account, however, and it does explain why there are so many different schools of thought in attributing different interpretations to these twenty-two Paths. Using the Tarot does give us an added advantage of being able to use pictures to symbolise each Path in an already complicated over-view of the Qabalah.

The Crowley Tarot, *The Book of Thoth* and *Liber 777* are used here because of the author's particular preference for this system, but using a different deck should not present too much of a problem since the designs of each Tarot are created for the individual seeker to interpret for him/herself. This empathy should be guided by the student's own particular Path and the writings of *bona fide* magical writers but, like all magical learning, the directions are not carved in stone and it is up to each seeker to identify with particular layouts of the cards and their place on the Tree.

Esoteric author, Alan Richardson describes the Tarot as being similar to trying to read a road map in thick fog and which will only become clear when it is aligned with some recognisable landmarks — i.e. the *sephiroth* in the Tree of Life. [*Magical Gateways*]

> *"No two students agree as to which of the major cards ought to fit on which path, or if they do agree on this then they disagree on the interpretation. Which is as it should be. It reminds us that there is no dogma within the magical tradition."*

Continuing to use the analogy of travel, we can now begin to see that, instead of being a confusing jumble of round-abouts, over and under-passes, there are clearly defined signposts to guide us along the Paths. Each Path, corresponding to one of the cards from the Major Arcana, is a straight carriage-way from one *sephiroth* to another. The Paths are the A-roads connecting the *sephiroth* (the cities); the three pillars are the motorways, while the four worlds are different counties. Like all journeys there is a beginning, middle and an end - and here we are merely mapping out the preparation for the journey. Just as you wouldn't set out on your travels without first checking that all the equipment and supplies were in order, so it would be inadvisable to set out on the exploration of the Tree of Life without making sure that you are not going to stall on the way and have no rescue service on call in the event of a breakdown.

Having spent some time studying the various correspondences and taking your own magical Tradition into account, the celestial/planetary god-forms, synonymous with each of the *sephiroth,* should now be firmly in place. These are your guardians and on arriving at each *sephirah,* you must be prepared to meet them face to face, according to the beliefs of your own people or Tradition. We have used the analogy of a road map but in reality your journeying will be taking you out onto the astral to navigate all manner of cosmic high-roads and by-roads.

NB: Remember *not* to pick up any parasitic astral travellers along the way!

You should already be familiar with the **Temple of Malkuth [Earth]** to which you now add an image of your own traditional deity whom you will invoke for protection. It cannot be stressed too strongly just how important it is for you to carry the mental picture of the Temple at all times. As we've said before, all workings begin with Malkuth and return to it when the journey is over; should you be interrupted or interfered with, instantly recall the Temple image of the blue light and you will automatically return to a level of safety.

In the *Atus of Tahuti,* the three paths leading from Malkuth are the **Aeon**, the **Universe** and the **Moon** - the latter giving the visual interpretation of the Gate and the World of Illusion and descent into Otherworld. Both the Universe and the Aeon represent the end and the beginning, as in a new era, but not *necessarily* in an up-beat form. These are the three doors in the eastern wall in the Temple, situated between the black and silver pillars.

The first door opens onto the **32nd Path - the Universe (Saturn/Earth)** - which joins Malkuth to Yesod. This card is symbolised by a naked woman floating in space; in her hands she manipulates a radiant spiral force in the form of the Serpent. The last card in the Major Arcana, the Universe brings everything to Nothing, thereby complementing the Fool at the top of the Tree and signifying the

199

completion of the Great Work. Here a wheel of Light reflecting the form of the Tree, showing the ten *sephiroth*, i.e. the ten principle bodies of the solar system. This is the Path of self-discovery. At physical death the spirit travels up this Path to Yesod; at birth the new soul travels down from Yesod to Malkuth. Seekers travel this path on many occasions and under many different circumstances since Malkuth is the Gate of Life and Death on both the Inner and Outer planes - so be prepared for both Light and Darkness … and Shadow.

The door to the left is the **31st Path - the Aeon (Fire/Spirit).** This link between Malkuth and Hod is pure Crowley symbolism and an adaptation of the Stélé of Revealing; it is the cornerstone of Thelemic practice, revealing the dawning of the New Aeon. The body of the sky-goddess Nuit, with her consort Hadit (as a winged globe of fire), flank the dual figure of Horus – it is often shown as the Angel or Messenger (or Judgement) in other Tarot systems. This is the Path of psychic evolution - subconscious 'past' memories, and although not necessarily remembered, influence our present actions; this Path represents the inflexible control our past has over our present and future. The way we choose to deal with others and our means of communication emanate from this Path, and because it is concerned with fire, we must beware of the manner in which we use the energies for our own sake and for others.

The door to the right is the **29th Path — the Moon (Pisces)** - and the pathway from Malkuth to Netzach and one of the most fascinating in the whole Major Arcana. This represents the Old Aeon, the resurrection of the Sun - not only from winter but from night as this card symbolises midnight. There is a brooding between-the-worlds landscape of barren hills and dark towers. "All prejudice, all superstition, dead tradition and ancestral loathing, all combine to darken her face before the eyes of men. It needs unconquerable courage to begin to tread this path," writes Crowley in *The Book of Thoth*. A guardian is there, however, in the double-form of Anubis and it is he who accompanies us on this journey of uncertainty. Crowley's viewpoint was endorsed by Dolores Ashcroft-Nowicki, who said: "Not that it is dangerous in the accepted sense, it is just that it is inclined to stir up things that most of us would rather leave undisturbed … In a nutshell, it is the path of sex." This is the Path of the 'Body' - not just the sex urge in its accepted sense but the whole primordial emergence from the slime to metamorphose into the ancient fertility cultos that underwrites all Mystery Traditions. The Moon, of course, has a tremendous influence on the physical plane in the eternal ebb and flow of tides in both natural and human terms. This is the domain of the moon-goddess and of Pan, in his ithyphallic guise; the world of Light and Darkness.

The Temple of Yesod [Moon] is reached by travelling from Malkuth via the 32nd Path; the walls shimmer with quartz, reflecting the misty violet colours of the veils. In this Temple there are four doors, including the 32nd Path which we have already travelled to reach Yesod. The door to the left is the **30th Path - the Sun (Sol)** the Lord of Light, Life, Liberty and Love. The twin children symbolise the male and female principles, eternally young, shameless and innocent, who are dancing in the light, but representing the next stage of mankind's development. This is the path of scientific discovery but also intuitive advancement; it represents enlightenment but of a more scientific nature than spiritual. Here we are travelling from the lunar influence into the 'disciplined sphere of the mind' which provides us with an excellent combination of 'scientific fact and inspire guesswork' = the sunlight of knowledge and the moonlight of intuition, according to Dolores Ashcroft-Nowicki.

To the left is the **28th Path - the Emperor (Aries)** - leading to Netzach and represented by a crowned male figure with imperial vestments and regalia. The Emperor is the alchemical symbol of Sulphur - the male fiery energy of the Universe, the swift creative energy that produces successful issue. If it is allowed to manifest for too long, however, it burns and destroys. The Emperor represents inspiration and aspiration and it also joins the symbol of a powerful man with the epitome of womanhood in Netzach. Nevertheless this is a path of tremendous creative power activated with the life-force emanating from Netzach but it is necessary to always maintain a sense of balance and proportion since we are still under the influence of Yesod, the *sephirah* of illusion.

The central door takes us out of the world of elements and action and into the world of Formation by way of the **25th Path - Art (Sagittarius)** - another of Crowley's strange but appropriate images. This is the path linking Yesod to Tiphareth and the 'county' border between Assiah and Yetzirah. This card represents the alchemical marriage with the black and white personages now united in the single figure of the androgyn. Here we also see fire and water harmoniously mingled in a crude symbol of the spiritual idea. "This state of the Great Work therefore consisted in the mingling of the contradictory elements in a cauldron," wrote Crowley. The 25th Path was described by Dolores Ashcroft-Nowicki as the second of the 'dark nights' in that this is the pathway of temptation – often depicted as the Star or Temperance. This temptation and subsequent passing through the mirror of illusion towards a new understanding is the test set out for us as the *sephirah* of Tiphareth is the realm of the sacrificial god.

The Temple of Hod [Mercury] is a world of brightness and learning with its book-lined walls broken by five doors, two of which are the 30th and 31st Paths already examined. The **27th Path - the Tower (Mars) -** is the first path that crosses the width of the Tree and refers to the manifestation of cosmic energy in its grossest form, and that in order to obtain perfection, all existing things must be annihilated. This is the overthrow of the confining Old Order and the establishment of the emancipated New Order. Described in *Liber 777* as 'the House of God'. Travelling along this pathway will shake your faith, courage and convictions in your ability to traverse the Tree and discover its Mystery. Many experienced practitioners reach a stage where they undergo a 'crisis of faith' in themselves and what they are doing
magically. The Tower is the destruction of confinement and the insurrection of liberating forces on a magical level which reinforce the faith in one's self if the journey is completed.

The first door to the left is the **26th Path - the Devil (Capricornus) -** associated with Pan and representing creative energy in its most material form - *Pan Pangenetir*, the All-Begetter. His creative energy is veiled in the symbol of the Wand of the Chief Adept, crowned with a winged globe and the twin serpents of Horus and Osiris. "In every symbol of this card there is the allusion to the highest things and the most remote," wrote Crowley. This path will prove to be a difficult one for those who cannot accept that which cannot be proven - here we must leave behind intellectual analysis and be prepared to 'go with the flow'. This is not the pathway of reason, because many of our most cherished beliefs will cast a distorted reflection, such as we would find in a Hall of Mirrors - and some of these images may not be pleasant.

The door to the far left is the **23rd Path - the Hanged Man (Water)** – and fraught with symbolism but despite its sacrificial theme the whole idea of sacrifice is a misconception of nature; it is the hope that lies in love and the lessons learned from the past. This is the pathway of clear reason; the ability to see things from every different angle. Here we also need to reflect upon the price that is always extracted for esoteric knowledge - and we never know in what coin that price will be paid for there is no room for negotiation.

The Temple of Netzach [Venus] is gleaming in green and copper and in the walls there are five doors. We have already travelled the paths to the left - the 29th, the 28th and the centre, the 27th Path, to arrive at this Temple. The first door to the right is the **24th Path - Death (Scorpio) -**

and another of the most fascinating in the Thoth Tarot. In alchemical terms, this card represents the concept of putrefaction - the technical term for a series of chemical changes which develops the final form of life from the original seed. The card represents the dance of death - the skeleton with the scythe wears the crown of Osiris and with a sweep of his scythe he creates bubbles in which are beginnings of new shapes taking form. This pathway represents letting go of something that is 'dead' - a reconciling of things past and how they will reappear in the future. A cycle of birth-death-rebirth at every level. Nearly all the esoteric Mysteries incorporate this formula within their initiation rites and so we need to reflect on the image from a more flexible viewpoint.

The door to the far right is the **21st Path - the Wheel of Fortune (Jupiter)** - which represents the Universe in its aspect of continual change and movement. At the top of the card is the firmament of stars. These appear in a variety of shapes and degrees of brightness and from them, the lightning churns the firmament into a swirling pattern of ten blue and purple plumes. Suspended in the centre is a wheel of ten spokes, according to the number of the *sephiroth*. Because of the powerful momentum of this path, it means that the traveller can be in for quite a few surprises, although it is also the path of choices. *"The Wheel of Fortune, round she goes; Where she stops, nobody knows"* is an old fairground call extorting us to try our luck. For the seeker it is often an opportunity to change tack when certain signs and correspondences present the chance to do so; here is the lesson about recognising the signs and knowing how to interpret them. This is also the Path of Destiny and we are given the chance to seize the moment - if we decide not to take it at that precise point in time, we cannot blame the gods for the direction our life takes afterwards.

The Temple of Tiphareth [Sun] is alive with intense, reflected brilliance. Three of the Paths (the 25th, 26th and 24th) are already familiar to us, which leaves a further five pathways to explore from this temple. Tiphareth is the main junction on the Tree and from here the going gets tougher as we reach out across another 'county' border and pass from Yetzirah, the World of Formation, into Briah, the World of Creation. The **22nd Path - Adjustment (Libra)** - reaches from Tiphareth to Geburah and is often referred to as Justice in other packs. The figure is a masked woman balancing upon tiptoe and crowned with the ostrich plumes of Ma'at, the Egyptian Goddess of Truth, Order and Justice. She holds the Sword of Magic in her two hands and balances the Universe with its spheres of light and darkness. Being the Path of Justice and karmic reckoning there is much to be apprehensive about and, according to Dolores Ashcroft-Nowicki, for the initiate it is the nearest thing to spiritual agony. For someone coming to the Path for the first time, it may present itself as a crossroads. The higher we progress, the more exacting the responsibilities placed upon us by the Old Ones. This may be the place to reflect on the Eastern adage: "If you want to know of your past life, consider your present circumstances; if you wish to know of your future life, consider your present actions."

The **17th Path - the Lovers (Gemini)** - is the long Path from Tiphareth to Binah and, according to Crowley, the most obscure and difficult of the cards in the Major Arcana. "Each of these symbols is in itself double, so the meanings form a divergent series, and the integration of the Card can only be regained by repeated marriages, identifications, and some form of Hermaphrodism ... The key is that the Card represents the Creation of the World." Avoid the misconception that this Path refers only to romantic involvement; the essences of the Lovers is Love in all its many splendid guises from the concrete to the abstract. The double meanings reflect that there are two sides to every experience - the gaining of knowledge can mean the loss of innocence. There is a duality in all of us and this is magnified in the fact that this Path links the Son (Tiphareth) with the Great Mother (Binah); and the underlying sexuality of this Path should not be overlooked.

The central door is the **13th Path - the High Priestess (Luna)** - which links Tiphareth with Kether. Clad in a luminous Veil of Light, the Path represents the universal symbol of the Moon which goes from the highest to the lowest, making a 'direct connection between the Father in his highest aspect, and the Son in his most perfect manifestation ... the purest and most exalted conception of the Moon'. On this Path we cross the Abyss and the mysterious *sephirah* of Daath - a continuance of the Path linking Malkuth with Kether and corresponding to all the chakras of the middle pillar. This is the channel through which the power descends down through Tiphareth, Yesod, and Malkuth and a seeker must be well-versed in Qabalistic learning if s/he is not to be seared by the current. Dolores Ashcroft-Nowicki warns that no one can take this Path and remain untouched by it and that a thorough contemplation should be undertaken before embarking on the journey. "It might happen that very little is felt for months, it may take that amount of time for it to rise from the depths of the mind."

The Path linking Tiphareth with Chokmah is the **15th Path – the Star (Aquarius)**, although this is more likely to be the Emperor in other packs. The Star in Crowley's system represents Nuit, our Lady of the Starry Heavens and for the full meaning behind the significance of the card, it is necessary to understand the first part of *The Book of the Law* on which Thelemic philosophy is based. Although most other systems do not place the Star on the 15th Path, it is interesting to note that the classic Hebrew symbol for the pathway means 'incoming light' or 'illumination' and contains the secret name of God. The Star is Sirius which plays an important role in nearly all mythologies and esoteric learning for both the masculine and feminine elements of Godhead.

The **20th Path - the Hermit (Virgo)** - is the Path which connects Tiphareth and Chesed. This card symbolises the Father who is Wisdom, the highest form of Mercury and the Logos, the Creator of all worlds. "Accordingly, his representative in physical life is the spermatozoan; this is why the card is called the Hermit ... the highest symbolism of this card, therefore, is Fertility in its most exalted sense." The Path represents the Wisdom of the Old Ones and is one of the pathways we travel when seeking their guidance through meditation. It is the responses we draw from them that are channelled along this path; and without meditation we cannot seek the Mysteries for they are not found in book learning. The Hermit lights our way.

The **Temple of Geburah [Mars]** is a place of fire and passion. We have already travelled the 23rd and 22nd Path. The **19th Path - Lust (Leo)** - is called Strength in many of the other packs but again this card has a particular significance for those on the Thelemic Path. Crowley changed the card because Lust implies not only strength but the joy of exercised strength, although not in a destructive way; it is vigour and the rapture of vigour. The card depicts a woman and a lion-serpent which was regarded with intense horror and fear when the design first appeared because the reference to *The Book of the Law* was not understood. This Path is dominated by the serpent of knowledge and here we face the complete truth about ourselves with no holds barred. "It is," Dolores Ashcroft-Nowicki writes in *The Shining Paths*, "a chance to face and conquer the dark twin that we carry within." This is controlled force, which, if unleashed, could become uncontrolled force and therefore utterly destructive. Our Lust, Passion and Strength must be rendered manageable if we are to safely navigate the Path and transmute it into creative force.

The **18th Path - the Chariot (Cancer)** - the design influenced by Eliphas Levi with the central and most important feature of the card being its focus - the Holy Grail of pure amethyst. This Path can be viewed as that leading from the Great Mother Binah to Geburah and 'is thus the influence of the Supernals descending through the Veil of Water (Blood) upon the energy of man, and so inspires it. It corresponds in this way, to the Hierophant which, on the other side of the Tree of Life, brings down the fire of Chokmah'. The general feeling of this Path is one of protection and stability that helps to re-align our focus which may have been knocked out of kilter by recent travelling. This is our Knight in Shining Armour on the Tree who helps to form a hard protective shell on our outer Self to shield the inner, higher Self.

The **Temple of Chesed [Jupiter]** is a bright place and we have already explored three of the paths (the 21st, the 20th, and the 19th) relating to it. The fourth door opens onto the **16th Path - the Hierophant (Taurus) -** leading from Chesed to Chokmah. The meaning of the word 'hierophant' is 'the one who shows the *hiera*, or holy things'. The principle reference of this card is that of all magic(k)al work - the uniting of the microcosm and the macrocosm. This Path allows us to probe the Mysteries of the Cosmos and discover the Divine Will that fuels all magical learning in terms of primal energy. As Dolores Ashcroft-Nowicki quite rightly points out, there is no avoiding the sexual imagery when working with the Tree of Life and if this is "upsetting or repugnant to anyone, then a study of the Qabalah is not for them, for the Tree is a Hymn to Creation in all its forms and beauty."

The **Temple of Binah [Saturn]** is an ancient, holy place and we have reached it by way of the 18th and 17th Paths. There are two doors to the right which will lead to the **14th Path - the Empress (Venus) -** the Path that unites the Father with the Mother and, although the Empress may be the complement of the Emperor, her attributes are much more universal, being one of the alchemical forms of energy: Salt. According to Crowley, this card may be summed up as the Gate of Heaven. This Path also represents the final 'county' boundary of the Four Worlds separating Briah, the World of Creation, from Atziluth, the World of Emanations. It is the ultimate balance which is the basis of all successful magical working, allowing us to incorporate both masculine and feminine energy in **All** - which, in itself, makes it one of great power.

And the **12th Path - the Magus (Mercury)**. The ideas connected with this symbol are so complex and multifarious that it is inadequate to try to give a clear, concise description of the Path in its entirety. This is the realm of the "Wisdom, the Will, the Word, the Logos by whom the worlds were created ... the Son, the manifestation in the act of the idea of the Father" - and the alchemical symbol of Mercury. This Path is the path of the realisation of our capability; *not* confirmation of our ability. The

Power of the Magus opens up the Universe in one gigantic panoramic view, as a glimpse of what *can* be attained with discipline and training. There are no short cuts; no quick-fix solutions; and certainly no books that will divulge all the secrets at a single reading.

The Temple of Chokmah [Zodiac] has a primitive feel. There are four doors but only one Path left for us to explore ... the **11th Path - the Fool (Air)** - representing the Nothingness above the Tree of Life; the source of all things; the Qabalistic Zero; the equation of the Universe; the initial and final balance of opposites. The whole picture is a glyph of creative light. This is the first and final Path on the Tree - the path that is both starting point and goal. From this vantage point the seeker can set out in any direction s/he chooses, carrying the seeds of creation to scatter along the way. The view of the Fool is best examined through the eyes of a child rather than the patronising scrutiny of the jaded magical practitioner.

As we can see, the whole symbolic system of the Tree is shot through with cosmic energies and correspondences that are basic shorthand for all and every magical operation ...

Magical correspondences

Just as the understanding of archetypal imagery is important to the magical-mystical seeker, so is a grasp of magical correspondences. In magical terms for example, in order for an image to be invested with a living spirit, it has to look a certain way and be consecrated in a certain way. The image, once properly prepared, set up, adorned, and decorated, becomes the focus of the spirit. It becomes what it is taken to represent.

As we've discussed earlier, magical practitioners use many of these associations to aid them in their magic, with each area being assigned its own set of individual correspondences relating to colour, perfume, flora, fauna, gemstones, etc., and a thorough grounding in these enables us to evoke the right 'essence' for a particular working. It is often obvious why particular correspondences are assigned their place but many are equally obscure. The various different sources will all have their own particular attributions and although Crowley's *Liber 777* has the most comprehensive listing, a degree of experimentation is permissible once we've learned the ground rules.

For the reasons of self-protection and preserving one's sanity we must also be fully conversant with the nature of the energies we encounter on the astral levels. We must, for example, learn to differentiate between the *individual* energy represented by Aphrodite (Greek), Venus (Roman), Hathor (Egyptian), Ishtar (Babylonian) and Astarte (Phoenician). In modern, eclectic paganism, all these energies would be identified as having one source, i.e. *the Goddess* - which is why much of what passes for 'pagan magic' is sterile. To understand the true power emanating from each source, we must understand what the indigenous peoples who worshipped them called upon, not what we read in today's dumbed-down, quasi-magical offerings.

If we study genuine magical material from the Golden Dawn, Dion Fortune or Aleister Crowley, we are instantly struck by the wealth of classical references in the texts. These were not scattered through the text at random to impress the reader, they were carefully controlled and contrived in order to produce the maximum effect in a particular instruction. God-power can be equally as destructive as demonic-energy if we haven't bothered to find out exactly what it is that we're channelling for magical purposes. Any problems stemming from this lack of recognition are the result of sheer arrogance on the part of the seeker, who believes he can control something that he isn't even on nodding acquaintance with.

As a result of this chapter, you've probably asked yourself the following question several times over: Why on earth do we need to have a wide knowledge of the myths and legends of different cultures to successfully practice magic? The answer, of course, is that the earthly reasons are negligible, it's the psychic levels that matter.

It might also come as a surprise to learn that myth, folk-lore and legend are now recognised as a vital part of the development of the human race, rather than just a confused jumble of ancient cultural children's stories. It is also accepted that at the roots of mythology and legend is a kind of serious philosophy that was *not* random and which had its own peculiar logic, even if this is not rationalistic logic that sits comfortable within the remit of modern society. For the seeker it is necessary to works through an irritating maze of analogies, allegories, symbols, correspondences - all of which means making connections between things which outwardly and rationally are not connected at all.

Myths that might, at first glance, seem merely products of childish fancy are very far from being merely fanciful and are the means by which ancient peoples expressed their fundamental notions of life and nature. These enduring myths are the *actual methods* by which they expressed certain ways of viewing the 'rules' of life and which were brought into existence by the manner in which life was regulated in their society: the myths reflecting the morality according to the lights of their time.

When we talk about the 'mythology of Egypt' for example, we are referring to the whole body of Egypt's divine, heroic and cosmogonic legends, together with the various attempts which have been made to explain these ancient narratives for the benefit of *modern* thinking. The real function of these myths, however, was to strengthen the existing tradition and endow it with a greater value and prestige by tracing it back to a higher, better, more 'supernatural' reality of ancient events. What men have thought, all over the world and throughout history, about the supernatural *is* important not only for what it may tell us about the Mysteries of life and death as the ancients viewed it, but for what it tells us about human beings today. If nothing else, it reveals what we have lost!

Very early in the history of conscious human thought, the various different priesthoods awoke to the reality that their religious stories (i.e. those that concealed the Mysteries) were in want of public explanation. As a result, the popular versions took over and the esoteric became exoteric. The myths of civilised peoples, the Aryans of India, the Celts, the Egyptians and the Greeks, therefore contained two elements: the rational and what to modern minds seems the irrational. The rational myths were those which represented the gods as beautiful and wise; but the *real* difficulties presented by mythology spring from the irrational elements, which to modern minds appear unnatural, senseless and often repellent. It is to these *irrational* elements that the seeker must turn if we wish to reconnect with stellar-wisdom and the ancient Mysteries, which still lie at the very heart of the Great Work. For the true seeker, the great classic myths remain 'true' stories; not because we think they really happened but because they contain certain 'universal truths' about humanity and life: truths that cannot be translated into plain statement.

The true star-seeker is never a linear thinker. This approach might be fine for other paths and traditions who like to have every ritual mapped out in chapter and verse - but for the true mystical seeker things are never that simple. We must think laterally, in spirals - so that when one end of the spiral is reached, it is found to be the beginning of another. Just as nothing in nature moves in a straight line so we must often re-programme our thoughts to accept that *all* magical/mystical thinking is a series of convoluted ideas and images which we as individuals need to grapple with in order to see what lies behind.

Like the Universe, magic is a system of illusion and what we *think* we see is only a tiny fraction of the whole. For example: for thousands of years, mankind's thinking was limited to our solar system. Now we *know* that there are other galaxies out there and many of them much larger than our own; that there are many more facets - not just a one dimensional system of circles, pillars and paths that make up the basic design of the Tree of Life.

As we have seen, each *sephirah* has its own additional levels or planes of existence, on which we can encounter all manner of entities or extra-terrestrial intelligences. Do we, for example, complete the Malkuth temple exercise and proceed to straight to Yesod … or do we plumb the realms of Malkuth? What other levels or planes of existence are there for us to contemplate at this lowly level? Before we even start to think about psychic dimensions, we need to be aware of the natural levels of existence that occur on planet Earth of which we pay scant attention in our quest for magical advancement.

"As above, so below" reminds us that there are forms of life = micro-organisms, that can exist under extreme conditions where we could not. There are those that thrive at temperatures above boiling point in the oceanic thermal vents; entire ecologies present in the frozen wastes of Antarctica; those living in the Earth's crust some eight kilometres below the surface; even those that thrive in nuclear reactors using enzymes to repair DNA damage. As one scientific writer points out: "There is scarcely any set of conditions prevailing on Earth, no matter how extreme, that is incapable of harbouring some form of microbial life." If that is the case, and "As above, so below", then how much more can we encounter on the psychic/astral level in the realm of Malkuth? Before we become too anxious to 'climb the Tree', perhaps we should spend more time investigating these different dimensions from our own eco-system and use path-working to investigate what other natural, elemental energies are available to us on a magical level, while studying the stars from the safety of the realm of Malkuth.

Another example of non-linear thinking concerns the black meteoric stones known as *baitulia* that were early objects of cult worship in ancient Greece from the earliest times, being invested with the divine, and animated by it since they had fallen from heaven. Once anointed with olive oil they were believed to work miracles on behalf of the supplicants. The sacred stone of Pessinus (the *agalma diipetes*) was a small, light black meteorite, which was regarded as the Great Mother and brought to Rome to be encased in silver – where it was substituted for the visage of the statue of Cybele. A contemporary writer of the time commented: "We all see it today put in that image instead of a face and un-hewn, giving the figure a countenance that is by no means lifelike." This sacred stone from the heavens was deliberately left un-worked because it was in this state that its sacredness resided.

This is what we mean by lateral magical thinking.

Reverse imagery

Similarly, the language of correspondences also takes into account the reverse meanings of certain symbols – the most well-known being the swastika. It is a symbol that generally takes the form of an equilateral cross, with its four legs bent at 90 degrees, and is still considered to be a sacred and auspicious symbol in Hinduism, Buddhism and Jainism. It has been used as a decorative element in various cultures since at least the Neolithic period, and the motif is found on a man's tunic depicted in a Roman mosaic in Sicily. It is recognised as an important symbol long used in Indian religions to represent 'auspiciousness' – and as such was adopted as such in pre-WWI Europe, even being used on the Scouting movement's Medal of Merit.

It's the *reverse* image (the symbol for chaos) that was appropriated by the Nazi Party prior to World War II and in many Western countries the swastika has been highly stigmatized because of these associations; since the 1930s the image has been largely associated with Nazism and white supremacy in most Western countries. As a result, its identity as a Nazi or hate symbol is prohibited in some countries, including Germany where, due to the stigma, many buildings that were decorated with the symbol have had it removed.

On a more pertinent level, however, according to archaeoastronomer, Reza Assasi, the "swastika is a geometric pattern in the sky representing the north ecliptic pole centred to Zeta Draconis". He argues that this primitive astrological symbol was later called the four-horse chariot of Mithra in ancient Iran and represented the centre of ecliptic in the star map, demonstrating that in Iranian mythology, the cosmos was believed to be pulled by four heavenly horses revolving in clockwise direction around a fixed centre, possibly because of a geocentric understanding of an astronomical phenomenon called axial precession. He suggests that this notion was transmitted to the West and flourished in Roman Mithraism, in which this symbol appears in Mithraic iconography and astrological representations.

One little symbol and so many universal meanings – from the holiest of holies to the most profane – and the seeker must be aware of all these different facets before being able to utilise them for his or her own use.

We must, however, also avoid the assumption that all reverse or negative symbolism is evil. Often esoteric writing will refer energies emanating from the 'Dark Side of the Tree' but this is a misnomer in as much as Dark does not = Evil. Magically speaking, 'dark' often refers to working with entities or energies of an uncertain temperament which, if not handled correctly can rebound and bite the practitioner on the arse! Let us take Demeter for example. The Universal Earth Mother is considered to be a kindly, caring and beneficent goddess, and yet the 'Wrath of Demeter' is well documented in the classical literature of Homer, Diodorus and Ovid, showing her to have unbridled violence concealed beneath the folds of her gown.

> *"Where the girl* [Persephone] *was she knew not, but reproached the whole wide world – ungrateful, not deserving her gift of grain ... So with angry hands she broke the plough that turned the soil and sent to death alike the farmer and his labouring ox, and bade the field betray their trust, and spoil the seeds ...The young crops died in the first blade, destroyed now by the rain too violent, now by the sun too strong. The stars and winds assailed them; hungry birds gobbled the scattered seeds; thistles and unconquerable twitch, wore down the wheat."* [*Metamorphoses 5*, Ovid.]

Here we see the dark side of the goddess, just as every spirit, deity, archetype and human conceals a 'darkness' within. This darkness can also be the realm of the Qliphoth of whom we have already spoken. As we have seen, these entities are not intrinsically evil but they inhabit the shadow world of the *sephirah*, waiting for some unsuspecting 'traveller' to wander past – waiting to be fuelled by any energy they encounter. Once brought through to the earthly realm where they can grow and develop into a more tangible form, any darker 'human' energy will quickly be magnified as the entity grows in strength.

Providing we remain alert to the existence of these reverse images, they will not impede our progress as we continue with our magical/mystical quest. Even if the shadows surrounding us feel heavy and oppressive, we know that if we cannot walk confidently in the darkness, we will never walk comfortably in the light. In truth, most of us are creatures of the light. It's not until we begin to actively seek out the Path to the Mysteries that we are willing to explore the 'darkness'. In *The Soul of the Night*, Chet Raymo wrote:

> *"In a dark time the eye begins to see. And this is the paradox: that black is white, that darkness is the mother of beauty that the extinction of light is a revelation ... Perhaps it is only in the dark times that the eye and the mind, turning to each other, can co-operate in the delicate and impassioned art of 'seeing'. Few people willingly choose to walk the dark path, to enter the dark wood, to feel the knot of fear in the stomach, or to live in the dark cave of the sleepless night. But then,*

unexpectedly ... the light of the mind returns bearing extraordinary gifts."

Although our general view of the heavens is one of bright lights and shimmering star-fire, in reality Deep Space is a very cold and dark place to be.

Simultaneous ideas

It has long been recognised by mystics and magical practitioners that there are 'universal truths' - ideas that crossed continents, peoples, cultures and religions, appearing in corresponding guises in circumstances where the obvious explanation – cross cultural pollination – makes no sense. It serves no purpose, for example, to claim that because the henges at Thornborough in Yorkshire were constructed before the Pyramids, that the Egyptians learned their sacred geometry from their Northern European cousins.

As we know, archaeoastronomy is the study of how people in the past have interpreted the phenomena in the sky, how they utilised them, and what role the sky played in their individual cultures. And nowhere else is this more evident than in Duncan Steel's suggestion of a valid explanation for the ancient pattern of pyramid building as resulting from the observation of the natural phenomena known as 'zodiacal light' – the diffuse triangular glow in the dawn sky that follows the path of the sun. In the fact that pyramid-building was confined to Mexico, East Asia, Babylonia, Egypt and Assyria, we cannot ignore the one thing these different civilisations had in common was their latitude – all near the Tropic of Cancer and despite them being aeons apart in terms of dating.

If we look at other astrological features that were clearly visible in the night sky right across the globe, then it is not difficult to see how each of them took on important mystical significance to the astronomer-priesthoods of different ancient civilisations. These distinctive shapes that followed a yearly procession across the velvet black of the heavens would quite understandably be viewed as mysterious and godly from wherever they were viewed in the world.

The most spectacular of all is, of course, the constellation of **Orion** with its distinctive placement of stars, seemingly to move between the Northern and Southern Hemispheres. The earliest depiction that has been linked to the constellation is a prehistoric mammoth ivory carving found in a cave in the Ach Valley in Germany, which archaeologists have estimated to have been fashioned approximately 32,000 to 38,000 years ago. The distinctive pattern of Orion has been recognized in numerous cultures around the world, and many myths have been associated with it.

Orion's astrological name derives from Greek mythology, in which Orion was a gigantic, supernaturally strong hunter of ancient times and a son of Poseidon (Neptune, god of the sea in the Graeco-Roman tradition). One myth recounts Gaia's rage at Orion's boast that he would kill every animal on the planet, and of her attempt to kill him with a scorpion's sting: which is why the constellations of Scorpius and Orion are never in the sky at the same time! Ophiuchus, the Serpent Bearer, revived Orion with an antidote. And this is said to be the reason the constellation of Ophiuchus stands midway between the Scorpion and the Hunter in the sky. The constellation is also mentioned in Horace's *Odes;* Homer's *Odyssey* and *Iliad*; and Virgil's *Aeneid*.

In ancient Egypt, the stars of Orion were regarded as a god, called Sah, and because Orion rises before Sirius, the star whose heliacal rising was the basis for the Egyptian calendar and the annual flooding of the Nile, Sah was closely linked with Sopdet, the goddess who personified Sirius. The god Sopdu was said to be the son of Sah and Sopdet. Later Sah was syncretized with Osiris, while Sopdet was syncretized with Osiris's wife, Isis. In the Pyramid Texts, from the 24th and 23rd centuries BC, Sah was one of many gods whose form the dead pharaoh was said to take in the afterlife.

In the ancient Near East the Babylonian star catalogues of the Late Bronze Age name Orion as 'The Heavenly Shepherd' or 'True Shepherd of Anu' - Anu being the chief god of the heavenly realms. The Armenians identified their legendary patriarch and founder Hayk with Orion. *Hayk* is also the name of the Orion constellation in the Armenian translation of the Bible. The Bible mentions Orion three times, naming it 'Kesil' literally - fool). Though, this name perhaps is etymologically connected with 'Kislev', the name for the ninth month of the Hebrew calendar (i.e. November–December and hope for winter rains.): Job: "He is the maker of the Bear and Orion." and "Can you loosen Orion's belt?" - and Amos: "He who made the Pleiades and Orion."

In ancient Syria the constellation was known as the *Nephilim*, a race of giants who may have been descendants of Orion; while in medieval Muslim astronomy, Orion was known as *al-jabbar*, 'the giant'; Orion's sixth brightest star, Saiph, is named from the Arabic, *saif al-jabbar*, meaning 'sword of the giant'.

East Asian antiquity: In China, Orion was one of the twenty-eight lunar mansions and known as *Shen,* literally meaning 'three', for the stars of Orion's Belt; the characters for the Shang Dynasty version are over three

214

millennia old. The *Rig Veda* refers to the Orion Constellation as *Mriga* (The Deer). It is said that the two bright stars in the front and two bright stars in the rear are the hunting dogs; the one comparatively less bright star in the middle and ahead of two front dogs is the hunter and three aligned bright stars in the middle is the deer; and three aligned but less brighter stars is the baby deer. The Malay call Orion's Belt *Bintang Tiga Beradik* - the 'Three Brother Star'.

European folklore: In old Hungarian tradition, Orion is known as the [magic] Archer, or Reaper. In recently rediscovered myths he is called Nimrod, the greatest hunter, father of the twins Hunor and Magor. The stars on upper right form together the reflex bow or the lifted scythe. In other Hungarian traditions, Orion's Belt is known as 'Judge's stick' or *Bírópálca*. In Scandinavian tradition, Orion's Belt was known as Frigg's Distaff (*friggerock*) or Freyja's Distaff. The Finns call Orion's Belt and the stars below it *Väinämöisen viikate* - Väinämöinen's scythe. Another name for the asterism of Alnilam, Alnitak and Mintaka is *Väinämöisen vyö'* – Väinämöinen's Belt; and the stars hanging from the belt as *Kalevanmiekka* (Kaleva's sword). In Siberia, the Chukchi people see Orion as a hunter; an arrow he has shot is represented by Aldebaran (Alpha Tauri), with the same figure as other Western depictions.

The Americas: The Seri people of north-western Mexico call the three stars in the belt of Orion *Hapj* (a name denoting a hunter) which consists of three stars: *Hap* (mule deer), *Haamoja* (pronghorn), and *Mojet* (bighorn sheep). *Hap* is in the middle and has been shot by the hunter; its blood has dripped onto Tiburón Island. The same three stars are known in Spain and most of Latin America as *Las tres Marías* (Spanish for the Three Marys). In Puerto Rico, the three stars are known as the *Los Tres Reyes Magos* (Spanish for the Three Wise Men). The Ojibwa (Chippewa) Native Americans call this constellation *Kabibona'kan*, the Winter Maker, as its presence in the night sky heralds winter. To the Lakota, *Tayamnicankhu* (Orion's Belt) is the spine of a bison. The great rectangle of Orion is the bison's ribs; the Pleiades star cluster in nearby Taurus is the bison's head; and Sirius in Canis Major, known as *Tayamnisinte*, is its tail.

Sirius, who follows the hunter, is the brightest star in the night sky and its name is derived from the ancient Greek, meaning 'glowing' or 'scorcher'. Sirius is also known colloquially as the Dog Star, reflecting its prominence in the constellation, Canis Major. Its heliacal rising of Sirius marked the flooding of the Nile in ancient Egypt and the 'dog days' of summer for the ancient Greeks; while to the Polynesians in the southern hemisphere it marked winter and was an important star for navigation around the Pacific Ocean.

Sirius is recorded in the earliest Egyptian astronomical records. During the era of the Middle Kingdom, Egyptians based their calendar on the heliacal rising of Sirius, namely the day it becomes visible just before sunrise after moving far enough away from the glare of the Sun. This occurred just before the annual flooding of the Nile and the Summer Solstice, after a 70-day absence from the skies. The hieroglyph for Sothis features a star and a triangle; when Sothis was later identified with the goddess Isis, who formed a part of a triad with her husband Osiris and their son Horus, while the 70-day period symbolised the passing of Isis and Osiris through the *duat* (Egyptian underworld).

The ancient Greeks observed that the appearance of Sirius heralded the hot and dry summer, and feared that it 'caused plants to wilt, men to weaken, and women to become aroused'. Due to its brightness, Sirius would have been noted to twinkle more in the unsettled weather conditions of early summer and to Greek observers, this signified certain emanations which caused its malignant influence. Anyone suffering its effects was said to be *astroboletos*, or 'star-struck' and the season was described as 'burning' or 'flaming' in literature. The season following the star's heliacal rising (i.e. rising with the Sun) came to be known as the Dog Days of summer when dogs had to go muzzled in case they became rabid.

The inhabitants of the island of Ceos in the Aegean would offer sacrifices to Sirius and Zeus to bring cooling breezes, and would eagerly await the reappearance of the star. If it rose clear, it would portend good fortune; if it was misty or faint then it foretold (or emanated) pestilence. Coins retrieved from the island from the 3rd-century BC feature dogs or stars with emanating rays, highlighting Sirius's importance. The Romans celebrated the heliacal setting of Sirius around 25th April, by sacrificing a dog, along with incense, wine, and a sheep, to the goddess Robigo, so that the star's emanations would not cause wheat rust on wheat crops that year.

Bright stars were important to the ancient Polynesians for navigation between the many islands and atolls of the Pacific Ocean. Low on the horizon, they acted as stellar compasses to assist mariners in charting courses to particular destinations. They also served as latitude markers; the declination of Sirius matches the latitude of the archipelago of Fiji and passes directly over the islands each night. Sirius served as the body of a 'Great Bird' constellation called *Manu*, with Canopus as the southern wingtip and Procyon the northern wingtip, which divided the Polynesian night sky into two hemispheres. Just as the appearance of Sirius in the morning sky marked summer in Greece, so it marked the chilly onset of winter for the Māori, whose name *Takurua* described both the star and the season. Its culmination at the Winter Solstice was marked by celebration in Hawaii, where it was known as *Ka'ulua*, 'Queen of Heaven'.

Ursa Major (Latin: 'Larger She-Bear'; also known as Charles' Wain) is visible throughout the year in most of the northern hemisphere and can be seen best during the month of April. It is dominated by the widely recognized asterism known as the 'Big Dipper', 'The Wagon' and 'The Plough', which is a useful pointer towards the north, and it has mythological significance in numerous world cultures. The constellation has been seen as a bear by many distinct civilizations, which may stem from a common oral traditions stretching back more than 13,000 years.

In Roman mythology, Jupiter lusted after a young woman named Callisto, a nymph in the train of Diana; Juno, Jupiter's jealous wife, transforms the beautiful Callisto into a bear. Callisto, while in bear form, later encounters her son Arcas, who almost shoots the bear, but to avert the tragedy, Jupiter turns them both into bears and places them among the stars, forming Ursa Major and Ursa Minor. In more ancient times the name of the constellation was Helike, ('turning'), because it turns around the Pole Star. In *Book Two* of Lucan it is called *Parrhasian Helice*, since Callisto came from Parrhasia in Arcadia, where the story was set. *The Odyssey* notes that it is the sole constellation that never sinks below the horizon and 'bathes in the Ocean's waves', so it was used as a celestial reference point for navigation. One of the few star groups mentioned in the Bible (Job 9:9; 38:32 - Orion and the Pleiades being others), Ursa Major was also pictured as a bear by the Jewish peoples, with 'The Bear' being translated as 'Arcturus' in the Vulgate version.

Ancient Finns believed the bear (*Ursus arctos*) was lowered to earth in a golden basket off the Ursa Major, and when a bear was killed, its head was positioned on a tree to allow the bear's spirit to return to Ursa Major.

The Native American Iroquois interpreted Alioth, Mizar, and Alkaid as three hunters pursuing the Great Bear. According to one version, the first hunter (Alioth) is carrying a bow and arrow to strike down the bear; the second hunter (Mizar) carries a large pot (the star Alcor) in which to cook the bear, while the third hunter (Alkaid), hauls a pile of firewood to light a fire beneath the pot. The Algonquin referred to Ursa Major as *maske*, meaning 'bear' – while the Lakota called the constellation *Wičhákhiyuhapi*, or 'Great Bear'.

In Hinduism, Ursa Major is known as *Saptarshi*, each of the stars representing one of the Saptarshis or Seven Sages viz. Bhrigu, Atri,

Angirasa, Vasishta, Pulastya, Pulalaha and Kratu. The fact that the two front stars of the constellations point to the pole star is explained as the boon given to the boy sage Dhruva by Lord Vishnu.

For the ancient Javanese these bright seven stars were known as *Lintang Wuluh*, literally means 'seven stars'. This star cluster is popular because its emergence is the start-time marker for planting. In Burmese, *Pucwan Tārā* is the name of a constellation comprising stars from the head and forelegs of Ursa Major; *pucwan* is a general term for a crustacean. While in South Korea, the constellation is referred to as 'the seven stars of the north', relating to the myth of a widow with seven sons who found comfort with a widower, but to get to his house required crossing a stream. The seven sons, sympathetic to their mother, placed stepping stones in the river; their mother, not knowing who put the stones in place, blessed them and, when her sons died, they became the constellation.

In Japanese Shinto belief, the seven largest stars of Ursa Major belong to Amenominakanushi, the oldest and most powerful of all *kami*, with the Big Dipper being called the 'North Dipper'(*hokutô*) and in ancient times, each one of these seven stars had a specific name:

Pivot - (*sû*) is for Dubhe (Alpha Ursae Majoris)
Beautiful jade - (*sen*) is for Merak (Beta Ursae Majoris)
Pearl - (*ki*) is for Phecda (Gamma Ursae Majoris)
Authority - (*ken*) is for Megrez (Delta Ursae Majoris)
Measuring rod of jade - (*gyokkô*) is for Alioth (Epsilon Ursae Majoris)
Opening of the Yang - (*kaiyô*) is for Mizar (Zeta Ursae Majoris)
Alkaid (Eta Ursae Majoris) has several names: Sword - (*ken* short for End of the Sword - (*ken saki*)); Flickering light - (*yôkô*), or Star of military defeat - (*hagun sei*), because travel in the direction of this star was regarded as bad luck for an army

The **Pleiades**, or Seven Sisters is a brilliant star cluster marking the shoulder of Taurus the bull, and is prominent on winter evenings in the northern hemisphere. The stars are named after the seven daughters of Atlas and the sea-nymph Pleione: Sterope, Merope, Electra, Maia, Taygete, Celaeno, and Alcyone. They were the sisters of Calypso, Hyas, the Hyades, and the Hesperides; they were nymphs in the train of Artemis, and together with the seven Hyades were nursemaids and teachers to the infant Bacchus. After Atlas was forced to carry the heavens on his shoulders, Orion began to pursue all of the Pleiades, and Zeus transformed them first into doves, and then into stars to comfort their father. The constellation of Orion is said to still pursue them across the night sky.

The mythology associated with the Pleiades is extensive and in Theosophy, it was believed that the *Seven Stars of the Pleiades* focussed the spiritual energy of the Seven Rays from the *Galactic Logos* to the *Seven Stars of the Great Bear*, then to Sirius, then to the Sun, then to the god of Earth (Sanat Kumara), and finally through the seven Masters of the Seven Rays to the human race.

Cassiopeia or 'The Queen' is easily recognised by its distinctive W-shape and is another of the circumpolar stars that are always in the sky – even in the daytime, although they are lost in the sun's brilliant light. Cassiopeia never sets, even passing overhead during daylight hours, only to reappear as the sun sets and the stars 'come out'. The Egyptians saw her as the goddess Tauret, represented by a hippopotamus.

The boast of Cassiopeia was that both she and her daughter Andromeda were more beautiful than all the Nereids, the nymph-daughters of the sea god Nereus. This brought the wrath of Poseidon, ruling god of the sea, upon the kingdom of Ethiopia. Trying to save their kingdom, Cepheus and Cassiopeia consulted a wise oracle, who told them that the only way to appease the sea gods was to sacrifice their daughter. Accordingly, Andromeda was chained to a rock at the sea's edge and left there to helplessly await her fate at the hands of the sea monster Cetus, but the hero Perseus arrived in time, killed Cetus, saved Andromeda and ultimately became her husband.

Since Poseidon thought that Cassiopeia should not escape punishment, he placed her in the heavens chained to a throne in such a position that referenced Andromeda's ordeal. As she circles the celestial pole in her throne, she is upside-down half the time. The constellation resembles the chair that originally represented an instrument of torture. As it is near the Pole Star, the constellation can be seen the whole year from the northern hemisphere, although sometimes upside down.

NB: Reference to the 'seven stars' occurs throughout history all over the world but we should not assume each culture is referring to the same star-grouping. Ursa Major, Orion and the Pleiades all have seven stars in their main grouping.

At night time, with a clear sky, it would have been easy to pin-point the location of the celestial pole around which all the other stars appeared to be moving. Homer was aware of the importance of the circumpolar stars which to him were ever visible. The 3rd-century Greek writer Aratus, in an astronomical poem, *Phaenomena*, describes the constellation of Ursa Minor: 'By her guidance the men of Sidon [Phoenicians] steer the straight course'. Traveller Pytheas of Massalia recorded details of a journey undertaken prior to 320BC – for example, the lengthening of the days as his journey proceeded northwards, and noting that there was no star at the exact pole. That knowledge of the importance of the celestial pole was widespread along the Atlantic seaways in early medieval times is shown by references to the pole star in Anglo-Saxon vocabularies and the Icelandic sagas. As Professor Barry Cunliffe remarks in *Facing the Ocean*: "In all probability this awareness goes back well into the prehistoric period. Indeed, navigation skills were needed even by land-based hunter-gatherer communities following herds in the Mesolithic period and earlier."

The ancients watched the stars from wherever they were in the world, and wove the stories and myths of their individual cultures around these predictable movements in the heavens.

How the Wisdom of the Ancients was Shared

Magic and mysticism, like mathematics, is a universal language and easily translated into a common tongue; similarly we are only beginning to discover just how well-travelled our ancient ancestors were in pre-historic times. Gone are the days when we believed that each civilisation grew, developed and expanded in a protective cultural bubble without interference or influence from its neighbours. Archaeology is repeatedly revealing that trade between Britain and the Mediterranean, for example, flourished in the centuries before the Celts and Romans turned up on these shores. And those shipping routes probably carried more than goods for barter and sale.

The world has always been an unsafe place for those of differing philosophies, beliefs or customs, and more than one dispossessed family would be fleeing from the despotic laws of their homeland. Persecution is responsible for thousands of years of cultural migration all over the world, and when people fled, they took their beliefs and their knowledge with them. Add to this the theory that Nature has a memory or instinct that can best be described as telepathic; that there is an interconnectedness among the living things within each species – the collective unconscious or racial memories.

Jung believed that we experience the unconscious through symbols that includes the medium of art, music and language, both communicated by hand and oral traditions. In *Viral Mythology*, the authors point out that given the astounding consistency in the underlying themes of these symbols, perhaps there is a collective memory being transmitted.

"Archetypal symbols are mysteriously transmitted throughout history and modernity. Nevertheless, it is not a question of specific inherited images as much as it is one of a unified conscious experience. The interaction between our individual perceptions, universal consciousness, and symbolism enriches life and promotes personal development and growth."
[*Viral Mythology*, Marie D Jones and Larry Flaxman]

There are also common themes and elements in ancient myths and legends, often recorded in art, architecture, iconography and images that retold the stories all over the world to describe various natural (or supernatural) phenomena, were often similar to one another, suggesting that certain themes were archetypal. Why did so many diverse civilisations, separated by thousands of miles and with no real means of communication, all tell the same story, using the identical symbolic imagery, and with only slight regional variations? Was there some outside influence spreading these common themes, or were these cultures tapping into a field of ideas and information that existed in the collective subconsciousness?

If, however, we look long enough at the ancient archaeological and astronomical monuments, the images seem to attempt to convey scientific knowledge through sacred geometry, and our thoughts must return to those massive remains of that huge African metropolis at Mpumalanga for some answers.

The clues rest with the research carried out by Professor Bryan Sykes, his findings reported in the best-selling book, *The Seven Daughters of Eve*, and the fundamental question of human evolution and mitochondrial DNA. We all know that modern *homo sapiens*, the species to which we all belong, originated in Africa. The main area of disagreement is the time-frame of this exodus. "The 'Out of Africa' school thinks there was a much more recent spread of humans from Africa, about 100,000 years ago, and that these new humans, our own *homo sapiens*, completely replaced the former *homo erectus* throughout its range," explains the Professor. "It showed quite clearly that the common mitochrondrial ancestor of all modern humans lived only about 150,000 years ago."

The fossil evidence supports the abrupt arrival in Europe about 45,000 years ago of humans with much lighter skeletons and skulls which were virtually indistinguishable from modern Europeans. These people were called Cro-Magnons and they brought with them one important gift – art.

"The Cro-Magnons had invented representational art. Over two hundred caves in France and northern Spain are adorned with their strangely beautiful and vigorous images of wild animals. Deer and horses, mammoths and bison decorate the walls of the deepest caverns, far from the light of day. These are not crude or child-like drawings but the expression of a mature and accomplished imagery, an abstracted and mystical representation of their world."
[*The Seven Daughters of Eve*, Bryan Sykes]

At some point, around 100,000 years ago, modern humans began to spread out of Africa to begin the eventual colonisation of the rest of the world, but according to Sykes, it could not have been a massive movement of people. "Had hundreds or thousands of people moved out, then it would follow that several African clans would be found in the gene pool of the rest of the world. But that is not the case …the numbers must have been very small. There was no mass exodus …"

All the evidence points to the Near East as the jumping-off point for the colonisation of the rest of the world since it was the only land route out of Africa, across Sinai. There is apparently good fossil evidence to support the arrival of *homo sapiens* in the Near East at least 100,000 years ago but only a faltering spread to the north and west into Europe, which finally succeeded only 50,000 years ago. "What held them up in the Near East for at least 50,000 years before that?" Professor Sykes asked.

Answer: Possibly the lush, green lands of the Euphrates-Tigris and Nile Valleys … recent discoveries show that beneath what is now the Persian Gulf, a once-fertile land mass may have supported some of the earliest humans outside Africa. At its peak, the flood-plain (now below the waters of the Gulf) would have been about the size of the UK before it began slowly shrinking as water began to flood the area. Then about 8,000 years ago, the remaining land was swallowed up by the Indian Ocean and the people became environmental refugees once again.

Around 100,000 years ago the Sahara, the Nile valley and the Euphrates-Tigris region would have been a vast green and pleasant land and Bryan Sykes' small 'Lara' tribe may well have thought they'd found the promised land after the long journey from the centre of the African continent. We have no way of knowing, of course, how and where the people of Mpumalanga were dispersed, or the true reason behind the decline of their once-great city but it is reasonable to assume that some of them survived, if only because of that powerful stellar-wisdom that manifested many aeons later in Egypt and the Near East.

But there was more to come … In 2012, Dr George Busby from the University of Oxford published an article that took the reality of global migration several steps further by citing three new studies published in *Nature*, and mapping the genetic profiles of more than 200 populations across the world. Although some scientists believe that all non-Africans today can trace their ancestry back to a single migrant population; others argue that there were *several* different waves of migration out of Africa. These migrations ranged further north into Europe, east across Asia and south to Australasia, eventually spreading north-east over the top of Beringia into the Americas; suggesting that on their way across the globe, our ancestors interbred with at least two archaic human species, the Neanderthals in Eurasia, and the Denisovans in Asia.

Two of the papers agree that the genetic bottleneck caused by the migration out of Africa occurred roughly 60,000 years ago, which is in line with dating from archaeological investigations. The research also manages to settle a long-running debate about the structure of African populations at the beginning of the migration. Was the small group of humans who left Africa representative of the whole continent at that time, or had they split off from more southerly populations earlier? The Simons Genome Diversity Project compared the genomes of 142 worldwide populations, including 20 from across Africa and conclusively show that modern African hunter-gatherer populations split off from the group that became non-Africans around 130,000 years ago and from West Africans around 90,000 years ago. A second study, led by Danish geneticist Eske Willersev, showed that the divergence within Africa also started before the migration, around 125,000 years ago.

Meanwhile, a third paper proposes an earlier migration out of Africa, some 120,000 years ago but only around 2% per cent of genomes can be traced to this earlier migration, which implies that this wave can't have many ancestors left in the present day. If true (and the two other papers find little support for it), this suggests that there must have been a migration across Asia prior to the big one about 60,000 years ago.

Migrating people don't only carry their DNA with them, their cultural/racial subconsciousness would have been in the baggage train too. If we go back to Gerald Massey's 1907 *magnum opus, Ancient Egypt: Light of the World,* we find he wrote: "It may be said that the dawn of African civilisation came full circle in Egypt, but that the earliest glimmer of the light which turned the darkness into day for all the earth first issued from the inner land ...the mythology, religious rites, totemic customs and primitive symbolism of Egypt are crowded with survivals from identifiable Inner African origins ... The Egyptian record when correctly read will tell us plainly that the human birthplace ... was a land of the great lakes ... from whence the sacred river ran to brim the valley of the Nile ... It is now proposed to seek for the birthplace of the beginnings in Central Africa, the land of the papyrus reed, around the equatorial lakes, by the aid of Egyptian astronomical mythology and the legendary lore ..."

And yet, even before the ancient Egyptians began building the pyramids, monumental construction work was already underway in northern Europe that was also aligned with the stars. The emergence of this distinctive Atlantic culture took place between 8000-4000BC when Britain was still joined to the continent. According to Professor Barry Cunliffe, the population grew rapidly 'generating an energy over and above that needed to ensure a constant and sufficient supply of food. The surplus energy was transformed into fine goods ... and into monumental tombs built to house and to commemorate the ancestors'.

By the beginning of the fourth millennium much of Atlantic Europe, including the off-shore islands of Britain and Ireland, had adopted a Neolithic life-style and the awesome astronomical building programmes were under way. At Newgrange in Co Meath, Ireland, for example, through a slot beneath a decorated lintel, at the dawn on the day of the midwinter solstice, the light shone along the passage and into the chamber at the end, lighting up a triple spiral carved into the stone.

It has long been believed that these megalithic structures were in some way related to the celestial cycle, and that the midsummer sun rose on the axis of Stonehenge was well known by the 18th-century. As Professor Cunliffe comments in *Facing the Ocean*: "Some of what has been written is completely spurious and some is unproven. Yet there remains the unshakeable fact that a number of our most impressive megalithic tombs were designed with immense skill to relate precisely to significant solar or lunar events."

A few examples will demonstrate the point: At Newgrange the passage of the monument was carefully aligned on the midwinter solstice; at nearby Knowth, the two separate passages in the monument are aligned exactly east to west, so that the west-facing passage catches the setting sun on the Vernal and Autumnal Equinoxes and the east-facing passage is oriented on the rising sun. Maes Howe in Orkney is aligned on the midwinter sunset and the Neolithic henges at Thornborough in England are aligned with Orion's Belt (*Before the Pyramids*, Christopher Knight).

With the benefit of hindsight, however, we can put ourselves in the mind-set of these ancient people through the shared knowledge of astronomy and magical application. To repeat Kenneth Grant's words of wisdom: "The answer is that the occultist understands that contacts with these energies may be established more completely through symbols so ancient that they have had time to bury themselves in the vast storehouse of racial subconsciousness. To such symbols the Forces respond swiftly and with incalculable fullness ... The magician, therefore, uses the more direct paths which long ages have mapped out in the shadow-lands of the subconsciousness."

Summary: Star-Fall

It is, of course, tempting to view stellar-power as 'lost knowledge' – the idea being that prehistoric times somehow represented a spiritual Golden Age when people lived in harmony with their environment, tapping currents of cosmic energy – a power accessible to our ancient ancestors but now lost to narrow-minded 20th-century thinkers. But this is not the case ....

The monuments of the past re-affirm our faith with the old stellar faith but it was not without its detractors. "The wisdom of the Egyptians," mocked St Augustine, "what was it but astronomy?" The answer is that it was not simply the science of astronomy in the modern sense, but astronomical mythology that was the 'subject of subjects' taught by the ancient 'mystery-teachers of the heavens' as the Egyptian Urshu, or astronomer-priesthood were designated.

"In this way the teachers who first glorified the storied windows of the heavens, like some cathedral of immensity, with their pictures of the past, are demonstrably Egyptian, because the Sign-language [hieroglyphics], the mythos, the legends, and the eschatology involved are wholly Egyptian and entirely independent of all who came after them. The so-called 'wisdom of the ancients' was Egyptian when the elemental powers were represented first as characters in mythology. It was Egyptian when that primeval mythology was rendered astronomically. It is also Egyptian in the phase of eschatology ... Egyptian mythology is the source of the marchen, the legends, and the folklore of the world, while the eschatology is the fountain-head of all the religious mysteries that ... were ultimately continued in the religion of ancient Rome. The mysteries were a dramatic mode of communicating the secrets of primitive knowledge in Sign-language when this had been extended to the astronomical mythology. Hence, we repeat, the Egyptian Urshu or astronomers were known by the title of 'mystery teachers of the heavens' because they explained the mysteries of primitive astronomy."

[*Ancient Egypt: Light of the World*, Gerald Massey]

Although all this speculation may be unfamiliar territory to us today, having become totally disconnected from the stars and their myths, it would have made perfect sense to people who had lived their lives under an unpolluted, open sky. And despite what often appear to be wild flights of fancy, there may be a way to re-connect with our ancient stellar past ...

The Greenwich Meridian

Around c150AD Ptolemy of Alexandria mapped the stars in *Books VII* and *VIII* of his *Almagest* in which he used Sirius as the location for the globe's central meridian, depicting it as one of six red-coloured stars. In1884, however, a north-south line running through the Royal Observatory at Greenwich was adopted as the Prime Meridian of the world in the name of international politics, navigation and commercial expediency, and became the central reference point for time and space on Earth. But what if this 'cutting edge of scientific endeavour' was not a modern concept centred on a first-rate astronomical observatory, but based on knowledge of a north-south axis thousands of years old?

The prime meridian is anchored at the Royal Observatory at Greenwich, near central London but it extends from pole to pole, entering England at the mouth of the Humber and exiting at Peacehaven on the south coast. One hundred miles across the English Channel it comes ashore near Le Havre, passing some hundred miles to the west of Paris where until 1884 the French had anchored their own line of zero longitude. The line continues south, across the Pyrenees into Spain and exiting at the Gulf of Valencia; down across western Africa crossing the Equator in the Bight of Guinea and following its watery course across the south Atlantic Ocean until it reaches Antarctica and the South Pole. But long before the formal agreement that the Greenwich Meridian would mark 0' longitude of the Prime Meridian of the world, this mysterious north/south alignment was laid out along an ancient 'line of power'.

It is under 200 miles from Peacehaven to the mouth of the River Humber and for much of the way the meridian is flanked by ancient monuments, historical and holy sites. In fact, many significant landscape features including earth works had been sited according to an older meridian that suggests it had a powerfully mystical influence. Or perhaps a conduit of natural magnetic energy, the knowledge of which was known to the ancient indigenous astronomer-priesthood.

For example, almost exactly due north of Greenwich, at the junction of two ancient roads – Ermine Street and the Icknield Way – is the curious bell-shaped 'Royston cave' positioned right at the intersection of two of the most important roads of ancient Britain as they led towards the North, South, East and West of the country – and almost exactly on the modern meridian. Ermine Street (leading to Royston) which is thousands of years old, runs virtually parallel to the Greenwich meridian line; the cave and the 12th century Royston Priory are both located almost exactly on the line. While the meridian actually runs *through* Waltham Abbey only a few feet from the traditional site of King Harold's grave – the last Saxon king of England.

"Some of the places listed so far are, of course, not located 'exactly' on the modern Meridian, but in the distant past astronomers did not have satellite Global Positioning Systems, lasers, telescopes or even accurate maps they could draw a ruler-straight line on. Although surveying techniques were highly sophisticated in antiquity, the central reference point for True North (and South) was determined by visual observation of the Sun and stars. Because of this there is much evidence to suggest that, over the ages, the original meridian ... was progressively refined to greater degrees of accuracy ... This is not so much different from the story of the modern Greenwich Meridian, which has been moved several times to achieve ever greater degrees of accuracy ..."

[*Axis of Heaven*, Paul Broadhurst]

Much of the Greenwich Meridian, however, avoids land-mass and lies under the waters of the northern seas and the south Atlantic. Nevertheless, at Fontevraud Abbey (0° 03'E) in the historic heart-land of Aquitaine, are the tombs of King Henry II, his wife Eleanor, and their son, Richard the Lionheart – forever linked to the Celestial Pole by the prime meridian. And if we look at the maps compiled by Barry Cunliffe for *Facing the Ocean*, we will find no shortage of ancient monuments following the 'line of power' down through western France to the Pyrenees.

The mysteries of the Prime Meridian are not confined to Europe. Where the line comes ashore on the North African coast in Algeria there is evidence of the early human occupation prior to the Neolithic period. Neolithic civilisation developed in the region between 6000 and 2000BC with a life-style richly depicted in the Tassili n'Ajjer cave paintings in south-eastern Algeria. The art is no older than 9–10 millennia, according to the dating of associated sediments, and depicts herds of cattle, large wild animals including crocodiles, and human activities such as hunting and dancing. Phoenician traders arrived on the North African coast around 900BC and established Carthage around 800BC.

This was the Africa Minor of the ancients, where the Prime Meridian crosses the Atlas Mountains and the Sahara - which was then dry savannah rather than desert. As the line crosses the Dogon country of Mali there are two places where ancient stellar-power is evident. The first is the area of the Bandiagara Escarpment (to the east of the line), still inhabited today by the Dogon people (see Chapter 2) with its impressive settlement dug into the base of the cliffs.

The second, starting out as a seasonal settlement, Timbuktu – of stellar-learning fame – (see Chapter 2) became a permanent community early in the 12th-century. After a shift in trading routes, Timbuktu (west of the line) flourished from the trade in salt, gold, ivory and slaves and became part of the Mali Empire early in the 14th-century. Like other important medieval West African towns, Iron Age settlements have been discovered in the area that predate the traditional foundation date of the town.

Here the Prime Meridian vanishes beneath the waters in the Gulf of Guinea until it reaches Antarctica but the line passes through what were assembly points for the movement of large numbers of people over thousands of years – both free men and slaves.

Ancient Polar Tradition and the Seven Stars

Even from the ancient Egyptian period, the celestial North has always been identified as 'the place of power' from which all magical and mystical energy emanates. "This 'still point of the turning world' has, since early times, accrued an extraordinary rich mythology and was an important factor in the design and layout of megalithic sites, ancient temples and churches," observed Paul Broadhurst in *Axis of Heaven*. "The concept of True North harbours many different layers of meaning, and, as we will come to see, there is a considerable amount of evidence that a 'polar religion' existed in antiquity, elements of which have filtered down into historical times."

The most important star in the heavens is, of course, the **Pole Star** or **Polaris**, although Polaris hasn't always been the Pole Star. Because of the effects of precession, the positions of the celestial poles are gradually drifting, and during the last 5000 years (including the time of the Pyramid Age) the north celestial pole has moved from **Thuban** in the constellation of Draco to now lie within 1° of Polaris, which will be at its closest to the pole around 2100AD. By 10,000AD the North Pole star will be **Deneb**, and by 14,000AD it will be **Vega**. The South celestial pole is marked by **Octantis**. At the time of Homer, however, **Kochab** and its neighbor

Pherkad were part of the famous asterism in the constellation **Ursa Minor**, the Lesser Bear and served as twin pole stars, circling the North Pole, from 1500BC until 500AD. Ancient Egyptian astronomers referred to them as 'The Indestructibles'. Neither star was as near to the celestial North Pole as Polaris is today, but they are still sometimes referred to as the 'Guardians of the Pole'.

The association of the Great and Little Bears, together with Draco (the *pen*-dragon) were firmly established in prehistoric times when bears were believed to be guardians not only of the heavens and earth, but represented ritual kingship. The familiar seven stars of Ursa Major – amongst the brightest in the sky – were central to one of Britain's most powerful primal myths: the cult of King Arthur. It has also been suggested that the famous insignia of the 'Bear and Ragged Staff' represented the seven guardian stars of the Great Bear of Ursa Minor; which is a very old symbol as witnessed by the rampant bear and ragged staff of the old Earls of Warwick [*Concise Encyclopaedia of Heraldry*] and alleged to have originally derived from the arms of one of the Conqueror's barons.

The title was next conferred upon the powerful statesman and soldier John Dudley, who was made Earl of Warwick in 1547. He was guardian of the young Edward VI and took the unprecedented step of having the old Tudor palace at Greenwich transferred into his own hands. Did the Earl know of the mythical power of the place and saw himself as the 'Great Bear' tethered to the Pole of the Heavens (i.e. the Sovereign) around which he circled? Robert Dudley probably later learned of this magic symbolism from Queen Elizabeth's astrologer John Dee and although both the bear and ragged staff were badges of the Beauchamp family - sometimes united to form a single badge - Robert Dudley, Earl of Leicester, wore them as a single device.

The origins of these emblems are lost in the distant past, but legend has it that Arthgallus, a knight of King Arthur's Round Table, whose name came from the Welsh *artos* or 'bear' and the ragged staff was chosen because his kinsman Morvidus, killed a giant with the broken branch of a tree. The bear and the ragged staff were first used by the Beauchamp family, who became Earls of Warwick in 1268, as a badge or mark of identity in addition to their own coat of arms. At first the emblems seem to have been used independently but in 1387 Thomas Beauchamp II (Earl from 1369 to 1402) owned a bed of black material embroidered with a golden bear and silver staff, which is the earliest known occurrence of the two emblems together. The bear and ragged staff have been used by subsequent holders of the Earldom of Warwick: the Dudleys and the Grevilles.

231

Walking the Labyrinth

Another widespread belief in many mystic pathways is symbolised by the sacred 'Mound' with its seven steps or concentric circles – Silbury Hill, near Avebury and Glastonbury Tor are prime examples of the ancient roots of the custom of climbing the Mound as part of some ritual or seasonal observance – similar to the seven layers of Purgatory's mountain, purging the seven cardinal sins that correspond to astrology's seven classical planets. In close proximity to the Mound is another universal symbol of the celestial centre - the labyrinth, or maze and these survived in many parts of Britain for use in seasonal rites and ceremonies. The concept of the Mound, Labyrinth, and Observatory were often combined in one location, being significant features in the ritual landscape; and 'telling the maze' is preserved in the shamanic elements of traditional witchcraft:

> *"Most* [labyrinths] *were of septenary design, for as the seven stars of the Great Bear circle the Pole they create a series of sevenfold concentric circles around the celestial centre. By walking the labyrinth one is led towards the centre and then away from it in emulation of the stages of life's [spiritual] journey, until ending up at the 'still point' ... According to the old shamanic beliefs, this is a ritual enactment of the soul's journey back to source."*
>
> [*Axis of Heaven*, Paul Broadhurst]

This ritual enactment was hijacked by the Church and the finest version of this sacred geometry is at Chartres Cathedral; but there even more esoteric layers concealed beneath the popular Greek, Roman and Christian smokescreens. Historically, magically and symbolically, the Cretan labyrinth is the oldest, and in Greek mythology it was an elaborate structure designed and built to hold the Minotaur, a mythical creature that was half man and half bull; in Minoan myth the Minotaur was known as Asterion, meaning 'starry' or 'ruler of the stars', which offers a completely different explanation of the symbolism of what we find at the heart of the labyrinth.

> *"In colloquial English, the word 'labyrinth' is generally synonymous with 'maze', but there is a distinct difference between the two. A maze is a complex branching passage through which the seeker must find a route via dead-ends and obstructions. In everyday speech, both maze and labyrinth denote a complex and confusing series of pathways, but technically the maze is distinguished from the labyrinth, as the*

labyrinth has a single through-route with twists and turns but without branches or dead-ends, and is not designed to be as difficult to navigate. A traditional witch understands the significance of these different aspects ..." [*Traditional Witchcraft and the Path to the Mysteries*, Melusine Draco]

Added to this we must also consider the points made by Michael Rice in *The Power of the Bull* that echo Karl Kerenyi's stellar reference [*The Gods of the Greeks*] to the Minoan name for the Minotaur as being Asterion - 'ruler of the stars'.

"The bull leads his followers into some very dark caverns; literally so, since the bull is a chthonic creature ... But the bull also leads on to the stars, in what is surely his most arcane epiphany. The bull is a celestial creature as much as he is terrestrial; his presence among the stars has for a very long time been an element in magic and forecasting the future ... "

And in ancient Egypt what was the hieroglyphic symbol used to depict Ursa Major in the Dendera zodiac? The right foreleg of an ox – the first portion the butcher would cut and use for offerings – that could also be interpreted as meaning 'strength'. The bear, of course, was not an indigenous animal to the Nile Valley, and so an animal of equal strength was chosen to represent this important northern constellation. During the Dynastic period of Egypt's history, Thuban (Alpha Draconis) was the Pole Star and it was this star that was aligned with the northern shaft in the King's Chamber of the Great Pyramid – while the northern shaft in the Queen's Chamber was aligned with Kochab (Beta Ursa Minor). All points of power facing north towards the Pole Star.

Focussing on the present Pole Star will not be a problem for any experienced magical practitioner since the North has been the 'place of power' since time immemorial, and we often begin, or end, there when casting the magical Compass for our personal use. Using the Tree of Life to gain access to the higher reaches of the mystical heavens, we can also draw upon our magical energies from the Celestial North that has been the driving force behind so many important events in world history – and rekindle the ancient Polar Tradition of the Ancestors and re-discover the mystical Thule that is situated at the end of the world.

Strabo relates (taking his text from Polybius): "Pytheas asserts that he explored in person the whole northern region of Europe as far as the ends of the world ... *Thoulē*, [Thule]," he says, "is the most northerly of the British Isles." Thule is described as an island of six days' sailing north of

233

Britain, near the frozen sea; that it has no nights at midsummer when the sun is at the summer solstice. He adds that the crossing to Thule starts at the island of *Berrice*, "the largest of all," which may have been Lewis in the Outer Hebrides.

In a collection of spiritual essays dating from 1897, *The Treasure of the Humble*, wherein the author writes about *Ultima Thule* – the extreme northern limits of the soul:

> *"We are here on the borderland of human thought and far across the Arctic circle of the spirit. There is no ordinary cold, no ordinary dark there, and yet you shall find there naught but flames and light. But to those who arrive without having trained their minds to these new perceptions, the light and flames are as dark and cold as though they were painted. This means that the intelligence, the reason, will not suffice of themselves: we must have faith."*

These sentiments are physically endorsed by the most northerly of the megalithic complexes on the Islands of Orkney. The stark landscape of the Islands offers a unique backdrop for these beautifully constructed sites, against which they take on an ethereal quality, as the builders must have been aware. The Neolithic immigration of the Orkneys began around 3,500BC, bringing with it the ancient stellar faith, and to finish their journey at the nearest northern land to both the Pole Star *and* the Prime Meridian (-2.9°). Was this, then, their *Ultima Thule?*

According to the ancient.wisdom.com/Scotland.orkneys website, "at the latitude of the Orkneys the major lunar standstill north becomes *almost* circumpolar, (*neither rising nor setting - with the effect that the moon 'rolls' along the horizon*). Because the Earth's axial tilt has changed by nearly half a degree since the majority of the stone circles were built, this effect is no longer accurate and the latitude today would have to be 63° north for a lunar standstill to be truly circumpolar, while a truly circumpolar moon would have been visible on the Orkneys at around 3,500 BC". Had our stellar travellers reached their final destination, leaving other megalithic builders trailing in their wake across mainland Europe?

For all its remoteness, the Orkney complex is no last, tattered remnants of a vanished civilisation, since the monuments reflect an extremely high standard of geological and astronomical alignment. The entrance to the Maes-Howe passage-mound, for example, is orientated towards the setting Winter Solstice sun behind the prominent Hills of Hoy in the distance. The chamber was placed so that for several days before and after

234

the winter solstice, the sunlight flashes directly into the passage not once, but twice, with a break of several minutes between each illumination.

"The passage is aligned facing Southwest, facing Ward Hill. For twenty days before the solstice and for 20 days after the solstice, the sun shines into the chamber twice a day. Every eight years Venus causes a double flash of light to enter the chamber. At around 2.35 pm on the winter solstice, the sun shines on the back of the chamber for 17 minutes, and then sets at 3.20 p.m. At 5.00 pm the light of Venus enters the first slot, lighting the chamber, and then at 5.15 p.m. it sets behind Ward Hill. But 15 minutes after its first setting, Venus reappears beyond Ward Hill, and the light enters the chamber for a further two minutes, before setting for a second and last time".

[ancient.wisdom.com/Scotland.orkneys]

It has been suggested that because the two Orkney stone circles have henges dug from the living rock, that the builders may have introduced this technique from elsewhere, where vast henges were dug, but usually into soil. Neither should any individual site be viewed as an independent structure because each was an integral part of a prehistoric, ceremonial landscape. Recent archaeological studies at the Ring of Brodgar, have revealed that the placement of the monuments share similarities with the 'ritual' landscape at Stonehenge. From the centre of Brodgar, the second largest circle in the British Isles, it can be seen how a mound was deliberately built at the same place the sun sets behinds the left-hand Hill of Hoy on the Winter Solstice. This attempt to replicate the horizon can be seen in several other megalithic sites in Scotland where it is also generally associated with astronomical observation.

There are also several features of the Orkneys constructions that have similarities to other megalithic structures from further south (i.e. Ireland, England, France), with all having similarly orientated passage-mounds, henges, stone-circles suggestive of astronomical observation. Also the structures themselves show strong cultural similarities through art, technique and design. As Barry Cunliffe explained in *Facing the Ocean*, a trend for migration along the western coast of Atlantic Europe can be seen from south to north with the Orkney complex representing the northerly most example of socio-astro-religious monuments. The fundamental similarities between the Orkneys complex and other contemporary sites along the western Atlantic coast provide a perfect example of what appears to be two essential components of many of the sites: a prominent mound and circle in close proximity. The sacred mound (on which principle ancient Egyptian temples were also built), can be seen as the 'primal hill', and is often repeated in the form of a passage mound, despite the regional variations at Avebury/Silbury.

> *"On the Orkneys, the monuments were constructed so as to merge with the landscape, in such a way that the stones compliment their backgrounds. The same sensitivity is seen at other megalithic sites, but nowhere is it realised quite so well as on the Orkneys. The creation of these large-scale civil constructions represents a form of higher communication between ourselves and the universe we live in. Their intimate connection with the living landscape into which we place them connects us to the earth, and their invariable orientation towards Solar and Lunar events brings us into time, with the visibly beating heart of the universe."* [ancient.wisdom.com/Scotland.orkneys]

Recent research by the University of Adelaide has also statistically proven that the earliest standing stone monuments of Britain, the great circles, were constructed specifically in line with the movements of the Sun and Moon, 5000 years ago. The research, published in the *Journal of Archaeological Science: Reports* (Douglas Scott), shows that the great stone circle, at Stenness on Orkney, is situated in a 'reverse' landscape. The project examined the alignments running from the centre of circle through the stones on the circle's perimeter and the stone holes where stones formally stood (as revealed by excavation) showed that the stone furthest to the right is oriented upon the last glimmer of a southern moon occurring only every 18.6 years; the second stone is aligned towards the winter solstice sunset and the stone furthest to the left is aligned to the moon as it sets into its most northern position every 18.6 years. These are astronomical events that could be seen 5000 years ago. Project leader Dr Gail Higginbottom observed:

> *"Nobody before this has ever statistically determined that a single stone circle was constructed with astronomical phenomena in mind – it was all supposition. Examining the oldest great stone circles built in Scotland (Callanish, on the Isle of Lewis, and Stenness, Isle of Orkney – both predating Stonehenge by about 500 years, the researchers found a great concentration of alignments towards the sun and moon at different times of their cycles. And 2000 years later in Scotland, much simpler monuments were still being built that had at least one of the same astronomical alignments found at the great circles."*

The stones, however, are not just connected with the sun and the moon. The researchers discovered a complex relationship between the alignment of them across the landscape. "This research is finally proof that the ancient Britons connected the Earth to the sky with their earliest standing stones, and that this practice continued in the same way for 2000 years," continued Dr Higginbottom. Examining sites in detail, it was found that about half the sites were surrounded by one landscape pattern and the other half by the complete reverse.

"These chosen surroundings would have influenced the way the sun and moon were seen, particularly in the timing of their rising and setting at special times, like when the Moon appears at its most northerly position on the horizon, which only happens every 18.6 years. These people chose to erect these great stones very precisely within the landscape and in relation to the astronomy they knew. They invested a tremendous amount of effort and work to do so. It tells us about their strong connection with their environment, and how important it must have been to them, for their culture and for their culture's survival."

Dotted with megaliths, settlements, and tombs, it seems as though Neolithic Orkney was well connected to the rest of its world; a religious complex and pilgrimage site whose cultural influence stretched far beyond its shores. Did those far-off megalith builders who worshipped the stars under the African sun, slowly spread throughout Europe via Egypt, as Bryan Sykes relates in *The Seven Daughters of Eve* – finally making their way north along the Atlantic coast as Barry Cunliffe describes in *Facing the Ocean*. Only to complete their spiritual journey on those wild, inhospitable islands where the North Sea and the Atlantic Ocean meet; the closest land to the both the Pole Star and the Prime Meridian. There was nowhere left to go …

Or far inland in a lush green glen of southern Ireland where the Fort of the Three Pillar Stones of Dún-Trí-Liag's passage tomb is reminiscent of the style commonly found in Brittany. The hill fortress is perhaps 6,000 years old and the passage tomb's construction is quite rare in the south of Ireland; its entrance faces north-west in line with the mid-summer sunset. A nearby cairn is positioned to give views to the east and south-west that are not obtainable from the tomb itself which is lower down on a slight northerly slope. The observation by Ó'Nualláin & Cody in the 1980s revealed a lunar alignment linked to the remains of another passage tomb on a nearby hill.

Finding our way in cosmic space and time is a journey each of us must make alone; your journey will almost certainly be different from mine. Our Paths may never cross but at the same time, hopefully, we will be able echo Aleister Crowley's sentiments: "Whatever horrors may afflict the soul, whatever abominations may excite the loathing of the heart, whatever terrors may assail the mind, the answer is the same at every stage: *How splendid is the Adventure!*"

Yet mark me closely!
Strongly I swear,
Seen or seen not,
The Face is there!
When the Veil is clearest
And sunniest,
Closest and nearest
The Face is prest;

From the *The Book of the Vision of Orm*, Robert Buchanan

SOURCES & BIBLIOGRAPHY
The Amateur Astronomer, Patrick Moore (Lutterworth)
Ancient Egypt: The Light of the World, Vol I, Gerald Massey (Reprint Series)
Astronomy Before the Telescope, ed. Christopher Walker (BMP)
Astronomy in Prehistoric Britain and Ireland, Clive Ruggles (Yale)
Axis of Heaven, Paul Broadhurst (Mythos)
Before the Pyramids, Christopher Knight (Watkins)
The Book of Vodou, Leah Gordon (BES)
The Complete Temples of Ancient Egypt, Richard H Wilkinson (Thames & Hudson)
Cults of the Shadow, Kenneth Grant (Skoob)
The Egyptian Book of Nights, Melusine Draco (ignotus)
The Extraordinary Voyage of Pytheas the Greek: The Man Who Discovered Britain, Barry Cunliffe (OUP)
Facing the Ocean, Barry Cunliffe (OUP)
Gods in the Sky, Allan Capman (4Books)
The Gods of the Greeks, Karl Kerenyi (Thames & Hudson Ltd)
The Heavenly Writing: Divination, Horoscopy, and Astronomy in Mesopotamian Culture, Francesca Rochberg (CUP)
A History of Astrology, Derek and Julia Parker (Deutsch)
History of Astrology, Peter Whitfield (Harry N. Abrams)
The Hollow Tree, Melusine Draco (ignotus)
Honey From Stone, Chet Raymo (Brandon)
Karahundj, The Armenian Stonehenge, Richard L Ney (article)
The Law is for All, Louis Wilkinson (New Falcom)
Lost Hall of Records, John van Auken and Lora Little (Page)
Magic Furnace, Marcus Chown (Vintage)
The Mystical Qabalah, Dion Fortune (Aquarian)
The Names of the Assyro-Babylonian Months and Their Regents, W. Muss-Arnolt, (Journal of Biblical Literature 1892).
The Origin of Humankind, Richard Leakey (Wedienfeld & Nicolson)
Popular Astronomy, The Zodiacal Temples of Uxmal, Stansbury Hagar (article)
The Power of Images, David Freedberg (Chicago)
The Power of the Bull, Michael Rice (Routledge)

The Setian, Billie Walker-John (ignotus)
The Seven Daughters of Eve, Bryan Sykes (Corgi)
The Soul of the Night, Chet Raymo (Prentice-Hall)
Stonehenge Decoded, G S Hawkins, (Fontana)
Stonehenge of the Kings, Patrick Baker (John Baker)
Temples of the African Gods, Michael Tellinger (Zulu Planet Publishers)
The Treasure of the Humble, Maurice Maeterlinck (Allen)
Traditional Witchcraft and the Path to the Mysteries, Melusine Draco
(Moon Books)
Viral Mythology, Marie D Jones and Larry Flaxmn (New Page Books)
Walking Zero, Chet Raymo (Walker)

Mélusine Draco's highly individualistic teaching methods and writing draw on historical sources supported by academic texts and current archaeological findings; endorsing Crowley's view that magic(k) is an amalgam of science and art, and that magic is the outer route to the inner Mysteries. Author of several titles currently published with John Hunt Publishing including the best-selling six-part Traditional Witchcraft series; two titles on power animals – *Aubry's Dog* and *Black Horse, White Horse*; *By Spellbook & Candle; The Dictionary of Magic & Mystery, The Secret People* published by Moon Books; *Magic Crystals Sacred Stones* and *The Atum-Re Revival* published by Axis Mundi Books. Her magical novels, *House of Strange Gods* and *Realm of Shadow* are part of the **Temple House Archive series** and available in both paperback and e-book formats on Amazon.

Web: www.covenofthescales.com **and** www.templeofkhem.com

The complete illustrated paperback version of *The Hollow Tree* by Melusine Draco and originally published by ignotus press contains the appropriate correspondences together with the Paths of the Tarot and planetary associations; limited copies can still be obtained from Coven of the Scales at www.covenofthescales.com – email for more information.

Milton Keynes UK
Ingram Content Group UK Ltd.
UKHW030931130824
446890UK00004B/74